ROOTED *in the* SPIRIT

ROOTED IN THE SPIRIT

Exploring Inspirational Gardens

MAUREEN GILMER

ℰℵℴ

Photography by Jerry Pavia

TAYLOR PUBLISHING COMPANY

DALLAS

ALSO BY MAUREEN GILMER
Redwoods and Roses • *The Complete Guide to Southern California Gardening* •
The Complete Guide to Northern California Gardening

In memory of my beloved agent,
SUSAN URSTADT
Vive velut rapto fugitivaque gaudia carpe:
Perdiderit nullum vita reversa diem.
Live as if you were rescued from death, and seize fleeting enjoyments,
and thus your recovered life will not have lost a single day.
SENECA
And to my editor, Holly McGuire,
who shared the vision and gave it form

ACKNOWLEDGMENTS

Jeanne Fredericks, Sisters of St. Louis, Nancy Ault, Sister Rose Ellen,
Sister Margeurite, Father Tom Hand, Father Breault

I believe that God is in me,
as the sun is in the color and fragrance of a flower,
the light in my darkness,
the Voice in my silence.
HELEN KELLER

Copyright © 1997 Maureen Gilmer

Published by Taylor Publishing Company
1550 West Mockingbird Lane
Dallas, Texas 75235
www.taylorpub.com

Designed by David Timmons

Library of Congress Cataloging-in-Publication Data
Gilmer, Maureen.
    Rooted in the spirit : exploring inspirational gardens / Maureen
Gilmer ; photography by Jerry Pavia.
        p.   cm.
    Includes bibliographical references and index.
    ISBN 0-87833-938-8 (cloth ; alk. paper)
        1. Gardens—Religious aspects—Christianity. 2. Gardens—
Religious aspects. I. Pavia, Jerry. II. Title.
    BT695.5.G565 1997
    158'.3—dc21   96-53544
                                                              CIP

Printed in the United States of America
10 9 8 7 6 5 4 3 2 1

CONTENTS

One

HALLOWED GROUND

WHY WE CREATE INSPIRATIONAL GARDENS

CIUNAS GAN VAIGNEAS. *Quietness without loneliness*
Gaelic, Orkney Islands

CONSILIA FIRMIORA SUNT DE DIVINIS LOCIS. *Councils are of higher sanction when taken in sacred places.*
Platus, 254–184 B.C.

e have often clung to the notion that buildings, such as temples, churches, and cathedrals were the only sacred places. In a cathedral it is often dark and silent, with candles flickering and footsteps echoing from the vaulted ceilings. Here the sense of the sacred is most palpable; we are inspired by such an aura to stop and pray.

Long before the cathedrals, cultures everywhere deemed certain places hallowed ground. The Druids of ancient Europe considered their tree groves temples. Beneath the leafy canopies they practiced their rites on earth so sacred that fires were to be kept burning continuously in homage to the spirits. In the Hebrew tradition today, we find similar sacred ground at the Wailing Wall in Jerusalem, the last ancient remnant of their great Temple. Jews from all corners of the globe make pilgrimages there to pray, to speak to God on ground considered different from anywhere else.

In that same city is the Church of the Holy Sepulchre, where Christians the world over believe Christ was crucified. This place, which was once nothing more than a rocky outcropping, later became the most potent of hallowed ground, and there fires are even today burning continuously. Christians

A secret garden of boxwood, clematis, and forget-me-not. *Chateau de Brecy, Saint-Gabriel-Brecy, France.*

Bridal Veil, Columbia Gorge, Oregon.

erence for the Earth is critical to both their material cultures and religious observances.

There is no official means of creating hallowed ground. The sense of the sacred, of a place set apart may be little more than the worshiper's perception and is therefore intimately meaningful. Worshipers may be entire religions, cultures, or simply individuals, and the meaning may be derived from events that once occurred there or simply from the emotional response that the place evokes. A friend of mine found a place in the Sierra Nevada where he claimed to feel a unique energy. He would retreat there for renewal when feeling overly stressed by daily life. Though there is no tangible evidence to suggest the place was different from any other, to him it was intimately special and thus became hallowed ground.

have recognized hallowed ground elsewhere, in Vatican City, Fatima, Lourdes, and Medjugorje. Their graveyards are officially hallowed by the church and blessed by priests as separate, places set apart.

The New World too had its own hallowed ground, with virtually every culture deeming certain places as homes of the spirits or as the places of origin of the people themselves. The Black Hills of the Dakotas were sacred, and the invasion of nineteenth-century Anglo gold seekers was considered the ultimate desecration by the native peoples there. For most aboriginal peoples of the Americas, there is even a much larger recognition of hallowed ground, applied to all the Earth, with its plants and animals. This rev-

The concept of hallowed ground is also an intrinsic part of a garden or landscape. Spaces arranged and planted in order to create a well defined sense of place can be more than just an aesthetic environment. We have lost our connection to the sacred, leaving the garden somehow vacant of a much deeper value. But when we open our minds and hearts to a new way of thinking, that a garden is much more than we ever imagined, then the sense of true hallowed ground becomes a reality.

Madame d'Andlau Garden, Remalard, France.

THE SACRED GARDEN

If a garden were being planned to surround a newly restored Colonial home, it would be created with plants of that period and in the style or arrangement of the day. The garden maker uses various tools to accomplish that end: the arrangement of space, selection of plants, and the addition of constructed elements to support the overall theme. In accomplishing this, the garden maker has created space which is profoundly linked to the building. What was once nothing more than bare ground becomes a statement of a period past, with its goals and aspirations reflected in every aspect of the garden.

Creation of a garden designed to inspire requires the same attention to layout, plants, and constructed elements as the historic garden. The process of creating any garden is a spiritual exercise in itself, because good design is always built upon a "big idea." This is the umbrella under which the intent and direction of the design are established. In this book there are gardens based upon big ideas, such as nature, water, the feminine, memorials, and the heavens. There are an infinite number of big ideas, and the one you choose will be meaningful and sacred to you.

Equal in importance to the big idea is the function of the garden. As the great landscape architect Thomas Church said, "Gardens are for people." His work was critical in the evolution of the residential garden from a visual showplace of the Victorian mind to the interactive, indoor-outdoor use of space so typical of the modern garden. So too should spiritual gardens serve the gardener in a most intimate way.

There are four basic characteristics which dictate the function of a garden. Your project may respond to one or all at the same time, depending on the scope. Understanding how each one works will be critical to how the garden is laid out.

Rest

People today suffer from decision overload. Every day, we spend time deciding which product to buy, where to park, which bill to pay, what to have for dinner. All these small, seemingly insignificant decisions add up until our minds revolt under the strain. Many believe that the stress-related maladies we see so often, such as migraine headaches, ulcers, and asthma, are signs of overloaded brains and nervous systems. Perhaps sensory-deprivation devices or even some forms of virtual reality appeal to us because they shut out the world and focus the mind.

A priest once told me of a man who came into the empty church at odd hours and remained there for long periods of time. He did not appear to be praying, and eventually the priest asked him about it. The man replied that he knew no prayers. "I just sit here," he said. "I look up at Him on the cross, and He looks back at me." That was all this fellow needed—the quiet church, without reading or speaking a word. He found the church a spiritual place closed off from the noise and confusion and myriad decisions of the outside world. The separation was critical to this man's peace of mind.

When I was young my father went through some difficult times which contributed to both an ulcer and asthma. He often talked of "peace" in those days, and the word took on a very powerful meaning to him. This is the same desire of many working women today who struggle to balance the needs of their families and their jobs. With little time for rest, they live on the ragged edge of life. The luxury of allowing just thirty minutes of uninterrupted time to do nothing, to stop and rest the body and the mind, would be worth more than pure gold to them.

To rest is to renew the self. We sleep at night to recharge the body for the coming day's challenges. Many Americans believe that to take a nap in the afternoon is a waste of time, while much of Latin America takes advantage of the *siesta* to recharge for the evening's work. The spiritual garden can be a place of rest, with a seat or chaise lounge for the body, plenty of beauty for the eyes, and as much quiet as we can manage for the mind.

Finally, there is the science of rest and peace. It is now widely known that brain waves exist in two forms, known as alpha and beta, and the technique of biofeedback is based upon these distinctions. Our conscious mind functions on beta waves most of the time. Alpha waves, on the other hand, occur when we are deeply relaxed, and it is in the alpha state that we are most creative.

I once worked in a landscape architecture office that employed some of the most talented people in the field. They faced very difficult and challenging design problems, which took much time and energy to resolve. Too often a person would announce upon arrival, "It came to me in the shower this morning!" Likewise, some claimed a brilliant idea occurred to them just before falling asleep at night. These two situations, in a hot shower or in the peaceful darkness and quiet of night, are both prime habitats prompting alpha brain waves, so it was in alpha states that they conjured up their greatest ideas.

The importance of rest to anyone in a problem-solving or creative profession is unmistakable. Denying this relaxation can hinder output and limit the mind's creative potential.

Reflection

For many of life's dilemmas, there are no simple answers. To many of life's mysteries, there are no clear explanations. The human heart and mind will forever ponder the nature of truth, the substance of love. St. John of the Cross said it so well: "Contemplation is nothing but a secret, peaceful, and loving infusion of God, which, if admitted, will set the soul on fire with the spirit of love."

Man is by nature a curious being, but what is deep and meaningful to one may be insignificant to another. We spend far more time contemplating our own lives than anyone imagines, because in the process of analytic thinking, we seek to organize our confusion. We continually probe our own behavior and that of others in an effort to explain the web of interpersonal communication.

Reflection is also an important part of understanding the writings of the mystics, such as Thomas Merton, and is critical to fully understanding biblical scripture. So much that cannot be expressed in words comes to us in impressions, feelings, and emotions, all of which gain focus under sufficient reflection or contemplation.

This introspection should not be confused with some forms of meditation which are based upon the emptying of the mind in a search for total peace. Certainly there is a value in such meditation as practiced in many Eastern religions, but the Western tradition is more of a sorting-out process, a mulling over of ideas, words, and situations which lead to truth or resolution. No matter what your reflection, contemplation, or meditation goals, the garden provides the most ideal environment for thought—particularly for those who work indoors each day.

Prayer

During times of grief and joy, desperation and thanksgiving, prayer becomes the cathartic act by

which we share these emotions with our Creator. There are as many types of prayer as there are people, for prayer is a very personal act. A friend told me once that he has two ways of praying, one active and one passive. First is the dialogue with God in which he asks for help. The second type of prayer is quiet, when he waits patiently for God to put the answers into his thoughts.

At parochial schools each day was punctuated with a bevy of prayers, which we all learned by rote. At that time we recited them in unison, paying little attention to the words or their meanings. It was only later in life I discovered why this sort of formal, memorized prayer exists and its value. After the death of my grandmother, I felt deep grief and tried desperately to pray. But in my sadness the words would not come, and I found myself staring at the crucifix in silence. Then the words to old classroom prayers came back to me, the same lines I recited countless mornings. They became my comfort. In particular, the rosary, the mantra of the Catholic Church recited from a string of beads, offered words that poured out of my heart in a torrent.

Among the many old religious sites, there are small shrines, appearing in the strangest of places, that are clearly sacred and remind us to stop and say a few words to the heavens. Throughout India there are roadside shrines that consist of nothing more than a stone or wall painted brightly to represent one of the Hindu deities, and passersby often stop to recognize that place by leaving incense or brightly colored paper. So too in the mountains of eastern Europe are roadside Christian shrines, where travelers stop and pray for a safe journey.

The garden provides a similar opportunity for us to draw apart from the rat race and pray. It takes great concentration to focus the mind upon prayer after a crazy day at the office, yet these are the times we need it most. This separation from the world and its effect is most visible to me at a little church on the tourist island of Balboa in southern California. Out on the main

Lani and Larry Freymiller Garden, Solano Beach, California.

street there are noisy crowds, jostling skaters, and bumper-to-bumper traffic, but while mass is being said in the chapel with the doors closed, there exists a separate reality achieved by blocking out the world. So too can our gardens provide us with this vital separation where we may compose our thoughts and formulate prayer. It is clear that through prayer we may discover answers that require no psychoanalysis, no self-help books, no seminars. It is a mystical experience that we cannot explain, but we know deeply how effective it can be.

Celebration

If you look up the definition of the word *inspire* in the dictionary, you'll find it means to "infuse animation, to quicken, to arouse, and to impel." Thus, an inspirational garden must urge us to respond in some way. It may ask us to stop and rest, to reflect on our lives, or to pray. There is another response, the urge to appreciate everything good and beautiful in our lives and give thanks. When most people see the wilderness here where I live, they see them as hills covered with trees and bushes. When I see the same hills, I notice that the trees grow on the hillsides, and grass takes over in the low spots where soil is deep. I notice the changes in leaf color and texture that separate the various types of shrubs. I see the exotic plants that have moved in and displaced the native species. I can pick out each and every different wildflower, however tiny.

Catmint (*Nepeta Mussinii*) and iris. *Ilmington Manor, Mr. D. and Lady Flower, Warwickshire, England.*

To sacramentalize earth, garden and fruits, and to supernaturalize governance and labor, calls not for number and size but for understanding and vision. Thus, the sowing and tending, too, of just one plant offers profound instruction in the fundamental principles, habits and responsibilities of our labor and stewardship for God's growing things.

JOHN S. STOKES, JR.,
Man in God's Garden

This quotation illustrates how the garden is an environment in which we control nature, and this wonderland of vegetation is the greatest miracle of all. Plants notify us of the season by flowering, fruiting, or losing their leaves. They show us dryness by wilting, they notify us of wind by swaying, and their lean points out just which direction the breeze flows. These are all miracles that happen around us every day, and the garden should call us to celebrate them as gifts of beauty and order from the heavens.

To create a garden inspired by our souls and spirits is to reclaim the origins of true inspiration known so well by artists, poets, and lovers. The gem beyond all price is the human heart. It is enriched by the simple things, the flowers and the birds, cooling shade, the sound of falling water, and every creation of earth and the heavens. To celebrate the garden rooted deeply in our spirits is the rediscovery of what has been known

Foxglove (*Digitalis*), lamb's ears (*Stachys byzantina*), variegated sage (*Salvia officinalis* 'Variegata'), and *Allium. Korbel Winery Garden, Guerneville, California.*

for thousands of years: that nature is the greatest cathedral of all, the most stunning of creations, providing us the ideal environment in which to cultivate our souls.

Iberis sempervirens. Cooney Garden, Birmingham, Alabama.

> For if delight may provoke men's labor, what greater delight is there than to behold the earth apparelled with plants, as with a robe of embroidered work, set with Orient pearls and garnished with great diversity of rare and costly jewels? If this variety and perfection of colors may affect the eye, it is such in herbs and flowers that no Apelles, no Zeuxis, ever could by any art express the like: if odours or if taste may work satisfaction they are both so soverign in plants and so comfortable that no confection of the apothecaries can equal their excellent virtue. But these delights are in the outward senses; the principal delight is in the mind, singularly enriched with the knowledge of these visible things, setting forth to us the invisible wisdom and admirable workmanship of Almighty God.
>
> JOHN GERARD,
> *Gerard's Herbal,* 1633

THE ACT OF GARDENING

We tend to view our gardens as finished products, but it is truly the act of creating and tending a garden that offers us the greatest benefit. We do not buy gardens—we create them, often later in life, when we are more deeply rooted in culture and have the leisure time to patiently watch our plants mature and flower. Once you begin a love of gardening, it steadily increases until the end of life.

One of the most unique qualities of a garden is that it is not static, but ever changing. When we build a home or decorate an interior, the accomplishment is completed—end of story. But gardens begin sparsely at first, when plants are small and young or when the garden making is undertaken one flower bed at a time. That young and gangly sapling will gradually become larger, cast more shade, and increase its overall

beauty. The same goes for most plants; as long as they live, they become ever more beautiful. It is this continual improvement of planting over time that makes garden addicts of us all, tied by invisible golden threads that promise an even more stunning display this year, and the year after.

Dr. L.H. Bailey, the late dean of American horticulturists, expressed one of the most profound truths of gardening: "A garden made by one's own hands is always the best garden, because it is a part of oneself. A garden made by another may interest, but it is another person's individuality. A poor garden of one's own is better than a good garden in which one may dig." In these words we realize that it is indeed the act of garden making that satisfies the soul. Mere viewing of another's work is a vicarious experience, but to feel the earth in our fingers, to see our tiny seeds become flowers, and witness the miracles revealed through the cyclical changes in season

A simple yet evocative garden shrine. *Sarah Hammond Garden, Bolinas, California.*

are the stuff of real peace. For there we find the greatest satisfaction of all, a returning of ourselves and our reality to nature, where the body and the mind will forever be rooted in the spirit.

THE GARDEN SHRINE

In the West the shrine has disappeared except within certain religious communities, yet it offers us one of the most powerful design elements in the garden. Just what constitutes a shrine? It is simply a place where we acknowledge spirituality or pay homage to anything or anyone that is meaningful to us. For example, we see shrines in the homes of Mexican-Americans, who surround images of Christ or Our Lady of Guadalupe with decorations. African-Americans frequently hang a picture of Martin Luther King, Jr., prominently in the home as a sign of their reverence for this important leader. In both cases the shrine serves as a reminder of religious and secular values.

A shrine is also a place to gather things that are meaningful to us and evoke positive images or memories. An older friend of mine tends a small planter encircled by a row of colorful stones, all about the size of a football. She has a story to tell about each, explaining that one was picked up on a trip to the Desert Southwest, and another was a gift from a relative's vacation. The planter has become a record of her life experiences.

A friend who has never left the state, since she cannot afford to travel, collects small stones brought to her from faraway places. These stones, quite ordinary to others, are special to her because of their origins. When I visited Stonehenge years ago, I brought her a small chunk of the chalk downs that surround this ancient monument. To Trina this rock became her link to the mysterious, and it sits with a handful of others beside her office computer.

Something as simple as a pebble can thus become special to us. A shrine becomes the place to gather these things together in order to help focus our thoughts on the memories, love, loss, and the future. The shrine itself becomes the selective environment where such mementos or images are ensconced, then embellished in a purely personal way.

There are no rules for design of shrines, but most include an altar of some sort. The altar becomes the official place where you pay homage to such memories and images by certain acts, such as burning candles and incense or offering sacred or symbolic food and cut flowers. These altars and offerings are found throughout the Bible from Genesis to Revelation. Altars are used most notably on the Hebrew holiday known as First Fruits, in which the first of the harvest is sacrificed to God upon an altar. In Asia the gods represented in little home or wayside shrines are also honored with gifts, often strips of brightly colored cloth or paper. Such materials are wrapped around statues, attached like flags, draped across as a banner, or simply placed upon the flat altar space as offerings.

The chief feature which distinguishes garden shrines from those indoors is their ability to stand up to the elements. We may draw upon a host of materials that offer a wide variety of colors, textures, and forms. They may be placed before the shrine, attached to its surface as decoration, serve as background, or simply arranged within. Most elements in a shrine can be classified as symbolic or purely decorative, proving there is a good deal of personal artistic expression involved.

Statues are the most common elements of shrines and the most outwardly religious. Made of ceramic, metals, finished woods, and plastics, they are often the central focuses of shrines.

These may represent gods or people or simply be lovely to look at. Actual pictures or art are frequently painted on ceramic tile, often made in Mexico or Italy. These usually depict the Virgin or Christ in bright glazes that never fade.

Other materials are used for both decorative and symbolic reasons. Stones connected with important places will always retain their meaning, as do those gathered during special events or on vacations. Consider placing stones such as obsidian, marble, and even fossils in the shrine as an offering or decoration. Those who look to the magical power of crystals enshrine them where they receive sufficient light to show off the many facets.

Metal objects may have meaning, as well, and others are so well crafted they suggest a reverence for mechanical design. Implements from a family farm long ago, an inheritance, even a tarnished silver vase that never quite fits with your interior decor—yet all may be intimately loved, and the shrine provides the ideal place to treasure them. Do not forget coins of aluminum, copper, and silver, foreign or domestic, as simple decoration or mementos of times and places past.

Even though glass is breakable, glass is the jewel of the sun and rightfully takes its place in brightly lit shrines. Beach glass, with its glinting colors and smooth contours, is ideal. Chunks of slag glass or old stained glass pieces all combine in the right light to make the shrine glitter. String glass beads together on fishing line into shining cords to dangle from tree limbs. Pile it up like sparkling riches or glue them onto the surfaces. Fill nooks and crannies of your stones with beads to make them shine.

As an amateur archeologist, I have a deep love for the artifacts of history I find around abandoned homesteads and historic sites. Each year I visit the old Emigrant Trail through the high country of the Sierra Nevada. There the wagons were unloaded and disassembled to scale these rocky heights in pieces. What remains of such great effort, iron hardware and shards of stoneware crocks, become my bit of the past, my recognition of those early days of the West. They are among my most cherished artifacts and are incorporated into my cactus rock garden, where they will always remind me of their origins.

Years ago my parish school tore down an old brick wall that dated back to the 1850s. The Knights of Columbus came up with the idea of cleaning the bricks and selling them as "holy bricks" to raise money for the school. The origins of the material, not the material itself, made it important enough to be marketable, and a home shrine created of these holy bricks was sacred to those who had memories of that school. This is similar to the marketing of chunks of the razed Berlin Wall, a silent testament to the triumph of freedom that occurred there. They are nothing more than pieces of broken concrete, but due to their origins they are among the lingering vestiges of a once oppressive nation.

The Grotto Shrines

Some of the most unique and inspiring garden shrines were created in the first half of this century by three immigrants, one from Italy and two from Germany, who shared the same eclectic style of construction and ornamentation. Perhaps this is a legacy of Europe brought to America by those with a strong back, an artistic eye, and the compulsion to create monuments to the things they most admired.

This grotto, created amidst the dry, swept yard, bears a statue of Mary with two large red votive candles. The overhead roof protects the statue, candles, and other items of devotion from the elements. (*Maureen Gilmer*)

At the base of Watts Towers is Sebastiano Rodia's artwork using a mosaic of discarded ceramics and a plaster signature. The date is just two years after he began this project, which spanned over thirty years. (*Maureen Gilmer*)

Anyone who grew up in Los Angeles or is familiar with American architecture can immediately recognize the Watts Towers. These landmarks were built by an Italian immigrant, Sebastiano Rodia, from 1921 to 1954. A mason and tile setter by trade, he created a sculpture garden, planted with cactus, fruit trees, and grapevines, in which he often sat reading encyclopedias, smoking cigarettes, and drinking homemade jug wine. Above it rose the towers, stretching to ten stories high, built single-handedly out of steel, cement, and millions of seashells, broken tile, and glass bottles. Here we see the direct implementation of the shrine materials discussed above, proving that you need not spend a lot of money to create a shrine of great beauty and lasting value.

Rodia's work was not just folk art, for there was indeed a theme, as he was an amateur scholar of history and great men of the past. In Rodia's words, "A man has to be good good or bad bad to be remembered," the thesis of his lifetime efforts to create monuments. The three towers that reach up to ten stories high were named the Niña, the Pinta, and the Santa Maria after the three ships of Christopher Columbus, a hero among Italians and finder of the New World Rodia so loved. Even though he did not create his towers and garden for religious purposes, it became a favorite place of baptism for a nearby Pentecostal church. The towers have been fully restored to become a cherished landmark of southern California.

Rodia's style was not unique, however, because there are two other sites that share this style of setting a patchwork of materials onto concrete to create marvelous outdoor shrines. Both of these were built by Catholic priests after settling down in Midwestern parishes, and both are dedicated to Christ and his church.

Thus the Grotto of the Redemption will continue to tell its story long after the builder has laid down his trowel, and will be a silent sermon expressing in permanently enduring precious stones the fundamental truths of Christianity.

P. M. DOBBERSTEIN

Father Paul Matthias Dobberstein was born in Rosenfeld, Germany, on September 21, 1872, and received higher education in the science of geology. Like Rodia, he immigrated to the United States in poverty—only twelve cents in his pocket. He received his calling to become a priest when the local bishop announced he needed young men who spoke German. Just before his ordination Father Paul fell ill with pneumonia, and he made a special agreement to the Blessed Mother than if he were granted renewed health, he would build a shrine in her honor.

After his recovery he settled down in West Bend, Iowa, where he began construction of a new school. During the process he stockpiled materials, and in 1912 he began construction on the grotto, a cave-like structure similar to those of Europe where shepherds often took shelter from storms and created small altars and decorations to help them pray. Forever a student of geology, Father Matthias took vacations to the Black Hills and New Mexico, where he gathered his beautiful rocks: crystals, quartzite, and stalactites.

After the grotto was finally completed, it contained a statue of the Blessed Mother and was officially named the Grotto of the Redemption. Many of those who came to see his handiwork returned time and again, bearing gifts of semi-precious stones and seashells. Some even brought Father Paul precious gems to be included in the shrines. This led the priest to continue his work, creating more grottoes and shrines there at his parish until, at the time of his death, the entire structure had reached the size of a city block.

It is most curious that another grotto-building immigrant, Mathias Wernerus, shared a name with Father Paul and was also born in Germany. He began attending the seminary there but finished his studies for the priesthood in America after his immigration in 1904. Father Wernerus came to the town of Dickeyville, Wisconsin, in 1918, probably because he spoke German. His project began at the end of World War I, when the parish sought to improve the cemetery for its sons fallen on the European battlefields. The priest proposed there be built a monument at the far end of the plot to honor the soldiers.

There were great rock ledges and quarries in the bluffs above the nearby Mississippi River, symbolic of the rock upon which Jesus built the church, and the actual rock Father Wernerus

would use to build his patriotic shrine to God and his new homeland. Developing his own special method of mixing concrete and without plans, he began his work in much the same style as Father Paul's Grotto of the Redemption. He gathered truckloads of stone from the Dakotas, Iowa, and Wisconsin. Just as we suggest collecting rocks for garden shrines because of the significance of their origins, Father Wernerus obtained stone from the catacombs of Italy and from the Holy Land. In his efforts to find even more beautiful rock, the priest became a spelunker, rambling about in caves in search of stalagmites and crystals.

But Father Wernerus was more like Rodia of Watts, for he also accepted shards of colored tile and glass from the kilns in Kokomo, Indiana. Many local people donated family heirlooms to his shrines, because this priest insisted that all members of the parish be included in the construction process. It was not his monument, but theirs. Even the local Native Americans from the Keshea reservation in Wisconsin became involved and donated arrowheads, axheads, and artifacts to the patriotic shrines.

Rodin, Father Paul, and Father Wernerus were all drawn to create shrines by passion and perhaps by early life exposure to the great traditions of European architecture and decoration. None of their shrines was made of expensive materials unless specially donated, with most decoration created with natural gifts of the earth: clay, stone, sand, and seashells. Collectively, they have proven that we may all create shrines, large or small, of such found materials. Through their great shrines, we have a blueprint for our own in which to honor the people and the concepts we value in a most unique, artistic way.

Visit the shrines

Watts Towers, 1727-107th St.,
Los Angeles, California

The Grotto of the Redemption, Box 376, West Bend, Iowa 50597

Dickeyville Grotto, 305 W. Main, Box 427, Dickeyville, WI 53808, (608) 568-7519

The exterior of the Grotto of the Redemption with a statue of the Sacred Heart. The arch is composed of white marble from Arizona. (*Maureen Gilmer*)

Two

THE BIBLICAL GARDEN

"*C*ONSIDER THE LILIES OF THE FIELD"

Matthew 6:28

ife began in a garden, and Christ was buried in a garden. Throughout the Great Book there are endless references to the earth, its botanical bounty, and its relationship to man. In the ancient Holy Land of the Bible, all people were closely tied to their crops and what was gathered from the wild. Plants provided food, clothing, shelter, tools, weapons, glue, incense, medicine, and almost everything else that was a part of the material culture. What was not grown was obtained from animals, who were equally dependent upon the plant kingdom. It is not at all surprising, then, that the Bible uses plants to teach its lessons, and we too may employ these same plants to teach ourselves and our children the fundamentals of Judeo-Christian principles.

The first few books of the Bible chronicle the beginnings of the Hebrew nation as God's chosen people and their subsequent wanderings. Clearly, the Israelites did not settle down until after their captivity and the ensuing forty years in the desert. They were finally rewarded with the Promised Land, where they made their home. Only then did they plant and harvest, taking up an agricultural life, where the home, hearth, crops, and livestock became the framework of rural households. They

Clay water jars such as this are mentioned throughout scripture and make ideal ornaments suggesting the festive wedding at Canna and its parable. *Lani and Larry Freymiller Garden, Solano Beach, California.*

Biblically inspired gardens for small spaces can contain a surprising diversity of plants. *Papete Bergman Garden, Santa Barbara, California.*

Bible gardens set apart from more active areas provide additional opportunities for meditation spaces. *Madame d'Andlau Garden, Remalard, France.*

started gardening very late, 446 B.C., in terms of world history: the Persians, Greeks, Egyptians, and other prosperous civilizations had been landscaping their countrysides for many centuries before the Jews.

Among the most beautiful of the Hebrew festivals which commemorates the abundance of this new land is that of First Fruits. In Leviticus 23:9–11 it is written, "The LORD said to Moses, 'Speak to the Israelites and say to them: "When you enter the land I am going to give you and you reap its harvest, bring to the priest a sheaf of the first grain you harvest. He is to wave the sheaf before the LORD so it will be accepted on your behalf; the priest is to wave it on the day after the Sabbath.'"

First Fruits comes on a moveable date dictated by the full moon, usually falling in either March or April, the season of harvest in the Holy Land. We see a harvest offering in almost

every culture, both pagan and Judeo-Christian, showing a universal human tendency to honor or give thanks for the plants and their miraculous ability to provide us with sustenance. In order to ensure the harvest's continuance through the benefits provided by God or the gods, festivals fall in almost every land at harvest time, although some peoples offer the first grain, while others offer the very last bit collected upon completion of the harvest.

It is important to understand how plants figured into the life of communities which struggled for survival in the desert or under near-desert conditions. Today we use the term *oasis* to refer to any lush place surrounded by dry country, and the Hebrews saw plants as the epitome of a sanctuary or well-watered place. They valued any species which could struggle through the dry season without irrigation and jealously guarded any crops they grew, which is well illustrated in many parables of the New Testament.

Among the gardens of the Bible is that of Eden, a paradisical concept of the garden as a holy creation of God. Though we do not know where it was, many speculate Eden was between the Tigris and Euphrates rivers. Lot described the Jordan Valley as a garden abundantly watered, again showing how water became the fundamental resource in support of plant and human life. This shows also that the concept of the garden was not necessarily of one cultivated by man, but simply a place where plants and trees grew.

In the Psalms are many garden references, mostly in a symbolic sense, as plants and trees are used as illustrative words of praise. Only Solomon's gardens are described in poetic verse amidst the pages of Song of Songs. We find in his words all the elements of the Hebrew idea of a garden, an orchard with herbs, and more important, a source of water.

> You are a garden locked up, my sister,
>   my bride;
> you are a spring enclosed, a sealed
>   fountain.
> Your plants are an orchard of pome-
>   granates

with choice fruits,
with henna and nard,
nard and saffron,
calamus and cinnamon,
with every kind of incense tree,
with myrrh and aloes
and the finest spices.
You are a garden fountain,
a well of flowing water streaming
down from Lebanon.

SONG OF SONGS 4:12–15

In the New Testament some of the great moments of Christ's life took place in gardens. He taught in gardens, prayed in gardens, and confronted his destiny in Gethsemene. But greatest of all was his resurrection in a garden. In her grief, Mary Magdalene mistook him for a gardener, which is believed to have symbolized his beckoning of man to return to Eden and the Father.

Among the few tangible legacies that remain with us of biblical times are the written word of God, the earth itself, celestial bodies,

This small pocket garden contains ornamental onion, lilies, and herbs which were common in the Holy Land. Ancient, yet at the same time projecting a very contemporary character. *Jack Larsen Garden, Long Island, New York.*

and plants. Though the peoples of the world have changed, the descendants of those plants which grew during the life of Christ are virtually identical, their genetic codes unchanged and thus linking us with this great book and God.

While the lands of the Old Testament were clearly arid, they were not as barren as those of the contemporary Holy Land. Some believe this was the result of poor land management. Today we know that forest land stripped of its vegetation can become a desert of harsh sun, soil erosion, and devastation. The once plentiful forests of cedar, palm, and olive which cloaked Israel were cut down over the ages by the native peoples and their many conquerors. The biblical references to forests and groves tell us that the trees were indeed once there, but only a handful remain today. No new replacement trees were planted in the wake of Solomon's lust for building materials with which to honor his God, and the groves he cut down gradually disappeared forever.

This deforestation is at the heart of how the land was known during the time of Christ. As groves disappeared, some of the only real tree-shaded areas were the orchards kept outside cities and the lingering palms clustered around isolated pools, wells, and springs. Later New

Christ as a Gardener Appearing to Mary Magdalene, woodcut by Albrecht Dürer.

Testament references concerning trees are within this context, limited mostly to those which provided fruit or wood for building, with others woven into parables and traditions.

The biblical garden for today's home is not about interpretation of Scripture. It is more of a botanical history that focuses upon species best suited to modern gardens and offering us the greatest benefit. Some Bible plants are obscure, their true meanings blurred by the fog of time. I include some plants for their products—the reed for mats and the wood for tabernacles. In sifting through the plants that were, might have been, or are today thought to be scripturally relevant, I picked out only those which can realistically be cultivated in a garden setting.

Entire books have been written about plants of the Bible, and for those seeking a much broader approach, it is best to consult the titles listed in the Bibliography. The creation of a Bible garden is an exercise in scholarship, and anyone making one finds the passages drawing one into an effort to discover their true meaning. Study and ultimate selection of plants is a creative act of faith, which results in sacred work to be embodied by the final garden scheme. Perhaps in the process we and our descendants, like the people of Israel, may find even more wisdom written between the lines of this holiest of books.

THE FLORA

Among the many species of plants mentioned in the Bible, there are annuals, perennials, vines, shrubs, and trees. In landscape design a palette of plants to be used in the proposed garden is assembled into these categories, then individuals are worked into a plan. The plants that make up your individual plant palette are further limited to those capable of growing in your local climate. While trees and shrubs must be sufficiently frost hardy, annuals, such as wheat, have finite life spans not always limited by winter conditions.

The plants that follow are just a few of the dozens mentioned in Scripture. It's important to know that long after the time of Christ, there evolved much folklore about Bible plants—folk-

The Rod of Aaron Blossoming on the Tabernacle, woodcut by Arndes Lubecker, *Lubecker Bibel*, 1494.

lore not accepted by biblical scholars. The Bible was only known by a literate elite, often church officials who read it in Latin or Greek. Before the first printing in the fifteenth century, books were copied by hand, a task that could take years. Entire monasteries were dedicated to copying sacred texts. The vast majority of the people, though, illiterate in their own languages, much less those tongues of science and literature. Therefore, more unconventional interpretations and beliefs developed in various cultures and became part of their relationship with the church and the Bible. Though not actually scriptural, these stories can be beautiful examples of faith and a testament to the times, often attempts to explain the mysteries of various types of plants.

Not all Bible plants are suitable for gardens, so I have included only the candidates most significant to Scripture, widely available, versatile, and attractive in the plant profiles that follow. It's important to understand the actual availability of the plant, as some are neither widely grown in the landscape trade nor available in seed form. When appropriate, a plant unavailable today may be represented by another species of the same genus, or by a different but related genus. This allows for more flexibility and increases the ability to create a Bible garden in difficult climates.

TREES OF THE BIBLE

Throughout the Old Testament there are references to rods and staffs carried by many important people. They are the precursors to the pastoral staffs carried by modern bishops. We find a curious traditional repetition of a theme concerning the staff, its miraculous transformation from common walking stick into a living plant bearing leaves and sometimes flowers. The first and best known example is the budding of Aaron's staff, which signified that he would be the next ruler of the Israelites.

The staff of Aaron thrown at Pharaoh's feet has a surprising lineage. Folklore states that Adam cut it from a tree in the Garden of Eden, and from him it descended to Noah. Then the heirloom was passed on to Abraham, Isaac, and Jacob, who gave it to Joseph. From him the staff eventually worked its way to Moses.

The LORD said to Moses, "Speak to the Israelites and get twelve staffs from them, one from the leader of each of their ancestral tribes. Write the name of each man on his staff. On the staff of Levi write Aaron's name, for there must be one staff for the head of each ancestral tribe. Place them in the Tent of Meeting in front of the Testimony, where I meet with you. The staff belonging to the man I choose will sprout, and I will rid myself of this constant grumbling against you by the Israelites."…The next day Moses entered the Tent of the Testimony and saw that Aaron's staff, which represented the house of Levi, had not only sprouted but had budded, blossomed and produced almonds.
NUMBERS 17:1–5, 8

Much folklore surrounding transformed staffs appeared later on during the Christian era. St. Christopher's staff of palm stem was transformed into a fruiting palm tree by the Christ child. Another example is the staff of Joseph of Arimathea, made of hawthorn wood native to the Holy Land. After Christ's death and resurrection, Joseph became a missionary to the far north. Upon landfall in Britain his staff took root and grew into the famous Glastonbury Thorn, described among the Christmas plants in chapter ten.

So powerful were some of these rods that medieval sorcerers took up rods to enact their own black magic, and such a wand is mandatory among modern performance magicians. Many believe this is also the origin of beliefs in the divining rod, made most often of hazel wood and imbued with special powers for finding water and valuable metals underground.

Phoenix dactylifera—Date Palm

On the first day you are to take choice fruit from the trees, and palm fronds, leafy branches and poplars, and rejoice before the LORD your God for seven days.
LEVITICUS 23:40

On the walls all around the temple, in both the inner and outer rooms, he carved cherubim, palm trees and open flowers.
I KINGS 6:29

The righteous shall flourish like a palm tree, they will grow like a cedar of

The date palm, in a nineteenth-century botanical work.

Lebanon; planted in the house of the
Lord, they will flourish in the courts of
our God.

PSALM 92:12–13

They took palm branches and went out to
meet him, shouting, "Hosanna! Blessed is
he who comes in the name of the Lord!"

JOHN 12:13

Few trees bear as rich a history and symbolism as
the palm tree, which is repeatedly depicted in
scripture from Genesis to Revelation. The palm
is of great value to cultures of arid lands because
it is capable of withstanding the extreme heat.
Palms are often the only trees in the isolated
desert oases of the Middle East from Persia
(Iran) through northern Africa. Their presence
indicates groundwater and therefore serves as a
vital symbol of life in a seemingly lifeless desert.

The desert palm is shaped much like an
open umbrella, bearing long, feathery fronds
which can provide considerable shade if trees are
growing close together, as they do today in
Middle Eastern cities. For the daily call to prayer
of Islamic peoples, vast outdoor plazas are planted in the form of a bosk, with trees set in a grid,
much like an orchard. The spacing between trees
has been set to allow them to touch canopy to
canopy for large scale shading.

Above all, palms were recognized as the
only crop in the barren wastes of the desert. The
vital life-giving ability of the palm has caused it
to become the symbol of Judea, and in 53 B.C.
the Romans took the palm as a symbol of their
conquering the peoples of that land. Later
Christians adopted it as a sign of their triumph

The catacombs of Rome contain the earliest Christian
burials. This image carved into a tomb bears a wreath
of olive to symbolize peace and two palm fronds to
symbolize triumph.

over the Hebrew hierarchy and the Romans.
During the centuries of Christian persecution by
the Romans, the palm also became a symbol of
the martyrs, with this plant showing the triumph
of faith over the destruction of the body.

The fronds of palm trees in biblical times
provided thatch for roofing, fibers for rope, and
weaving material for baskets. In addition, the
dates they produced were eaten fresh, dried,
ground into sugar, and the seed pressed for oil.
In those days it grew far more abundantly in the
Holy Land than it does today, with many scriptural references to very large groves, one nearly
seven miles long.

The name of the date palm genus, *Phoenix*,
is rooted in the name *Phoenicia* (modern
Lebanon and Syria), translated as "land of
palms." The biblical city Bethany translates into
"the house of dates," attesting to the prominent
role of palm trees there. The most well-known
reference to palms in the Bible is that of the triumphant entry of Jesus into Jerusalem, but the
Jews had used palms much earlier in their Feast
of Tabernacles.

Other Christian legends are attributed to
the palm as well, but are not part of scripture.
During the flight of Mary, Joseph, and the Christ
child into Egypt, Jesus requested that the tree
bend down to allow Mary to reach the dates after
Joseph had refused to climb for them. The palm
did so willingly, and as a reward Jesus blessed it
and deemed it a symbol of salvation for the
dying, promising to return triumphant with a
palm frond in his hand on Palm Sunday.

There is even more to the palm, which was
sometimes called the Tree of the Virgin. Legend
has it that just before the death of the Virgin
Mary, an angel brought her a palm branch from
the Garden of Eden. It was so holy the leaflets
sparkled like stars of the morning. In medieval
times people marveled that the palm tree always
grew perfectly erect no matter how much it was
battered by wind and rain. As a result, it became
a symbol of triumph over adversity.

Perhaps the most interesting palm tale not
mentioned in the Bible but attributed to its people concerns Cain. After he killed his brother,
Abel, he carried the body around for many days,

ℐT. CHRISTOPHER'S PALM

St. Christopher with his palm staff carrying the Christ Child.

St. Christopher is no longer an official patron of the traveler, the modern church having found that his charming legend is probably more fiction than fact. Yet the tale is so well loved, he will never disappear: he has simply moved out of official sainthood and into folklore.

The story begins with Christopher, a pagan who made a living by carrying people across a river on his back, lest they get wet or could not swim themselves. He always steadied himself in the current with a staff made of palm. One day a small child approached him and asked to cross over, so Christopher hoisted the lightweight boy onto his back to begin the crossing. As they forded the waters the boy grew heavier and heavier, which surprised Christopher, but he continued on. Upon reaching the far side, Christopher asked the boy who he was and added, "Had I carried the world on my shoulders, the burden could not have been heavier."

The child replied, "Do not wonder, Christopher, for you not only bore the world, but him who made the world as well. You offered me charity, and I accepted; and in so doing I accepted you. Plant your staff in the ground, and it will sprout leaves and fruit." Christopher did so, and immediately it flourished into a palm tree bearing huge clusters of dates. He then found the child had disappeared and fell upon his knees and worshipped Christ.

not sure how to dispose of it. At last he came up with an idea inspired by the actions of a raven, who scratched a hole in the ground and pushed in and buried another raven's dead body. With his dilemma solved, Cain dug a hole at the foot of a palm tree and there buried his brother. Forever after, the palm's fronds would droop in sadness. As Cain did so, however, the raven also observed the man, then flew off to inform Adam of the murder and burial of his son. From then on the raven would be the symbolic bringer of bad tidings and a sign of evil omen.

The palm was a symbol of elegance and grace in these and many pagan cultures. Among the remnants of Egyptian temples, their stone columns have capitals carved as palm trees. Among the Greeks palms represented riches, procreation, victory, and light and were often dedicated to the god Apollo.

The biblical date palm is grown commercially in the American Southwest, where it fruits prolifically in the intense heat while its roots feed upon irrigation and sometimes groundwater. The tree is not frost hardy and thus is unsuitable anywhere but relatively frost-free climates. Desert palms are very large trees, growing to thirty feet tall with trunks three feet in diameter—definitely not suited to small spaces.

A close relative, the Canary Island date palm, *Phoenix canariensis*, is visually similar but far more attractive, with thicker fronds and a very strongly textured trunk. The Canary Islands are located off the west coast of Africa, which points to some geographic relation to the other palm. Its fruit is not edible, but it is highly ornamental, and the trees do exceptionally well as a widely available ornamental.

Even the Canary Island palm may not live

A windrow of olive trees as they might have appeared in the time of Christ. *Mr. and Mrs. Brewer Garden, California.*

too far north, but in its place may be substituted palms that are more hardy and smaller in stature. Among the most cold tolerant are the windmill palm, *Trachycarpus fortunei,* and the Mediterranean fan palm, *Chamerops humilis.* These will survive to single-digit temperatures and provide all the educational and religious symbolism of their larger relatives.

Olea europea—Olive

> When the dove returned to him in the evening, there in its beak was a freshly plucked olive leaf!
>
> GENESIS 8:11

> Command the Israelites to bring you clear oil of pressed olives for the light so that the lamps may be kept burning.
>
> EXODUS 27:20

> But I am like an olive tree/flourishing in the house of God;/I trust in God's unfailing love for ever and ever.
>
> PSALM 52:8

> These are the two olive trees and the two lampstands that stand before the Lord of the earth.
>
> REVELATION 11:4

The olive tree was critical to the development of the earliest civilizations because it was the source of precious oil. We tend to take vegetable oils for granted these days since there are so many other sources, both natural and synthetic, but olive oil was responsible for a great improvement in living conditions because it was edible and useful in so many other ways. The tree was also capable of living in arid conditions, which made it one of the valuable plants of the Mediterranean region. It has been traced back 5,000 years to ancient Egypt and Crete, where the earliest known evidence of the "olive culture" has been found.

The gardens in biblical scripture usually refer to olive orchards, not ornamental gardens, as we know them. These trees were the reason for the name Mount of Olives, or Mount Olivet. Virtually every Holy Land village or town had an olive grove and the presses to extract the oil. Also, when an olive crop was harvested, the pickers always left some of the fruit behind for the poor, strangers, orphans, and widows to gather for themselves.

The olive tree became a symbol of light because it was oil, pressed from the fruit, that yielded fuel for lamps. Until the oil was discovered, people had only their hearth fires and candles for light after sunset. It is believed that olive oil gave the Greeks and the Romans the edge which fueled their great civilizations. Scriptures of both the Old Testament and parables in the Gospels often involve oil because this precious commodity provided light, as well as a variety of cosmetics and the stuff of anointment in religious ceremony.

The olive is also significant as a symbol of peace because of the story of Noah, who sent out the dove, which returned with a sprig of olive in its beak. A German legend suggests that the olive first sprang from the tomb of Adam, and it was from this tree that Noah's dove obtained its sprig. A Middle Eastern belief held that only a peaceful man would plant an olive orchard, because the trees grew so slowly the planter would have to live a long life to see them bear the first crop.

Other legends, many of which are believed to have appeared during medieval times, relate the spiritual lineage of the olive. It is said that the angel guarding the gates to the Garden of Eden gave Adam's son Seth three seeds, one each of olive, cypress, and cedar. After Adam died Seth planted the three seeds in Adam's mouth, and they grew up into a single tree of three trunks, one olive, one cypress, and one cedar. The tree was later cut down by King Solomon but was not suitable for lumber, so it was cast off into the marsh. There it floated and provided the Queen of Sheba with a footbridge. Ultimately, it was reclaimed by the Romans and made into the cross of the Crucifixion.

Pagan civilizations also revered the olive tree and wove their mythology through its branches and leaves. The Greeks believed in a tale of Athena, the goddess of Wisdom, who argued with Poseidon, the god of the Mediterranean, over the name for a newly founded city. The other deities upon Mount Olympus decided that whoever was able to provide Greece with the greater gift would be allowed to name the city. Poseidon struck the earth with his trident, and a horse appeared. Athena in turn struck the earth, and an olive tree sprang up. The other gods decided that the olive, a symbol of peace and light, was more important to civilization and so allowed the city to be named Athens after the goddess.

The olive we grow today in American orchards and gardens is the very same species that grew wild around the Mediterranean and was domesticated by civilizations there. Its unique characteristics include the ability to stump-sprout vigorously, defying the woodsman's ax by springing up again after the tree is cut down. When used in an ornamental sense or in a biblical garden, the trees will fruit heavily, becoming a problem in some cases. New fruitless cultivars offer better choices for the Bible garden, and combined with an aviary filled with living doves make a beautiful testament to Scripture. Of course, a ceramic dove perched in the branches is also wonderfully symbolic.

Ficus carica—Fig

During Solomon's lifetime Judah and Israel, from Dan to Beersheba, lived in safety, each man under his own vine and fig tree.

I KINGS 4:25

Seeing in the distance a fig tree in leaf, he went to find out if it had any fruit. When he reached it, he found nothing but leaves, because it was not the season for figs.

MARK 11:13

There are more biblical references to the fig than any other plant because it was such an important food crop to peoples of Palestine. It was well known by rich and poor alike, which broadened its appeal. Anyone fortunate enough to have land or a garden of trees always grew at least one fig tree in the corner of the yard. The expression "to sit under one's own fig tree" is still a common way to suggest peace and prosperity in the Holy Land.

There are many references to the crops of figs, which are borne by the trees twice a year, a smaller crop with the first leaves of spring and a heavier one in the fall. As the leaves emerge, a tiny fruit accompanies them, ensuring a harvest. Figs can be fickle, though, and sometimes simply refuse to bear, despite vigorous foliage. Some

Rapid growth, attractive fruit, and flowers makes fig trees ideal for espalier.

believe that the references to barren fig trees in the New Testament symbolize people who refuse to accept the Gospel of Christ; no matter how much they are coaxed into believing, they never bear the fruit of Christianity.

In the Garden of Eden after their fall, Adam and Eve began to cover their nakedness with the leaves of a fig tree. Many believe that this points to the fig as the original tree of knowledge, rather than the more widely accepted apple. Such use of the fig leaf to cover more controversial portions of the human form persisted down through the ages in fine art depiction of the first couple and others.

The fig tree once grew wild throughout the Middle East and was often found near wells. Even today we find them here in the West growing along river courses, their foliage baked by rocky cliffs while the roots reach deep to tap into limitless groundwater. In Palestine virtually every home has a fig tree because of its carefree habit, resistance to the hot, arid climate, and double crop of fruit.

The fig is an ideal shade tree if properly cared for and makes a good background for Bible gardens where climate permits. Though the genus *Ficus* is very large and includes dozens of commonly cultivated trees, there are only a few varieties of edible figs, and many will not bear in mild climates.

Punica granatum—Pomegranate

> On the capitals of both pillars, above the bowl-shaped part next to the network, were the two hundred pomegranates in rows all around.
>
> I KINGS 7:20

Virtually all of the references to the pomegranate in the Bible are from the Old Testament, and both the fruit and flower are clearly the inspiration for much detailing in Solomon's temple and upon temple robes. The fruit's end bears a small, crown-shaped extension called the calix, which also influenced the shape of Solomon's crown. The imagery has lasted throughout many ages, appearing in the crowns of European royalty thousands of years later.

There are far more legends and references to the pomegranate in pagan mythology than there are in the Bible. The Egyptians held the pomegranate sacred, and it appears frequently in hieroglyphics and murals depicted in pharaohs' tombs. A Syrian and Babylonian god known as Ramman ruled over thunder, wind, and storms. It is believed that the pomegranate tree symbolized Ramman, and the tree today still bears the name *rumman* in Arabic. Pomegranate-inspired decorations have been found on the Persian royal scepter.

The pomegranate, a very ancient tree, is one of the few succulent fruits that will grow in arid climates. Biblical peoples relished it fresh, as wine, or as cooling drinks. Its red, fleshy seeds are borne inside a hard outer covering, and the sheer numbers of them have always come to symbolize fertility among many cultures. It is the custom in Turkey for the bride to cast a ripe pomegranate to the ground and the number of seeds that fall from the fruit will tell the number of children she will bear.

Today there are numerous varieties of pomegranate, but all bear a similar shrubby appearance, with thin, twiggy growth and vigorous suckering that springs from the base of the trunk. Trees make fine landscape specimens due to the tangerine-colored flowers and the attractive red fruit that hangs on the tree very late in the season. Dwarf varieties make equally fine landscape plants, more confined in size, with smaller fruit that is ornamental. Deciduous and drought tolerant, pomegranates are easy to grow in the biblical garden.

Cedrus libani—Cedar of Lebanon

> "By your messengers you have heaped insults on the Lord. And you have said, 'With my many chariots I have ascended the heights of the mountains, the utmost heights of Lebanon. I have cut down the tallest cedars, the choicest of its pines.'"
>
> ISAIAH 37:24

"'Consider Assyria, once a cedar in Lebanon, with beautiful branches overshadowing the forest; it towered on high, its top above the thick foliage. The waters nourished it, deep springs made it grow tall; their streams flowed all around its base and sent their channels to all the trees of the field.'"

Ezekiel 31:3–4

The story of biblical cedar trees is one of immortality and destruction. The cedar, native to the Holy Land, grew in the mountains of Lebanon at the higher elevations. The wood of all species of the genus *Cedrus* has unique properties: it is fragrant and resists decay. This fragrant oil, the scent so familiar in cedar chests and lined closets, repels moths and thus early became vital in the preservation of cloth goods. The wood itself was valued during biblical times as the only sizable timber, and it would not rot as other kinds of wood did if exposed to earth or the elements. As a result, it became symbolic of the infinite nature of God and was avidly sought out for the building of Solomon's temple.

The cedar groves were decimated very early on, the trees mercilessly logged for the building of palaces and temples. By the fifth century B.C., the original groves had nearly disappeared, with the only remaining cedars in difficult high points upon the mountaintops. For Solomon's temple, thirty thousand Israelites were sent to Lebanon in shifts over seven years to log the great cedar forests. Solomon's temple took thirteen additional years to build and used so much cedar it was called the House of the Forest of Lebanon.

Such was the demand for cedar wood, for everything from chariot construction to ship masts, that the destruction of forests as well as the native palm groves caused massive erosion in the Holy Land and rendered it the desert we see today. Though the cedar was once a majestic tree which symbolized vigor, beauty, and age, it was destroyed, and biblical scholars often mention the parallels between the loss of Lebanon's cedar groves and the destruction of the temple and the Israelites under Roman rule.

Other peoples of biblical times, namely the Egyptians, greatly valued the wood of the cedar, which is frequently found in tombs. Cedar

The true cedar of Lebanon, *Cedrus libani* 'Green Prince'.

mummy cases not only resisted decomposition, they repelled insects that could spoil a fine embalming job. The softness of the wood, its fragrance, and its lasting quality made it the first choice for those who carved icons or idols in many cultures of the Mediterranean.

The cedar of Lebanon is one of the most versatile trees in the biblical garden plant palette because it is quite cold hardy, disease resistant, and widely available. It can serve many practical roles, from windbreak to shading. There are many other species of the cedar genus as well, providing more options for gardens in difficult climates.

Suggested species:

Cedrus atlantica—atlas cedar (zone 6)
Cedrus deodora—deodar cedar (zone 7)
Cedrus libani—cedar of Lebanon (zone 5)

Cupressus sempervirens—Italian Cypress, Gopher Wood

Genesis 6:14 Isaiah 41:19 Isaiah 60:13
Ecclesiastes 24:13, 50:10

This is the familiar tall, thin cypress that has come to be most associated with the Italian

The most common oak of the Holy Land, *Quercus ilex.*

countryside and can be seen in the backgrounds of paintings by the old masters. Its wood was valued for its aromatic quality and was used to create tabernacles and in the temple. Perhaps its most famous application is as gopher wood to build Noah's ark, and it was a common material for boat building among the Assyrians and Egyptians.

There is much confusion over references to junipers and other conifers native to the Holy Land. This cypress is a pencil-thin columnar tree, but other cypress species exhibit differing silhouettes. Any one or all may be part of temperate gardens, but the Italian cypress may not be compatible with snow accumulations, which cause the pointed tip to split apart at the top like a banana peel.

Suggested species:
Cupressus sempervirens—Italian Cypress (zone 7)
Cupressus arizonica—Arizona Cypress (zone 7)
Cupressus bakeri—Modoc Cypress (zone 5)
Cupressus macrocarpa—Monterey Cypress

Quercus spp.—Oak

GENESIS 12:6, 13:8, 14:13, 18:1 & 8, 35:4,8 38:28,30 EXODUS 25:4, 26:1, 28:33, 34:13, 35:23, 39:24 LEVITICUS 14:4,6,51-52 NUMBERS 19:6, 24:6 DEUTERONOMY 11:30, 12:2-3, 16:21 JOSHUA 24:26 JUDGES 3:7, 6:11, 9:6 2-SAMUEL 18:9-10 1-KINGS 13:14, 14:23, 18:19 2-KINGS 17:10,16, 18:4, 21:7, 23:6,14, 1-CHRONICLES 10:12, 2-CHRONICLES 2:7,14, 3:14, 28:4, PSALMS 1:3, ISAIAH 1:18,29,30, 2:13, 6:13, 27:9, 44:14, 61:3, JEREMIAH 4:30, 10:3, 17:8, EZEKIEL 6:13, 20:28, 27:6, 31:14, DANIEL 4:10-12, HOSEA 4:13 AMOS 2:9, MICAH 7:14, ZECHARIAH 11:2, HEBREWS 9:19, REVELATION 18:12.

Long before the Hebrews settled in the Promised Land, peoples throughout the Mediterranean worshipped their gods in groves of trees. In many cases the trees themselves became the abodes of the spirits and were thus sacred. Such was the case in the Holy Land, and for that reason worship of the Hebrew God in groves was strictly forbidden. Above all, the most sacred of the pagan trees was the oak and would remain so for centuries after Christ's death.

Oaks mentioned in scriptural references are believed to be of a number of species. The kermes oak, *Quercus coccifera*, was grown in the Holy Land as a source of red dye from the scale insects that infest this species. The Valona oak, *Quercus aegilops*, is also mentioned and was also a dye source, no doubt due to the tannin content. And certainly, the cork oak, *Quercus suber*, was harvested for its thick, spongy bark.

The holm oak, or holly oak, *Quercus ilex*, is the most famous of all because it continually appears in myth and Scripture. Christian legend has it that all the trees of the forest refused to give their wood for the cross except the holm oak. Despite this, Christ forgave the little holm because it was willing to die with him, and it was beneath its canopy that Jesus met with his disciples after the Resurrection.

Suggested species:
Quercus agrifolia—California live oak (zone 9)
Quercus alba—White Oak (zone 4)
Quercus coccinea—Scarlet Oak (zone 4)

Quercus falcata—Southern Red Oak (zone 5)
Quercus ilex—Holly Oak, Holm Oak (zone 9)
Quercus laurifolia—Laurel Oak (zone 7)
Quercus libani—Lebanon Oak (zone 7)
Quercus palustris—Pin Oak (zone 4)
Quercus robur—English Oak (zone 5)
Quercus rubra—Red Oak (zone 3)
Quercus suber—Cork Oak (zone 7)
Quercus virginiana—Live Oak (zone 7)

Acacia seyal—Acacia, Shittim Tree

EXODUS 25:5,10,13,23,28, 26:15-16,26,32,37, 27:1,6, 30:1,5, 35:7,24 36:20,31,36, 37:1,4,10,15,25,28, 38:1,6 NUMBERS 25:1, 33:49 DEUTERONOMY 10:3 JOSHUA 2:1, 3:1 ISAIAH 41:19 MICAH 6:5

The vast majority of acacia species hail from either Africa or Australia and as a rule are not particularly frost hardy. Bible gardens in extreme climates to the north may not be able to cultivate this tree, but this genus offers quite a few ornamental varieties which make fine landscape specimens and groves elsewhere.

Suggested species:

Acacia baileyana—Bailey acacia (zone 10)
Acacia dealbata—silver wattle (zone 9)
Acacia melanoxylon—blackwood acacia (zone 10)

Pinus pinea—Italian Stone Pine

LEVITICUS 23:40 NEHEMIAH 8:15 PSALMS 74:5-6 ISAIAH 41:19, 60:13

Pines are often confused with fir trees in Scripture. It is believed that a direct reference to pine or the wood of pine trees called "thick trees" are the Italian stone pine, *Pinus pinea*, which grows to monumental proportions. Italian stone pines become massive when mature, with broad, flat-topped canopies on tall, unbranched trunks.

Although just two species of pine are mentioned here, a

Italian Stone Pine, *Pinus pinea*

garden inspired by Scripture may contain virtually any pine or true fir, depending on climate. In temperate zone gardens the frost hardiness of the tree is paramount, so locally adapted species may be more realistic than obtaining a plant more comfortable in warmer climates. These trees also provide plentiful Christmas greens, and a symmetrical individual may be planted out in front of home or church to be decorated with outdoor lights for the holidays. Don't forget the star of Bethlehem on top!

Pinus halepensis—Aleppo Pine

2 SAMUEL 6:5 1 KINGS 5:8,10, 6:34 2 KINGS 19:23 2 CHRONICLES 2:8 PSALM 104:17 SONG 1:17 ISAIAH 14:8, 37:24, 41:19, 44:14, 55:13, 60:13 EZEKIEL 27:5, 31:8 NAHUM 2:3 ZECHARIAH 11:1–2

Biblical scholars believe that the references to the fir tree in the above scriptures is really the Aleppo pine. Aleppo pines are bushy trees commonly grown in desert communities of the Western states, where they are one of the few that tolerate this harsh climate similar to that of the Holy Land. It is purely up to the garden maker whether to follow this tendency or to prefer a more strict translation, which would indicate a member of the true fir genus, *Tsuga*, as the correct choice.

Populus alba, Populus euphratica—Poplar

GENESIS 30:37 LEVITICUS 23:40, 26:36 2 SAMUEL 5:23-24 1 CHRONICLES 14:14-15 PSALM 84:6, 137:2 ISAIAH 7:2, 65:3 HOSEA 4:13

Just as there is confusion over pine and fir in Scripture, so is there difficulty separating out passages that use willow to describe poplar from those that are true willow references, as all are known to inhabit watercourses of the Holy Land. When choosing plants for the biblical garden, it's a good idea to closely review Scripture, because the references can vary from one version to the next. Among the poplars, the following suggestions will prove widely available. Many poplars today lack true species names or even varietal names, yet they make fine landscape trees. They should be planted only where the roots won't damage paving or underground utilities, though.

Suggested species:
Populus alba—White poplar (zone 3)
Populus balsamifera—Balm of Gilead (zone 2)
Populus fremontii—Fremont cottonwood (zone 7)
Populus nigra 'Italica'—Lombardy poplar (zone 3)
Populus tremuloides—Quaking aspen (zone 1)

Salix spp.—Willow

JUDGES 16:7–9 JOB 40:22 ISAIAH 15:7, 44:4
EZEKIEL 17:5 AMOS 6:14

It is important to clear up one misconception about willows in the Bible. A widely known Christian legend says that the willows of Psalm 137:2 were the ones upon which the captive Jews hung their harps as they wept for Zion. It goes on to state that the once-erect willow tree, weighted down with the harps, was so saddened that its branches hung forever after in weeping form. This was so widely believed until the last few centuries, even Linnaeus gave the weeping willow the species name *babylonica* to honor what we now know as a fictitious role in the Bible.

Unfortunately, the weeping willow, native to east Asia, never grew in Babylon or any part of Palestine, and those found in the Holy Land today are later introductions. There are over twenty species of willow native to Palestine which grow clustered along stream banks, in marshy lowland, or around water sources.

Since it is difficult for anyone but the most well-trained botanist to identify all these willows, the door is open to use any species available locally to represent the willows of the Old Testament.

Suggested species:
Salix alba—White willow (zone 2)
Salix babylonica—Babylon weeping willow (zone 6)

Salix caprea—goat willow, pussy willow (zone 4)
Salix matsudana 'Tortuosa'—corkscrew willow (zone 4)

OTHER PLANTS OF THE BIBLE

Vitis vinifera—Grape

My loved one had a vineyard
on a fertile hillside.
He dug it up and cleared it of stones
and planted it with the choicest vines.
He built a watchtower in it
and cut out a winepress as well.
Then he looked for a crop of good grapes,
but it yielded only bad fruit....
The vineyard of the LORD Almighty
is the house of Israel,
and the men of Judah
are the garden of his delight. ISAIAH 5:1–2,
5:7

"I am the true vine and my Father is the gardener. He cuts off every branch in me that bears no fruit, while every branch that does bear fruit he trims clean so that it will be even more fruitful." JOHN 15:1–2

There are more references to the vine, grape, and wine than any other food or botanical topic in the Bible. They are as frequent in the Old as in the New Testament, and to list them all would be tiresome. Rest assured that the grapevine was truly the most precious plant in Palestine besides the olive, for it was the source of the drink "which cheereth both gods and men" (Judges 9:13). This vine is the center of the most loved of Christ's parables and was the first plant to be cultivated, according to Genesis 9:20.

Grape growers of the Holy Land once allowed their vines to sprawl upon the ground or drape down slopes or rocky ledges. This plant became the central focus of life, with whole families coming into the vineyards from the countryside for the harvest. Vineyards also became a place for weary travelers to rest and camp.

Old manuscripts tell us that the east wall of

This lovely arbor with its stone columns supports a carefully pruned grapevine. Such an arrangement is ideal for outdoor ceremonies. *Rodmarton Manor, Mr. and Mrs. Simon Biddulph, Gloucestershire, England.*

the great Temple of Jerusalem was once adorned with a golden sculpture depicting a grapevine, bearing clusters of fruit made of precious stones. After the Romans conquered Jerusalem and destroyed the Temple in A.D. 70, their general, Titus Flavius Sabinus Vespasianus, seized the sculpture and carried it back to Rome.

No garden is complete without the grape arbor, where climate permits the growing of grapevines, which is all but the very far north. Virtually any of today's table or wine grape cultivars will suffice. If the local climate is too cold,

wild North American grape species transplanted into the garden are likely to do better than named varieties.

Anemone coronaria—**Anemone, Windflower**

Nehemiah 1:1 Esther 1:2 Psalms 45, 60
Matthew 6:28–30 Luke 12:27–28

You are likely to find widely differing beliefs concerning the exact plant referred to in the Gospels as the "lilies of the field" (Matthew

THE "LILIES" OF THE BIBLE

Lilies mentioned throughout the Scriptures may be one of a wide variety of flowering perennials native to the Holy Land. Using those below as well as the anemone, you can create a garden based strictly upon the theme of lilies of the Bible—a very attractive way to honor Scripture in church or home landscaping.

Hyacinth	Water lily	Fritillaria	Iris
Narcissus	Cyclamen	Ranunculus	Chamomile
Madonna lily	Tulip	Violet	True lily

Anemone coronaria 'De Caen'.

6:28). Scholars have opined it to be a species of hyacinth, the true lily, the Madonna lily, tulip, violet, cyclamen, and dozens of others. Early translators of the Bible knew of only a few local flowers and tended to use their names when translating flower names in the Bible, making it more understandable to their audience in a particular language. The most persuasive argument for the anemone is that it was plentiful in the Holy Land. Like the fig, olive, grapevine, and other plants of parable and history, the Lord would have chosen them for just this familiarity. Christ spoke to the uneducated masses, and only through the most widely known plants could he successfully weave his teachings.

Artemisia spp.—Wormwood, Sagebrush

> DEUTERONOMY 29:18 JOB 30:4
> PROVERBS 5:4 JEREMIAH 9:15,
> 23:15 LAMENTATIONS 3:15,19
> HOSEA 10:4 AMOS 5:7, 6:12
> REVELATION 8:10–11

The most significant aspect of wormwood is its very bitter taste, which is believed to be the source of "bitter gall" in the Bible. Wormwood is the source of the drink absinthe, once popular among nineteenth-century Parisians, namely artists. Most often it is used in a symbolic or

medicinal sense, for the oil can repel insects and mask offensive odors.

Arundo donax—Giant Reed

> 2 KINGS 18:21 JOB 8:11, 40:21 ISAIAH
> 19:6, 35:7, 42:3 JEREMIAH 51:32
> EZEKIEL 29:6–7, 40:3 MATTHEW 11:7

Biblical references to reeds can be to any number of semiaquatic plants, such as bulrushes, cattail, or papyrus. Since most gardens lack such habitat, the giant reed, which has naturalized all over North America, is the ideal choice. Also known as Persian reed, it is native to the Holy Land. Very tall and similar to bamboo in length and culm (stem) strength, it is easy to transplant, but this vigor also makes it somewhat invasive and best grown in a pot or a confined space.

Brassica nigra—Mustard

> MATTHEW 13:31–32, 17:20 MARK 4:31–32
> LUKE 13:19, 17:6

Biblical references to mustard occur only in the New Testament parables of Jesus. Where there is no frost to cut these plants down, they grow to treelike proportions in the Holy Land, where birds do make their nests in the sturdy branches.

Artemisia 'Abortasnum × Absinthium'—absinthe wormwood.

Arundo donax—giant reed.

Brassica nigra—mustard.

Hyssopus officinalis—Hyssop

EXODUS 12:22 LEVITICUS 14 NUMBERS 19
KINGS 4:31–33

Hebrew used hyssop sprigs to mark their doors with the blood of paschal lambs just before their exodus from Egypt. Most other references suggest hyssop was a plant of cleansing, particularly associated with purification ceremonies of Mosaic law. In the scriptures of Leviticus and Numbers, it is used to cleanse after contact with the dead or with lepers. This is related to its later medicinal value as a purgative and cathartic.

Hyssop is a mandatory plant in biblical herb gardens, but it is not used today as a culinary flavoring and thus is absent from many kitchen plots. Perhaps its ancient value as a symbolic cleansing agent may be due to its astringency and ability to cover offensive odors. In the Middle Ages, when bathing was rare, hyssop's aromatic quality merited it a place among the strewing herbs tucked into beds and spread out along corridors to mask lingering odors of daily life. It was also potent enough to use with meats that had been around a bit too long.

Myrtus communis—Myrtle

NEHEMIAH 8:15 ESTER 2:7 ISAIAH 41:19,
55:13 ZECHARIAH 1:8,10-11

Myrtle is a beautiful evergreen landscape shrub with fragrant flowers and foliage that becomes aromatic when crushed. It has long been used as a perfume, for its scent is potent and capable of masking less desirable odors.

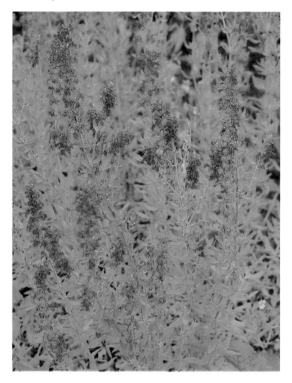

Hyssopus officinalis—hyssop.

Myrtus communis 'Variegata'—variegated myrtle.

In the scriptures, myrtle is frequently a sign of divine generosity. It is part of the celebration of the Feast of Tabernacles, commemorating the time when the children of Israel sat beneath the myrtle trees calling to widows, orphans, and strangers to dispense with sorrow and rejoice in the Lord. Since even today myrtle is used in this feast as a decoration, it would make a fine landscape plant for temple grounds, ensuring a plentiful supply of ornamental foliage. Myrtle also takes well to formal shearing and may be used as a hedge.

Triticum spp.—Wheat

The many species of wheat growing in the Holy Land during ancient times were not the only grains. There were barley and millet as well.

A Hebrew herb garden does not require much space nor much care. Here a variety of plants are clustered together at the center of a courtyard. *Villa Garden, Designed by Marianne Faulkner, Charlotte, North Carolina.*

A HEBREW GARDEN OF HERBS

Herbs were of such great value during biblical times that some were counted among the plants tithed by the Pharisees. The following, the most well known of the lot, constitute the palette for a Hebrew herbal.

Anise, Dill	*Anethum gravolens*	culinary
Coriander	*Coriandrum sativum*	culinary
Cumin	*Cuminum cyminum*	culinary
Garlic	*Allium sativum*	culinary
Hyssop	*Hyssopus officinalis*	symbolic, aromatic
Leek	*Allium porrum*	culinary
Mandrake	*Mandragora officinarum*	narcotic
Mint	*Mentha* spp.	culinary, aromatic
Mustard	*Brassica nigra*	symbolic
Onion	*Allium* spp.	culinary
Rue	*Ruta graveolens*	medicinal
Wormwood	*Artemisia* spp.	symbolic, aromatic

Despite the references to "corn," this New World plant, *Zea maize*, or Indian corn, was as yet undiscovered. The name *corn* was used to describe the grain seed itself separated from the chaff on the threshing floor, then ground by millstones into flour, both methods mentioned repeatedly. Because wheat was used in both the Old and New Testaments and was the stuff of unleavened bread—still used today in both Christian and Jewish ceremonies—it is an essential plant of the Bible garden.

Wheat is as simple to grow as grass, and you can simply buy the dried wheat used by flower arrangers and plant a crop from the seeds. Gardeners who use bale straw for mulch will find an occasional seed head, as well. Some seed houses are now offering unique wheat varieties from the dozens that are no longer cultivated because newer, more productive strains have taken their place. For example, *Triticum durum*, or black tip wheat, is highly ornamental, with white glumes, which hold the seed, and black awns, which are the spikes that stick out at the tip of the seed head. Simply plant the seed in early spring either in small bunches about the size of a sheaf, or in blocks, where the effect is more like the biblical grainfields.

GARDEN DESIGN TIPS

For the true goal of the biblical garden is not necessarily to study plants through the Bible, but to impart the teachings and values of the Bible through plants.

There are many ways to create a Bible garden, some more instructive, others symbolic and less tied to the written word. For example, a Bible garden created on church grounds to help Sunday school students better understand Scripture must have a clear link to the written word. In this case a diversity of plants, each accompanied by a symbol or an entire verse from the Bible, ensures maximum educational value. To offer such information, place small weatherproof markers beside each plant.

Another approach may be to plant the garden with biblical species in order to recreate the environment of the Holy Land, not directly linking Scripture to each and every plant. The garden may be limited to plants that symbolize a specific theme, such as peace, resurrection, or fertility. A Bible garden may be simply a small part of the churchyard dedicated to this use, or it may encompass the entire site, depending on the scale desired. The way the garden is to be used and plant choices both influence the design scheme.

Do not feel obliged to plant an entire garden, either. The prominence of trees makes it much simpler to create a special grove made up of important species. This often works well on church grounds where the grove may be planted around the turf fields used for sports, bringing these scriptural trees into the realm of soccer and baseball. They also serve a practical purpose by offering a shaded place for spectators to sit during hot summer months, at the same time providing a teaching opportunity.

Similarly, gardens may be composed of other groups of selected plants which express more specific subthemes. A Holy Land herbal garden would contain all the herbs and aromatic plants of the Hebrews. These are fundamental in the various Jewish holidays, such as the bitter herbs of Passover. Such a garden on temple grounds would make this important celebration even more poignant, educating the young in these ancient rites.

Consider a garden dedicated exclusively to the plants of the New Testament, such as those which figured largely in Christ's teaching described in the Gospels. Perhaps a garden on church grounds could be designed to produce the altar decorations which coincide with important feasts, such as Palm Sunday and Easter. Frost-hardy Bible evergreens, such as boxwood, pine, and cedar, are not only scriptural but make ideal Christmas greens for altar and sanctuary. Even the simplest approach honoring the Eucharistic mysteries can be profoundly important: just a grapevine and an annual crop of wheat would well underscore this central focus of the Christian faith, the body and blood of Christ.

BIBLICAL GARDEN DESIGNS

A Biblical Arboretum

Throughout both the Old and New Testaments, trees are the plants that most often appear. Trees are also our most powerful design element, due to their size and their ability to moderate climate. If you wish to create an educational experience as well as a functional landscape for church or temple grounds, a biblical arboretum is an ideal way to highlight the tree's importance in scripture.

An arboretum is a collection of labeled trees. Specifics concerning their origins are often included. In a biblical arboretum, labels offer not only the scriptural names of the trees, but the biblical books that hold the references for student study. In this design, the arboretum is arranged around a sports field, so that meaningful tree species will shade spectators. Only nine different types of trees are shown here, but there are many others to choose from. Best of all, an arboretum helps heal the environment in many ways.

A Hebrew Garden of Herbs

The people of Israel lived in a harsh, arid climate that discouraged the cultivation of any plant that was not useful. A plant's use was sometimes part of ritual, such as the use of hyssop sprigs to mark a doorway with blood on the night commemorating Passover, or of myrtle in the Feast of Tabernacles. Other plants, such as herbs, were so highly valued they were considered suitable as a tithe at temple.

This Hebrew garden of herbs can be laid out in a very small space, so there is minimal care required. Since these plants appear in both the Old and New Testaments, the garden should appeal to both Jewish and Christian sites. Small enough to be made in a courtyard, it can become part of the celebration at feasts and ritual gatherings.

The space is divided into two similar halves, representing the Old and New Testaments. They hinge upon a single date palm in the center, which represents eternal life in the Bible and the eternal nature of faith. There are twin paved areas, one on each side, which are connected by a series of large stepping stones so that the center may be entered on both sides. The pavements are framed by an overhead arbor

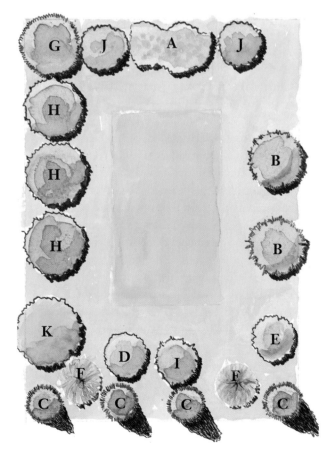

A Biblical Arboretum

A.   *Acacia melanoxylon*—Blackwood Acacia
B.   *Cedrus libani*—Cedar of Lebanon
C.   *Cupressus sempervirens*—Italian Cypress
D.   *Ficus carica*—Fig
E.   *Olea europea*—Olive
F.   *Phoenix dactylifera*—Date Palm
G.   *Pinus halepensis*—Aleppo Pine
H.   *Pinus pinea*—Italian Stone Pine
I.   *Punica granatum*—Pomegranate
J.   *Quercus ilex*—Holly Oak
K.   *Salix babylonica*—Weeping Willow

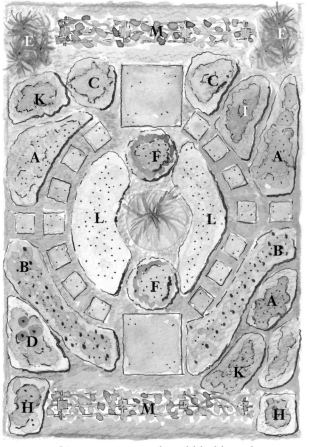

A Hebrew Garden of Herbs

A. *Allium*—Ornamental Onion
B. *Anemone coronaria*—Windflower
C. *Anethum gravolens*—Dill
D. *Artemisia*—Wormwood
E. *Arundo donax*—Giant Reed
F. *Brassica nigra*—Mustard
G. *Coriandrum sativum*—Coriander
H. *Hyssopus officinalis*—Hyssop
I. *Mentha*—Mints
J. *Phoenix dactylifera*—Date Palm
K. *Ruta graveolens*—Rue
L. *Triticum*—Wheat
M. *Vitis vinifera*—Grapevine

covered in grapevines and could hold an altar, which, if expanded, could make an ideal site for outdoor weddings. The spaces may include something more symbolic, such as tall terra cotta clay water jars to suggest the wedding at Canna, a saint's statue, or a more elaborate shrine. They are left empty here to allow you to develop ideas that are specifically suited to your church or temple. The giant reed suggests the vegetation of the Nile in the story of Moses' childhood and shows up in scenes of the Crucifixion. To emphasize this, there are two clumps of reeds, one at

each end of the grape arbor.

The plants shown present diverse forms and textures and can be easily grown. Most of all, these species are deeply rooted in scripture and present great educational opportunities. Among them are annuals, such as wheat and mustard, which must be replanted each year from seed. Grapevines can live to a great age in most climates, and where winters are too cold native grapevines may be planted instead. The planting of the mustard and wheat each year can become an educational tradition, as can the training of the grapevines.

The bulk of the planting is composed of scented herbs of the Holy Land, such as hyssop, rue, mints, and wormwood. Anemone, the proverbial lily of the field, and ornamental onion offer beautiful flowers and deep symbolism. You may want to mark each plant with a sign that indicates both its present name and the one used in scripture for immediate cross-reference.

THE WATER OF LIFE

FONS VITAE

*A*LL PRAISE BE YOURS, MY LORD, THROUGH SISTER WATER,
SO USEFUL, LOWLY, PRECIOUS AND PURE.
St. Francis of Assisi, "Canticle of Brother Sun"

here there is water, there is life. Except for fire, its elemental opposite, water is the single most powerful aspect of nature and the most essential. A human being can live for weeks without food but only a handful of days without water. Among the desert Arabs it is more precious than gold, for without it even the richest man is ensured a painful death. Water is the most miraculous gift from God, falling from the heavens, bubbling up through springs, and filling the oceans that cover well over half our globe.

The need for fresh water dictated exactly where humans could live, so it was beside water bodies that permanent settlements first appeared. Even now the Nile is the essential river of life in Egypt, and it was in the fertile valley between the Tigris and Euphrates rivers that civilization is thought to have begun.

WATER, THE LIFE GIVER

Water ensured life, and this relationship became fundamental to most early religions. In almost all of them, there are defined rites of rain making to end droughts that ravaged the land. Even before the

Springs thought to produce healing waters were usually capped off, and the water channeled into a fountain such as this to make the waters more widely available to pilgrims seeking cures. *Chalice Well, Glastonbury, England.*

The early pagan wells of Britain, into which the Celts cast their offerings to the spirits of the water, appeared much as this one. *Guillaume Pellerin Garden, Vauville, France.*

advent of agriculture, drought had such devastating effects upon wild food plants and game that entire civilizations were threatened with extinction. Thus, water became the most important commodity for peoples all over the globe, and every primitive belief system included rituals and gods that could influence the availability of water in every form.

Part of the beloved 23rd Psalm reads, "He makes me lie down in green pastures, he leads me beside quiet waters, he restores my soul." Here we see that the ancient people who resided in the dry country of the Middle East, Asia Minor, and the Mediterranean perceived green grass and pools of water as restorative symbols that applied not only to the body but to the spirit as well. It is also clear that religions of Greece and Rome believed that mythological nymphs and sprites resided in every well, spring, lake, and river. The feast of Fontinalia (the fountains) was celebrated each year by the Romans during the Ides of October to honor these mythological creatures.

To these and other ancient peoples, the fear of a well running dry was all too real, and to appease the water nymphs who controlled the ebb and flow of this precious substance, they offered gifts of all kinds. Pagan religions of Europe and Britain also gave each body of water a spirit. Among the Celts there was the unique practice of petitioning the water spirits by casting valuable gold figures into the waters. Over the centuries the value of the gifts declined, until it was reduced to pins because all metal was valuable. Today we carry on the tradition by throwing coins into wishing wells.

When the Romans conquered the tribes of Europe, they knew the Celts had been filling their sacred waters with gold and silver. Once the Romans seized the land, they auctioned off each body of water to the highest bidder, who then promptly desecrated the holy waters by gathering the accumulated offerings.

There are still examples of pagan holy wells in Britain and Europe, but they have been given Christian names, such as the Norse well of Thor renamed for St. Helen. St. Bridget widely supplanted the earth goddess of pagan religions during the early Christian era, and her name comes up repeatedly throughout early European folklore concerning holy wells.

Many wells were once dedicated to Druid

Lindisfarne Holy Well, over which an entire monastery was erected, is now in ruin. *Lindisfarne Abbey, Holy Island, England.*

gods, and an oak tree beside a spring marked the holiest of hallowed ground. It was a common custom to dip a piece of fabric in one of these holy wells in the very early morning before sunrise, then tie it to a nearby tree as an offering. Roman chronicles tell of finding many such trees, draped in abundance with the accumulated gifts, creating an eerie scene, which no doubt left many centurions ill at ease. Some believe that the decoration of Christmas trees can be traced back to such practices. But the link between trees and water in this act is clear, a logical practice among people who believed their gods resided in both the oaks and the waters.

When Christianity first crept across pagan Europe, there came the inevitable struggle of the church to replace the old ways. The result was often a strange mingling of faiths. The Catholic use of holy water, or ceremonial water blessed for certain occasions, evolved out of reverence for magical holy wells—the early church wisely adopting some of the ancient customs in order to overlay the new faith upon the old. Today holy water supplies are blessed each year during the Easter Vigil mass to be used in the coming baptisms, marriages, and funerals.

We find similar relationships of wells to healing and saints throughout Britain. St. Augustine's Well at Cerne, in Dorset, is one. Its legend states that after a long journey through the countryside, Augustine grew thirsty but found no water to drink. Discouraged, he pressed his staff into the earth at his feet, and suddenly the water began to flow. Folktale explains that St. Milburga's horse struck a stone with its foot and caused water to flow, and there she founded Wenlock Abbey. The water continued to flow even in dry weather and was thought to have the ability to heal diseases of the eyes. In Yorkshire St. Chad, abbot of a monastery, is linked to a number of wells. The most notable of these is at Lichfield, where in the seventh century he did penance by praying for hours on end while standing naked in the icy water. This well became the favorite of medieval pilgrims seeking healing. After the Reformation, when the links to saints fell out of favor, a health spa was built, and

Spring water is piped into this beautiful pool. *Kerdalo, Prince Wolkonsky, Traguier, France.*

later the mineral salts in the water were believed to be the source of benefit, not St. Chad.

A more contemporary example of magical springs is found in the story of Lourdes, a town in France where in 1858 a poor, uneducated girl, Bernadette Soubrious, saw a vision of the Virgin Mary in a grotto called Massabielle. There were many apparitions visible only to Bernadette, but the people still did not believe that the girl had seen anything supernatural. Then on the ninth apparition, the Virgin commanded Bernadette to dig in the dry dirt floor of the grotto. After she groveled in what had become damp mud and rubbed it on her face, the crowd grew disappointed and thought she'd lost her mind. Then a stream of water began to flow out of the ground, down the hill to the river, and today that same spring produces 30,000 gallons of water a day.

The people became convinced that the vision was indeed an act of God, and many miraculous cures have been attributed to that holy spring. Today Lourdes is a bustling center of pilgrims who travel from all over the globe to touch the waters that might heal their afflictions, just as pagan believers once traveled long distances to touch the water at St. Winifred's Well in Wales. For those who cannot travel, Lourdes water is bottled at the spring and sent to the sick worldwide.

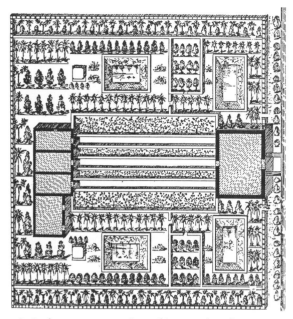

A single square reservoir pool is central to this
Egyptian home orchard.

The River of Life

Who makes the herb for cattle
And the fruit tree for mankind,
He gives life to the fish of the river
And to the birds under the heaven.

EGYPTIAN PAPYRUS

Egypt, the haunt of pharaohs and eternal land of
the Nile, was like no other civilization before or
since. Here was an entire culture which based
every aspect of life upon the ebb and flow of the
great river, the year organized into a cyclical calendar of flooding that governed agriculture, religion, and death. The Nile could also wreak
havoc when it flooded too deeply or when it did
not flood enough.

Since the wealth of Egypt was linked to the
abundance of its fertile floodplain fields, the
behavior of the water became the work of Hapi,
god of the Nile. This god is always depicted in
the colors of green and blue to match the flood-
waters. He was continually offered sacrifices and
gifts by the Egyptians in order to appease his
fickle nature. He was also associated with fertility, which depended upon the silt deposits after
flooding. To encourage this renewing layer of

earth, the ancients threw all sorts of offerings
into the water—from amulets to female fertility
statues, food, and drink. Casting gifts into the
water was shared later by the Celts, the Maya,
and many other peoples who also saw water as
the most essential part of life. It was believed
that Hapi was responsible for the moist dew that
came down onto Egyptian gardens at night, for it
was the god's divine sweat that made the flowers
glisten in the morning sun.

Thus, water, land, and religion became a
vital triad fueling the great civilization. The Nile
provided a food supply unlike any other place in
the Middle East or northern Africa. Egyptians
clung to the verdant strips that divided the vast
desert into two banks of the River Nile, and
from that situation grew an advanced knowledge
of the cosmos.

It is not difficult to understand why a people who lived amidst an endless desert coveted
plants and flowers. These green, growing things
soothe the eye, cool and scent the air, and generally compensate for the dry, dusty conditions that
are typical of all this nation, except along the
river, where there is water. When entertaining
guests an Egyptian host would serve fragrant
flowers as we do fine wine, but not for drink: to
enjoy for their beauty and sweet scent. We find
examples of this love for flowers in the hieroglyphics on the walls of their temples and tombs,
where the spiritual symbolism is all too clear.

To the Egyptian, who had neither forests
nor cool meadows in which to enjoy nature, the
pleasure garden, totally separate from agriculture, became the sole expression of his affinity
for the landscape. The home of a wealthy
Egyptian was usually located near the river and
composed of a house attached to a much larger
vineyard and garden. Private homes were quite
modest in size and design compared to the massive royal gardens, but all were protected by
walls from the sandblast of hot desert winds.
Such a garden illustrates why the Persians and
King Solomon saw paradise as a walled garden
where conditions were much more pleasant than
inside stuffy buildings beneath a merciless desert
sun. We know today that the concept of the heat
island, which occurs in modern cities during

summer, was at work in Egypt, as well. Masonry walls, bare earth, and sand combined to create high temperatures, which lingered unabated even at night.

Just as the shade of street trees cast upon paving can reduce this accumulation of heat from reflective surfaces, so did the plants of these gardens make the entire area cooler. This was more than mere shading; it was the respiration of plants which humidified the dry air and thus could modify climate. It's strange how we rediscover these old ways known thousands of years ago in Thebes, claiming our revelations as "new techniques in environmental engineering." Pharaohs long before the time of Christ were planting their cities with trees to achieve this same effect on a communitywide scale.

The proximity to the river ensured that the water table was high enough to charge the rectangular pool that was an essential part of the residential garden. It provided not only visual beauty but a water source with which to irrigate the plants. The pool was stocked with colorful fish, and in it grew lilies of all sorts and papyrus reeds. The Pharaohs also built great pools surrounding their palaces, and Amenhotep III had a great body of still water measuring one and a half kilometers long and over three hundred meters wide (about 5,000 by 1,000 feet). Imagine the fantastic reflections seen in its mirrored surface of the surrounding gardens and temples in all their gilded, colorful majesty. Such appreciation is expressed in an inscription on many eighteenth-dynasty tombs, which shows that even in the underworld the dead pharaoh sought the refreshment of water:

> That I may each day walk continuously
>   on the banks of my water,
> That my soul may repose on the branch-
>   es of the trees that I have planted,
> That I may refresh myself under the
>   shadow of my sycamore.

Just as we today lounge around swimming pools in our leisure hours, so did the Egyptian spend his time enjoying this cooling water. He and his family found tranquillity in all bodies of water, both natural and ornamental. Without tanks and pools, there would be no garden. In the residences along the Nile, we find more than anywhere else the great power that water has to modify the environment to provide a better quality of life. There lies a great truth: in civilizations where food is abundant, there is time to investigate matters of the spirit. Although the Nile was unpredictable, it made the ancient Egyptians rich and powerful compared to their seminomadic neighbors in the surrounding barren lands.

The Rivers of Paradise

The water-centered Egyptian garden eventually spread into nearby kingdoms. An example of this

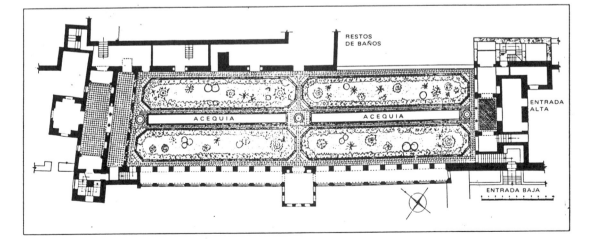

This plan of an historic Moorish garden at the Alhambra in Granada, Spain, shows the four-quadrant layout so fundamental to the Islamic vision of paradise. It also depicts the traditional narrow canals, used to water plants.

Jeanne Lee Garden, Baton Rouge, Louisiana.

adaptation were the Hanging Gardens of Babylon built by King Nebuchadnezzar in 605 B.C. His Persian wife had grown homesick for the beautiful gardens of her homeland—elaborate gardens connected to the Zoroastrian religion. To appease her Nebuchadnezzar built a great terraced garden, using massive retaining walls, columns, and arches. These were not just plain terraces, but a labyrinth of underground wells and mechanical pumps watered the plants, following the traditions of the Persian garden. Earth was hauled up and deposited in great masonry cavities large enough to contain shade and fruit trees. Upon these beds were grown plants of every kind, shading and spilling down the walls in a riot of color.

The Persian garden later evolved into the Islam vision of a heavenly paradise, as described in the Koran. For any people originating in the dry Middle Eastern deserts, the chief feature of paradise was and is always water. Without it there would be only wasteland, so images of Eden or Paradise gleaned from the Koran were always connected with water.

When the Muslims invaded Persia in A.D. 637, they found an immense network of underground canals that irrigated this arid land. It is logical that most of these irrigation systems were geometric in design for greater efficiency, and trees planted along these lines lent a decidedly formal, geometric character to individual gar-

dens. The basic layout was composed of a central pool that fed canals flowing in four directions to water the entire garden. This happened to correspond to the rivers of Paradise described in the Koran. The Islamic universe was divided into eight sections, which fit perfectly into the four quadrants of the Persian garden. Where the Egyptians utilized the reflection pool to its greatest advantage, the Muslims added engineering that spouted water into the air in concentrated streams, where it would maximize the sound of water and cool the air.

Classical Gardens

The Greeks were inspired by the gardens of Egypt and Babylon, and with their endless mythology they proved their deep love and respect for nature. From Greek legends we obtain a surprising number of plant names. For example, *crocus, cypress, iris, hyacinth, myrtle,* and *narcissus* are all rooted in the names and legends of Greek gods.

Before the great temples Greeks worshipped their gods out in the open, beneath the spreading canopies of natural tree groves. When they began to build stone temples, the trees already growing there became linked to the gods through mythology. One of the first temples to Apollo was built at a grove of laurel trees where he had long been worshipped, and the myths say the first crown of laurels was bequeathed by Apollo to all victors of Greece. Hence came the title *baccalaureate*, which means "laurel berries." Eventually the connection to tree groves disappeared, and temples were built wherever the elect deemed they were needed or appropriate.

The Greeks retained their love of nature in a land where winters were mild and summers warm and dry. Plato built his Academy near Athens, and the classrooms were *al fresco*, shaded by avenues of plane trees, *Platanus occidentalis*, the favorite of Greece. Among the pavements, trees, and statues of the gods, teachers and their pupils walked the paths sharing knowledge. Growing into the greatest complex of learning in classical times, the Academy included various types of indoor-outdoor gardenlike spaces.

Other school layouts gave rise to the three

concepts that made up later gardens and components of the Roman home: the tree-covered avenues of the Lyceum of the Peripatetics (school of the wanderers), the Portico of the Stoics, which was an avenue of columns covered with a roof but open on the sides, and the Garden of the Epicureans, which was more like a traditional courtyard.

As the power of Athens faded, mighty Rome grew into a massive warrior empire. As students of Greek learning, Romans adopted the building elements of the Greeks, their porticos and courtyards essential to comfortable living. We see for the first time a formula for garden spaces in the typical Roman house, which were built throughout Europe, Britain, northern Africa, Asia Minor—wherever Roman legions conquered peoples who were to be governed by the empire's administrators.

Like the Egyptian garden, the Roman house turned its back on the street or desert and focused its living space inward. Often the house was a single row of rooms surrounding an open courtyard at the center. This made sense for those living amidst hostile cultures resentful of Roman taxation and savage retribution. Thus, the rooms of the house became like a fortress protecting those who lived inside while they could still enjoy the sunshine and fresh air.

The Roman house was frequently set upon a site where a well or spring already existed. If no such spring or well could be found, Roman engineering ensured that a small aqueduct was constructed to bring water to the household, where it bubbled up into a simple pool or fountain. This water source became the focus of the central courtyard, where daily life occurred, and with the Romans this frequently included bathing, unlike many other cultures of the time. With such fastidious concern for hygiene, these people appreciated the fragrances of plants, particularly those which contained aromatic oils and were pungently scented. In the open courtyard the plantings were laid out in geometric patterns much like those on the mosaic floors so often found in Roman ruins. Among the most common aromatic plants depicted were rosemary, lavender, laurel, and myrtle.

Stone grottoes and other ruins are often found at sites of springs. The Romans found spring water ideal for their ablutions. *Kerdalo, Prince Wolkonsky, Traguier, France.*

Amidst this garden the family honored its favorite household or family gods, known as Lares, in small shrines and altars called *lararia*. Upon these altars offerings could be made daily or on the many special feast days of the Roman calendar. The Lar representing Venus was the most common as she was the Roman protector goddess of the garden, who was later replaced by the Madonna in Christian Rome. To a lesser extent Flora, goddess of vegetation, was also represented, as was Diana, goddess of the moon, tree groves, and farm crops. Strangely, the majority of household gods were female, which suggests that in the Roman mind there was an important link between life and women and the garden. There were a few male Lares, usually Dionysus or Bacchus—both gods of the grape— plus less commonly Hercules and Mars.

Isis, ancient mother and creator in Egyptian mythology, was often added to the Roman garden *lararia* as a symbol of fertility, which in dry climates could not be separated from water. Thus, it was Isis who became the goddess of the water source, either natural or manmade, in Roman homes, bringing the assurance of life in all its forms. These lararium idols were so precious that when the people fled the city of Pompeii as Vesuvius erupted, they took many of them with them.

Wherever the Romans went with their knowledge of irrigation, gardens appeared not only in the home courtyard, but all over the countryside in fields and orchards. This culture's love of vegetable foods ensured good health. The legions ranged far and wide creating colonies for Rome, collected new plants that bore crops and provided medicinals so well described by the famous doctor, Pliny the Elder. We may credit the Romans not only for discovering new plants, but also for their network of roads and trading arteries, which brought the plants back to be propagated.

We know the Romans cultivated flowers, including pot marigolds, narcissus, snapdragon, lilies, hyacinth, violets, pansies, and poppies. From the Far East wild roses were gathered, particularly those species which contained aromatic oils in the foliage, not just the flowers. These old species were so pungent they were cultivated and harvested for the oil, known as attar of rose, the fundamental scent of the perfume trade. The Romans also grew in abundance the pomegranate, lemon, apricots, oranges, plus a wide variety of grains and legumes.

WATER THE CLEANSER

The Spirit of God was hovering over the waters.

GENESIS 1:2

Water is the consummate symbol of cleansing, purification, and healing. It figured largely in the religions of the past and is still widely used today. In Greek, Roman, and Persian religions, there are frequent references to sacred water sources and their remarkable abilities to heal the sick and wash away the stain of death after battle. Among Jews, ritual cleansing before meals and other practices are still observed today, and the Pool of Siloam outside Jerusalem remains sacred for its unique healing abilities.

The origins of baptism are also found in the Jewish faith. At the Jordan River baptisms were performed as rituals of forgiveness and rebirth. There in the Jordan Jesus was baptized by St. John the Baptist in the traditional Hebrew rite. With the advent of Christianity came a new appreciation for baptism, which takes on various forms, depending on the church. There also arose some unusual practices, perhaps lingering vestiges of old pagan spring fertility water rites combined with Christian ritual, that are still practiced in eastern European countries. In most cases, they boil down to the essential themes of cleansing, renewal, and healing.

For many, on Easter Day all running water is especially blessed. This is because the Risen Lord sanctified all life-giving elements on that day, bestowing upon them special powers. In French Canada, Old World Catholics go out to the countryside and wash in the rivers and streams made temporarily sacred on Easter. They also bottle up the water, which is believed to retain its healing ability throughout the following year. The Irish, who also believe in this Easter water rite, once kept samples to use against witches and evil spirits. Similarly, after Easter on Trinity Sunday, all hoped for rain. This "Trinity rain" was thought to ensure health and fertility and make magic flowers blossom at midnight.

A related belief widespread in medieval times said that the water in wells and fountains was equally blessed on Christmas Eve. St. Gregory of Tours, in his book *Libri Miraculorum* (*Book of Miracles*, A.D. 594) told of a miracle related to Christmas at the Well of the Magi outside Bethlehem. The locals gathered there during Christmas week and bent over the opening of the well, covering themselves and the opening with thick blankets to block out the sunlight. Then they peered down into the dark well. According to legend the Star of Bethlehem would be seen moving slowly across the water— but only by the pure of heart.

Water has always played an important role in Western spirituality. It can be considered the haunt of pagan spirits, or be blessed and thus holy, or simply recognized as a force of the earth. Perhaps the water is there to remind you that it is indeed the most fundamental element of life, thus playing a vital role in every garden.

Tierra Bendita, The Blessed Earth

From the earth I was made,
And the earth shall eat me;
The earth has sustained me,
And at last the earth I shall be also.

OLD CATHOLIC MISSION HYMN

There are many examples of healing springs in
the New World which were recognized by the
pre-Columbian civilizations. Some are no longer
water bearing, but the people cling to their faith.
It is believed that these dry springs remain hallowed ground and the mere grains of soil contain
the ability to cause miracles of healing.

In sixteenth-century Mexico the Maya were
known to make pilgrimages to sulfur springs outside the town of Esquípulas in times of illness.
There they drank the water and ate the earth—as
well as made offerings and sacrifices to the gods
of the springs. Catholic missionaries viewed the
site an opportune place to show how baptism
with water was as mystical as the powerful gods
of the springs. In 1578 a church was built, and
local peoples were converted. Just as the Maya
had once offered silver effigies to the spring gods,
the newly Christian community pooled their
resources and bought a crucifix for the church.
Carved of orange wood and inlaid with silver, it
was named the Black Christ, *El Cristo Negro de
Esquípulas*. The crucifix was credited with miraculous healing, just as were the sulfur springs.

Even though the sulfur springs eventually
dried up, people still came to eat of that earth, a
practice which is not uncommon and is attributed to benefits derived from minerals in soil.
Aztecs had long consumed meals coated with
muck from the lake bottoms which surrounded
Mexico City as part of their religious rites, which
probably freed them from the effects of mineral
deficiency. Even now pilgrims make the long
journey to the springs, wearing handwoven straw
hats with wide brims to protect them from the
sun. When returning, they trim their hats with
wreaths of Spanish moss and yellow fruit from
the gourd family called *chichitas*. This announces
to anyone they meet that the pilgrims had ful-
filled their vows to visit the shrine of the Black
Christ.

True lotus plants can be distinguished by their round
leaves borne well above the water level. Their foliage
makes them attractive even when they are not in
flower.

THE ETERNAL FLOWER

The priests of ancient Egypt as far back as 2000
B.C. were buried amidst a shower of fresh lotus
flowers. When Egyptologists opened the sar-
cophagus of the Ramses II, they found a wreath
of lotus petals laid around the mummy's neck. In
other Egyptian burials the entire bodies of the
deceased have been literally covered with several
layers of this stunning flower of the Nile.

These flowers are found among the
Egyptian dead for purely symbolic beliefs of
death and rebirth and immortality. An Egyptian
creation myth describes the lotus flower as rising
up out of the primordial night with its petals
tightly closed. There appeared a strong light
inside the flower, which gently pushed the petals
apart to allow the first sun to rise into the sky.

This symbolism is closely linked to the
remarkable ability of the lotus to withstand the
seasonal rise and fall of the Nile. When waters
recede after the annual flood, the plants wither,
then become dormant, their life sequestered in
the edible fleshy root. Seed also remains viable,

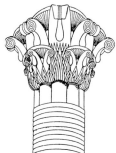

These capitals on columns in Egyptian temples illustrate the direct architectural inspiration derived from the lotus plant. It also became the model for the Roman Ionic capital.

waiting in the earth for hundreds of years until conditions are right for germination. When waters begin to rise again, the lotus quickly sprouts from the muck of the river bed in an almost supernatural resurrection and grows into a stunning flower. Add the fact that the root and seed were valuable food sources, and it's easy to see why ancient people from Asia to Europe saw this flower as a powerful symbol.

Lotus flowers and their unique large seed pods appear in architectural ornament and provided the direct inspiration for the Ionic capital depicted in Egyptian papyri. These ancient peoples cultivated three species: one that

Nelumbo nucifera 'Maggie Bell Slocum' is one of the many new lotus cultivars which offer flowers with far more petals than the original species. The unusual cone at the flower's center is the ovary; it will enlarge to many times this size as it matures.

flowered blue, another white, and, the most sacred of all, the red flowering rose lily of the Nile, or "sacred bean." To honor a guest the Egyptian host would wind the flower's long stem around the guest's head so the bud hung down upon the forehead, close to the nose, where its fragrance was most appreciated.

The plant was always used to crown the Egyptian god Osiris, lord of the underworld and ruler of the dead. After being murdered by another god, Set, Osiris rose from the dead wearing water lilies or lotus, flowers of the morning, and this rebirth was linked to the rising sun. This led all pharaohs to wear a wreath of such flowers to symbolize their own immortality. Another god of the Egyptians, Horus, is often seen sitting on a lotus.

Greeks too had a passion for the lotus. One myth tells of a beautiful nymph who was deserted by Hercules and so threw herself into the Nile, where her body was transformed into a pure white lotus flower. In the *Odyssey* Homer describes a nation that lived entirely upon lotus, which left them in an intoxicated, dreamy state. The true diet of the lotus eaters is subject to debate since the lotus did not grow in Greece at that time.

Lotus figures largely in the Buddhist and Hindu faiths, as well. To Buddhists lotus symbolizes man, with his head held high above the water in sunlight, while his roots are buried in the murky world of experience. The lotus flower is also considered a symbol of India. The nation is represented by the immature seed pod at the center, which is surrounded by petals, the neighboring cultures.

Lotus accommodates winter frost by sending its rootstock deep into mud, where it is insulated from the cold. This is ideal for large natural ponds but not in contained water gardens. Since plants grown in submerged containers of soil are portable, they can be lifted from the pond and kept moist at about 40 degrees for the winter, when they will die back naturally, just as they do when the Nile recedes. There is much confusion between the true lotus and the water lily. They are two distinctly different aquatic plants. The genus of the lotus, the taller plant of the two, is *Nelumbo*, while the genus of the lower growing water lily is *Nymphaea*.

The lotus can grow very large, with leaves reaching up to two feet across. It is ideal for naturalizing, but only dwarf lotus varieties are suitable for small pools. The stems average about five feet long on standard species, much less for dwarfs. The flowers rise far above the water to bloom for just three days, unlike standard water lilies, which bloom very close to the cluster of leaves. Lotus tubers can be purchased by mail from most water garden suppliers, and there are dozens of cultivars to choose from in a wide variety of colors.

Lily of the Waters

The genus name for the true water lily, *Nymphaea*, is rooted in the Latin, *Nymphe*, the mythological beings which the Romans believed haunted every body of water. Among the many strains of water lily are both day-blooming and night-blooming varieties, the latter making striking additions to moon gardens. Day-blooming lilies were thought by the Egyptians to close their flowers and disappear beneath the surface of the water until the next morning, when they would rise again and open. This was of great interest to these great tomb builders, who linked this mechanism to the powers of the morning star.

These clusters of water lilies in bloom illustrate just how shallow the water level can be and still support floating plants. *Butchart Gardens, Victoria, British Columbia, Canada.*

The many species of water lily are native to almost every continent, and the water lily appears in many legends worldwide for the same reason as the lotus. The European species was honored by St. Peter, who legend had waiting at the golden gates of heaven to judge souls. This legend suggested that all flowers have souls, which was probably a holdover from the pagan belief that all plants contained spirits. The story describes the water lily as having no fragrance at all, which rendered it pure and sinless, thus suitable for landscaping the gates of Paradise. While there the water lily became the judge of all flowers, deciding which ones would be allowed to enter heaven. To do so she asks just one question, "What use did you make of your God-given scent while on earth?" If she judges the flower worthy, it enters heaven to bloom on forever, while a wasteful flower must return to earth. There it would be transformed into ripening seeds, which show how forgiving the water lily was, for these would sprout into new plants, giving the flower a second chance to enter Paradise.

Native Americans revered the yellow lotus, which is native to the temperate states. The

CHRISTIAN FISH

Besides the crucifix, the simple drawing of the fish is most often used to symbolize Christianity. This is a remnant of the early church, when Roman persecution forced the people underground. This was both literal and figurative, as they held most functions in the catacombs, the subterranean burial tombs of the Romans. The figure of the fish was simple, and in it were written five Greek letters. Each letter represented a word to express the fundamental belief of Christianity, that Christ was the son of God.

I = Jesus	X = Christ	O = of God	Y = Son	C = Savior

In using water in the symbolic garden, those wishing to evoke thoughts of Christ may find that fish in a pool serve as a living reminder. The fish also represents baptism because the church saw this act of initiation and cleansing of original sin as being as essential to human life as water is to the survival of a fish. Not only are fish soothing to watch, be they in an aquarium, fish tank, or koi pond, but their fluid motion is conducive to peaceful thoughts, meditation and prayer.

Dakotas called it *tewape* and relished the fleshy tubers roasted in an open fire. Their legend says that in the Red Strawberry Moon, which falls in the month of June, an old chief was sleeping outside his tepee. He dreamed that a Star-maiden stood beside him asking for counsel, explaining that she was tired of holding her torch in the sky every night and wanted to come to earth and live among the Dakotas. Since she could not become a mortal, she asked the old man what form would be best for her.

Before he could answer her, the old chief woke up to find an unusually bright, golden star hovering above a distant hilltop. The chief consulted his shaman, the Wise One, about his problem and was told to sleep on it. In his dreams the Star-maiden came again, asking the same question, "What form should I take?"

This time the chief woke up to see another bright star in a treetop, which then drifted over to rest on the lodgepole of his tepee. This awakened the chief's son, who came running out to find the source of such bright light. The chief, not sure what to do, said, "Son, paddle down the river and fetch the Wise One; he should see this."

As the boy ran to his canoe, the star fol-lowed him and rested on the bow, lighting his way. The boy was very excited and paddled as hard as he could, but he failed to see a nearly submerged log lurking in the dark waters. He hit it so hard the canoe tipped over and dumped the boy and his star into the water, where they both vanished beneath the surface. There was nothing left in the morning except a golden yellow water lily floating on the still waters, for the Star-maiden had finally found her form. It's interesting to note that other Native American tribes have legends to explain the presence of the water lily. Strangely enough, most involve stars which turn into the flowers.

While the lotus is available in only a few colors, water lilies have been bred into a veritable rainbow of blossoms. They provide a much more varied water garden scheme than the lotus but do not bear the large ornamental seed pods. Water lilies can be very hardy, since some are native to the temperate zone. There's another large group of tropicals, including the giant nocturnal Amazon water lily, *Victoria cruziana*. The pads or leaves of this species are large enough to support up to 150 pounds, and the highly scented white flowers are the size of a dinner plate.

The Egyptian Paper Rush

Clustered in the shallow waters on the edges of the Nile, the reed known as papyrus once came to represent Egypt just as the palm was the symbol of Israel. In both cases, it was because the plant provided so much to a desert people that it could never be separated from the culture.

Papyrus gave Egypt a unique surface upon which to depict their sacred writings. This reed was stripped and pressed into the first official paper in the West. Upon it was painted the spiritual life of this civilization through sacred hieroglyphics, which have survived well over two millenniums with their beauty and message intact. Some of the early manuscripts of the Bible were written in various languages on either papyrus paper or parchment made of very thin animal hides. Surely some portions of the New Testament were first written on papyrus, and other ancient papyrus texts are still being discovered in the caves around the Dead Sea.

> When she saw that he was a fine child, she hid him for three months. But when she could hide him no longer, she got a papyrus basket for him and coated it with tar and pitch. Then she placed the child in it and put it among the reeds along the bank of the Nile.
>
> EXODUS 2:2–3

It's probably the story of Moses which gives us the greatest insight into the value of this plant in the history of the Hebrew nation. Moses' mother kept him from being murdered by Pharaoh by giving him up in a basket of papyrus, which we know is already resistant to decomposition in the water, but which she made even stronger by a coating of pitch. "The reeds along the bank of the Nile" were primarily papyrus as well, but most of these have disappeared since the completion of the dam at Aswan, which reduced flooding on the Nile and limited the plant's wetland habitat.

Papyrus grows much like cattails and tules, but it is not frost hardy and so cannot grow too far north. Avid water gardeners find its tall, graceful stalks and fluffy heads most graceful, but they die off with the onset of winter. Come spring, papyrus puts on a powerful growth spurt, reaching six to eight feet in a single season. Some people grow them in tubs which can be brought indoors for the winter. Papyrus has the same impact on a water garden as the lotus; it is the epitome of the Nile, a glimpse back at the ancients and their insatiable quest for immortality.

This tiny pool supports the three most beautiful and traditional semiaquatic plants of the ancients: lotus, water lily, and papyrus. *Beverly Stidham Garden, Columbia, South Carolina.*

The *Fleur de Lis*

The iris is truly a plant of the margin, growing in both water and upon dry land. This characteristic evolved to adapt to the rise and fall of water over the seasons, and colonies of irises are commonly found along the edges of streams, ponds, and lakes.

Like all irises, the common yellow flag bears a flower with three distinct parts. This

The lavender flowers of *Iris engata*, an iris which prefers the shallow margins of this pond. *The Coster Garden, Designed by Connie Cross, Cutchogue, New York.*

During a military campaign Clovis and his army became trapped at the Rhine River at Strasbourg in the midst of a heated battle with the Alemanni, a pagan Germanic tribe. Clovis and his men were hopelessly outnumbered, with no choice but to be defeated or flee across the river, taking their losses in drowned men. In a final desperate act, he resorted to praying to his wife's Christian God for the first time. While doing so his eye rested upon the yellow flag, *Iris pseudacorus*, which was growing far out into the waters of the Rhine. This revelation proved that the river was probably shallow enough to ford, and in doing so, his army escaped to safety.

Clovis returned home and was promptly baptized by St. Remigius. While praying later with his wife in a private chapel, an angel appeared to them and laid at his feet a blue banner embroidered with three irises. This experience so inspired Clovis that he redesigned his coat of arms by replacing his three toads with

triad has appealed to many faiths, which see this number as symbolic. The ancient Egyptians took them to be faith, valor, and wisdom and placed an iris at the end of the royal scepter and upon the forehead of the Sphinx. In ancient Greece the goddess Iris was believed to be in every rainbow or colorful prism of refracted light, so this flower, with its many different hues, was named after her. Irises were often planted beside graves because this goddess also guided souls after death.

The magic iris also became a part of Christian images, although its only link is the tale of the conversion of Clovis. The tale dates back to about A.D. 500 and the Franks, who lived in what is today northern France. Their leader, the famous Clovis, King of the Franks, was married to a Christian woman, the Princess Clotilda. Daily she prayed for his conversion, but to no avail.

The wild iris of Europe, *Iris pseudoacorus*, just as King Clovis saw it pointing to the salvation of his army.

three iris blossoms, representing faith, wisdom, and valor. After Clovis took up the iris, he was never again defeated in battle. Coincidentally, just a few years later, the Empress Theodora, the wife of the Byzantine emperor Justinian, added the iris flower to her official crown, as well.

The iris flower appeared hundreds of years later in 1137 during the Crusades. Louis VII dreamed of an angel, who reminded him of the benefits King Clovis received after adopting the iris as his symbol. Taking it on himself, Louis and his armies left France under long banners studded with many irises, each symbolizing the Holy Trinity. The name of such a symbol was first *fleur de Louis*, "flower of Louis," but evolved into *fleur de luce*, "flower of light." The *fleur de lis* we know today is still seen in the French national coat of arms, dating from the twelfth century, as gold symbols arranged upon a royal blue field. Later it became a part of various European heraldries. The name *flag* evolved from the frequent depiction of the *fleur de lis* on medieval heraldic flags and banners.

A charming medieval tale adds to the iris folklore. In it, a knight who had led a wicked life suddenly changed his ways after experiencing a holy vision. He went to a monastery and begged the monks to allow him to join the community, but no matter how hard he tried to remember their voluminous prayers, he recalled only two words, "Ave Maria." It was these two words that he prayed continually until his death. The monks buried him in their monastery garden and carved the two words on the knight's headstone. The morning after the burial, the monks found a tall plant growing upon the

grave, each of its blossoms marked with those two words of the knight's pitiful prayer, "Ave Maria." Intrigued, the monks dug up the grave and found that the body had disappeared. They then realized it had been transformed into the flower.

There is a unique link between this story and the spread of Islam. The Muslims believed that the dead appreciated a sweet perfume. Because the root of the iris bears a pleasing fragrance, they planted the flower in their graveyards. In doing this the Moors helped to spread the Florentine iris throughout the Mediterranean region.

The yellow flag can be found in many early paintings of the Virgin Mary and was dedicated to her. The word *iris* is thought to have once meant sword lily, probably inspired by the bladed foliage, symbolizing the pain Mary felt during the crucifixion.

The kingdom of the iris includes many different species from around the globe. Among them are those native to the very dry soils of arid California and others which thrive in the wet southern bayous. The iris species planted around water gardens are considered "marginals," the amphibians of the plant world, because they will remain growing, unlike the lotus, as waters recede during the dry season. Our gardens need not be limited to the yellow flag, for many other marginal iris species offer brilliant flower colors. When grown in clusters, Kaempferi hybrids are known as "butterfly irises" because their lovely blossoms suggest a flock of butterflies alighting on the plants.

Florentine iris.

The Willow

Since ancient times the family of willows, which consists of over four hundred species, has come to represent the tenacity of life. They are hydric wetland trees, uniquely adapted to inundation by flood waters during the growing season, a condition that denies oxygen to the root zone for long periods. Without root-zone oxygen most

Water in the garden need not support plants or fish and may be far more easy to maintain without them. Here, natural changes in grade are used to create the many steps of this waterfall, which eventually reaches the double pool. *Chalice Well, Glastonbury, England.*

plants quickly die, but the willows have the ability to alter their photosynthetic process, obtaining oxygen not from the roots but through the leaves. Willows are a bold advertisement that there is groundwater close to the surface, and in the dry season they are often the only green plants for miles. They line the banks of streams and rivers, playing a critical role in bank stabilization.

Early people saw another facet of the willow that proved its tenacity. This plant could be cut back drastically, sometimes to a tiny stump, and yet spring forth again with rampant, whip-like growth. The flexible nature of its wood allowed willow to be used for a variety of purposes, from wattle fencing to basket making. When healing was still closely tied with religious beliefs, the pain-relieving ability of willow bark made it a common element in early medicine. At some point the willow became associated with witchcraft, where it was the preferred material for magic wands. A lesser known common name, tree of Enchantment, attests to this fact, and many believed it was used as the binding for witch's brooms. Today practitioners of these ancient arts tie a knot in a willow whip when casting spells, and once the magic takes effect, the knot is then undone.

The combination of tenacity, flexibility, and the ability to renew itself even after the entire plant is devastated made it an important symbol of the Gospels of Christ. For the New Testament survived, just as does the willow, no matter how much is cut away, suggesting that the martyrdom of many saints failed to suppress the Gospels. The weeping willow has appeared often in fine art, where it also symbolizes the tears shed for those who have passed away, and it became a popular graveyard motif in the eighteenth and nineteenth centuries.

SYMBOLIC WATER IN THE GARDEN

Not all uses of water in the garden are like the reflection pools of the Egyptians, though any water does mirror skies and flowers, making the visual image of the garden seem that much larger. This same reflective surface brings to our eye an appreciation for weather conditions in various seasons as its surface is rippled by the wind, is speckled with raindrops, or darkens to black with an impending storm.

There are many ways to add water into the garden, and not all include aquatic plants and fish. Some people don't want the maintenance chores of a true water garden but enjoy the sound of falling water or its reflective quality. Pools and fountains with circulating electric pumps are ideal, and in the heat, when algae blooms are more common, you can simply add a little bit of chlorine, and the problem disappears.

For examples of styles, look to the reflection pools found in Moorish architecture. These troughs so common in the old palaces of Spain are similar to today's popular lap pools, which are also narrow but long. If the bottom is finished with black plaster, this increases the reflective quality of any swimming pool and adds drama.

More ideas come from Spanish tier or wall fountains, which maximize the visual and sound quality of very small amounts of water. Above all, the water feature must blend with its surroundings in order for the overall garden to reflect a well thought-out and integrated scheme.

The formal pool provides the most striking environment for water lilies and other aquatic plants, but the free-form rock edge can be just as beautiful. In many ways it reflects the holy wells of the Celts, where nature is the theme. Even a half a wine barrel can be made into a fine garden. Such a small-space alternative is most appreciated by those in the city with only a small outdoor place to enjoy plants and fish.

To build a traditional water feature in the garden as a symbolic gesture, you must apply all the nuts-and-bolts criteria to planning its final location and means of construction. Although we cover the fundamentals here, you should purchase a pond-building book and learn more about year-around care before attempting such a project.

For best results with aquatic plants such as water lilies, the pool must have direct sunlight for *at least four hours* per day. This is also important for winter use of living spaces around the pool so they will be in the sun for greater com-

fort. In hot climates, morning sun is preferable over afternoon exposure. It's also important to avoid placing the garden beneath the canopy of large trees, because their litter can cause problems with water quality.

The pool must hold water, because if water seeps out or evaporates off the surface, you'll be refilling it daily. Therefore, above all, the pool must be lined with a waterproof material, usually a rubber or PVC sheeting or a prefabricated rigid plastic or fiberglass shell. The flexible sheeting is best for a naturally free-form pool because it can be fitted into irregular, curving edges. The rigid liners can also come free-form, but you must dig a hole the right size and shape to contain it.

A young child can drown in just a few inches of water, which makes issues of accessibility to the pool and safety important if you have children around. You must keep a free-form pool shallow or slope the sides gradually, so that if a toddler falls in, he or she may climb out again easily. Be aware of local ordinances, which may require you to erect a safety fence if the pool is over a minimum size.

For a pump or filter, you will need access to electrical outlets suitable for all-weather usage. A long run of extension cords is not a

The open character of this natural-appearing pond ensures that the water receives plenty of sunlight to support lilies. *Batsford Arboretum, Gloucestershire, England.*

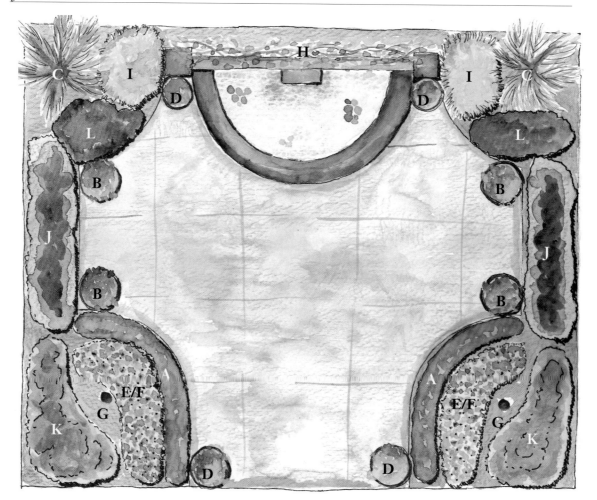

good idea. Have an electrician extend conduit to the pond site if it is too far away. This also helps to support night lighting or a fountain.

When you first fill the pond, it is not immediately suitable for fish. Let it stand a week or so to allow the temperature to even out. This also allows any chlorine in the water supply to evaporate. Be sure the fish you choose are hardy enough for your local climate and are compatible with one another.

Water lilies in the wild have root systems anchored in the mud, but your pool may not have a similar bottom. Plus, if you're in a colder climate, you may have to keep your water lilies warm in the winter. The solution everyone uses is to plant the lilies in a container, which is then submerged to sit upon the pond bottom just like a dry-land container garden. Be aware that normal potting soils won't work here, so it's important to use a designated aquatic soil mix to

A Garden of Reflections

A. *Buxus microphyllus*—Boxwood
B. *Canna* Hybrids—Canna Lily
C. *Chamerops humilis*—Mediterranean Fan Palm
D. *Equisetum hyemale*—Horsetail Grass
E. *Iris*—Bearded
F. *Iris*—Bulbous
G. *Laurus nobilis*—Grecian Laurel
H. *Parthenocissus tricuspidata*—Boston Ivy
I. *Phyllostachys nigra*—Black Bamboo
J. *Prunus laurocerasus*—English Laurel
K. *Punica granatum* 'Nana'—Dwarf Pomegranate
L. *Rosmarinus officinalis*—Rosemary

ensure it won't jeopardize water quality. Those little white foam balls called perlite float! Once the pool is planted, keep about two thirds of the water surface clear of aquatic vegetation for maximum reflective quality.

A WATER OF LIFE GARDEN DESIGN

Perhaps the most vivid legacy of the Egyptians, Arabs, and Romans was their love of using a pool of water to reflect the surroundings on its mirrorlike surface. This type of water garden is contemplative, and its simple beauty connects us all. The inspiration for this garden plan is that of a courtyard one might have found in ancient Greece or Rome, planted in the semiformal style with fragrant Mediterranean species and potted plants. It is enclosed by hedge plants and walls that keep the garden a secret place separated from the outside world.

The water feature can either be a true water garden filled with lilies, lotus or papyrus, and colorful fish or a small dipping pool filled with warm chlorinated water. The water is placed near a vertical wall, which has a thick masonry column at each end. Just as the Romans displayed household gods prominently in their gardens, these columns feature shelves to display statuary. If the water feature is raised, a thick edge can provide ideal seating in every season.

The palette here is predominately green, from the bright yellow-green of bamboo to the deep emerald of laurel. Foliage textures provide interest—the fans of palm fronds, the needles of rosemary, and a formal hedge of boxwood. There are pots at the base of each column in which to grow horsetail or other types of lilylike reeds. The other pots contain dwarf canna lilies, a seasonal plant known for its tropical flowers and lush, broad leaves. The twin beds composed of blue, purple, and white bearded iris could be combined with seasonal bulbous iris to resemble the flags that proved to be the salvation of King Clovis. These iris may be set out in more pots around the rim of the water garden.

ENCHANTING THE LANDSCAPE

ALL EARTH IS A CHURCH, ALL WOODS A SACRAMENT.
Spanish Missionary, Guatemala City, 1775

WE ARE STARDUST, WE ARE GOLDEN…AND WE'VE GOT TO GET OURSELVES BACK TO THE GARDEN.
Joni Mitchell, "Woodstock"

In the Judeo-Christian tradition, the Bible placed Adam and Eve in a garden called Paradise. God chose a garden as the most desirable place in which to live, a place of beauty and abundance for his beloved creations. Thus we find the most compelling truth: that no great house or gloriously ornamented cathedral can compare with the garden. Our return to this simple gift of God is our destiny, be it the wild countryside, a hushed forest, or a garden cultivated by our own hands. Because in nature we will find the earthly paradise that is as close to Eden as we can get while still being grounded.

MIRACLES OF FINDHORN

To love where I was, love whom I was with, and love what I was doing.

PETER CADDY, quoting the Rosicrucian Prime Rule of Life

It was during the frigid winter of 1962 that Peter Caddy, his clairvoyant wife, Eileen, and their two

Bridal Veil, Columbia Gorge, Oregon.

sons moved into a tiny trailer in a run-down park overlooking the Firth of Fornay in Scotland. Theyoung family had no money to live on, and conditions were poor there, with persistent cold wind and infertile, sandy soil. Their desire to return to the land, however, was so great that they survived that first dark winter while discovering their spiritual link to a supreme intelligence, which they called "Unlimited Power and Love."

After much meditation through long nights of solitude in the trailer park's communal bathroom, Eileen sought out a new spiritual name that would become the starting point for life at Findhorn. The name Elixir came to her repeatedly, and she saw visions of a garden and a community of peace and light where the beat-up trailers sat. It was then that both Eileen and Peter discovered the spirits of nature, which spoke to them of natural ways to grow plants, and both claim these spirits have guided them every step of the way.

Through their tireless efforts and perhaps the benevolent hand of fate, the Caddys began to fortify their sandy, gravel soil with all sorts of organic materials, composting everything they could find. When pests threatened their plants, wood ashes and other natural means of control were suggested by the spirits, and the plagues were halted without chemicals. The soil at Findhorn soon began to produce in abundance, with cabbages and other crops growing to incredible proportions. Gardeners from all over Britain came to see for themselves that the legends were true, and soon the garden not only supported the Caddy family but a host of similar-minded young people, as well.

Much has been written about Findhorn and how it inspired communal groups all over Europe and North America to follow the same approach. For many, this little Scottish garden remains a spiritual mecca, from which vibrations similar to those felt by Eileen Caddy imbue those seeking guidance with a deep sense of communion with the earth. There they discover how the unlimited intelligence within all creation is attributed to the garden's success. For others, it is simply a pilgrimage to one of the most famous organic food gardens of today,

where the fruits of the earth and its abundance are clearly seen in the produce.

Although we cannot all expect to be so finely tuned to nature as those at Findhorn, there remains far more to the garden than simply earth, plants, water, and sun. The garden becomes the conduit through which we can rediscover subtle changes, tiny organisms, and the miracle of life. The interaction of plants with insects, birds, mammals, and reptiles is remarkable, but we rarely take the time to stop and appreciate it. Our lives have become separated from nature by urban sprawl and work which keeps us sequestered indoors for much of the day.

By creating and tending gardens, we are all assured a new view of life, one that is as slow as plant growth, as bright as the sun, and as refreshing as water. Good gardeners are those who take the time to inspect each of their plants as they would children, in order to assess their individual needs and problems. For creation of gardens fills our instinctual yearning to return to Eden, where we may cast off the chains of our complex lives and rediscover that childlike sense of wonder in all things. Often I think this is the soul of the hippie movement of the 1960s, the searching for a more fundamental sense of belonging, the need for reattachment to the earth whence we all have come.

Years ago, before I began my sojourn into the vast world of plants, I saw my surroundings in unremarkable ways. I saw a forest, a mountain, a stream, or a desert. These were single, unbroken elements. Now I have discovered the intimate qualities of nature that Thoreau surely found at Walden and many others before and after will equally appreciate. To me nature is like a family comprised of different members of many generations, and no matter where I go, my family of plants is always around me. I am never alone.

When I see a forest, I see it as a community and can pick out virtually every species that is visible, and there are others I know are there, although they remain invisible. The forest that surrounds me here in the Sierra Nevada is filled with trees, some pine, some fir, many oaks, cedar, and dogwood. I see the mosses and fungi cling-

Nardozzi Garden, Vermont.

ing to the rotting bark, clumps of mistletoe that suck life from their host plants, and the poison oak snaking up into the branches for support. These and dozens of others—the grasses and native shrubs, tall broadleaf weeds, and ferns in the moist stream bottoms—are all a part of that big picture, the forest.

To come to know nature and the garden is to learn about all these plants, discover their unique place in the larger scheme of things, find out their value to people both in a practical and spiritual sense, and make them as familiar as your best friend. For once you become intimate with nature, you too will never be alone, no matter what year it is, what continent you stand upon, and what forest wraps you in its loving, leafy arms. You are always among friends.

TREE OF KNOWLEDGE, TREE OF LIFE

This is the forest primeval,
The murmuring pines and the hemlocks,
Bearded with moss, and in garments
    green, indistinct in the twilight
Stand like Druids of old, with voices
    sad and prophetic.
        HENRY WADSWORTH LONGFELLOW,
        Evangeline

The forest primeval shows how central the tree was to early peoples. In legends and folklore of almost every culture we find a tree, usually a certain species, defined as the Tree of Life or the Tree of Knowledge. Except for the hills and mountains, trees were the largest things to exist upon the land. They also lived a very long time, most longer than a single human's life span, perhaps longer than the combined lives of multiple generations. The genealogical family tree evolved from this multigenerational concept.

To primitive man the ability of a deciduous tree to apparently die over the winter, then resurrect itself in spring by leafing out again was truly magical. The ability of certain evergreen trees to remain in leaf while the deciduous trees had lost theirs to the cold was equally magical. Even more profound is the ability of the palm to thrive in a waterless desert, which makes its image all the more powerful.

The symbology of the World Tree took root in Norse mythology with an ash named Yggdrasil, from which Odin created the first man, Askr. This tree represented the earth, the mother and source of life that explains all aspects of nature and the cosmos. Its roots extend deep into the earth, linking them to the netherworld. The branches rise up to support the heavens and are cloaked in clouds of foliage studded with fruits, which represent bright stars. Another version of Scandinavian creation myth explains that dwarfs, supernatural beings of the forest, carved two figures out of trees. They were found by Odin and his brothers, who endowed them with life and understanding, naming them Askr and Embla, the first human beings.

These myths of trees as part of man's origins are also prevalent in the New World, which is amazing, considering its complete isolation from Old World cultures. Yurucases Indians of Bolivia believe that in ancient times all the people were killed by an enormous fire. The god Tiri then opened a tree and from it drew out all the various tribes, then closed up the tree again.

The Trees of Life and Knowledge in the Garden of Eden, Leeu, 1486.

In the biblical story of Adam and Eve, we find references to two trees, one the tree of life and the other the tree of knowledge. The concept of a tree of life can be found in creation mythology of many cultures, for it represents immortality. To the Druids it was the oak, the Assyrians chose the date palm, and the Egyptians saw it as the sycamore fig.

In contrast, the tree of knowledge shown in Genesis is a symbol of mortality, the assurance of eventual death and decay. Early translations of the Bible depict this as an apple tree, but in truth it could have been any tree bearing fruit. Many believe that it was in fact a fig, as this was the kind of leaves used as clothing by Adam and Eve after they had sinned.

Scholars first see the apple in Latin Bible translations made from Greek by St. Jerome. Others think the apple came to civilized Europe much later, during the Germanic invasions, which began in the sixth century. The Nordic

peoples retained many myths about their sacred tree, the apple, which probably crept into Christian literature during the Middle Ages.

Perhaps the Norse apple and the tree of knowledge were combined to fashion the mythical Apple of Sodom, a giant tree which Europeans thought grew on the land that once held the infamous cities of Sodom and Gomorrah. It was believed that any traveler who was foolish enough to pick its fruit would find it turning to smoke and ashes the minute its stem was detached from the branch. Such a reaction is rooted in the biblical story of Lot and the destruction of these twin venues of sin.

In the New World the Maya designated the ceiba tree, *Eriodendrum vesculifolium*, sacred, and whenever forest is cleared, these trees are carefully preserved. It is called the "tree of council" since there is one in most villages. There meetings are held beneath its canopy to elect elders, and on special feast days its roots are decorated with fresh rose petals, and copal is burned there. Like the Norse beliefs, this tree also had represented the universe, with roots in the earth from which descended their race, trunk above the horizon, and top in the sky.

Certain clans in Guatemala mark their traditional dress with symbols relating to their status and rank. Among some of the most high born are those descended from "the land of the pine tree," and their traditional blouses, richly embroidered *huipiles*, bear designs depicting this tree, which became a symbol of longevity.

The Oak, Thunder, and Oracles

Groves were planted to console at noon
The pensive wanderer in their shades.
At eve
The moonbeams, sliding softly in between
The sleeping leaves, is all the light he wants
For meditation.

UNKNOWN POET,
from *Forest Folklore and Mythology*

One of the very earliest forms of religion in the Old World was the worship of trees and vegetation. Long before the Greek and Roman civilizations, most of Europe and Britain was cloaked in ancient forests of majestic hardwood trees. The tribes that inhabited these lands developed religions centered upon these groves, and many believed that every tree contained a spirit. The largest specimens were thought to be the most powerful, and the oldest, darkest groves were considered hallowed ground.

The oak tree is unique because it is more often struck by lightning than any other species. The bark of many oak species is rough and irregular, covering extremely dense wood. Often the heartwood at the center of an oak rots away, leaving the outer sapwood to support the trunk and branches. In the heartwood cavity, water accumulates, and today firewood cutters often encounter such pockets deep within the trees. When struck by lightning, this water, combined with moisture in the wood itself, expands so rapidly, the oak literally explodes into a grand spectacle, which was no doubt a source of both amazement and fear to primitive peoples.

It's logical, then, that the gods of thunder—Zeus among the Greeks, Jupiter of the Romans, and Thor to the Nordic tribes—are most often believed to inhabit oak trees. In ancient Greece any tree struck by lightning was immediately designated as a sanctuary to Zeus, and the charred trunk was fenced in and protected. Temples to the gods were also placed around sacred oaks, which stood long after the trees had died. Because rain often followed thunderstorms, rain-making rituals dictated that the priests of these civilizations dip oak boughs in water. Sometimes priests would climb into the trees and bang metal gongs to imitate thunder in hopes it would gain the god's attention.

The god of thunder bears two names by Greco-Roman cultures, Zeus and Jupiter. He is shown here with a bundle of lightning bolts in his hand.

The most famous oak grove of ancient Greece is that of Dodona, in the Chaonian Forest in Epirus, where it is believed that thunderstorms rage more often than anywhere else. A temple was built there beneath a giant tree dedicated to Zeus, which became an oracle. Through the rustling of the leaves, the priests were thought to hear the words of the god and interpret their meaning. Bronze gongs were hung from the trees surrounding this sanctuary, so that wind would imitate thunder. A sliver of wood taken from these sacred oaks was built into Jason's ship, the *Argo*, as a powerful talisman on his journey to capture the Golden Fleece.

The mighty oak.

Of all the people of pre-Christian Europe, it was the Druids, the priests of the Celts, who are best known to venerate trees, and above all they respected the oak. In fact, it is believed that the word *druid* translated means "oak man," which attests to the relationship between this religion and the tree.

Druid priests chose certain groves in which to place their temples because it was unlawful to worship under roofs. The groves at the centers of forests, those cloaked in gloom beneath massive canopies, were chosen and guarded diligently, lest some unholy foot enter the holiest of holies. At one sacred Druid grove a circular area was enclosed with one or two rows of stones set perpendicularly in the ground—much like the stone circles found throughout Britain. The circular area constituted a temple within which stood an altar where sacrifices were made. Often a fire was kept burning day and night, fed by the wood of the most sacred trees. Only fire tenders could touch this wood. The punishment for fire tenders who failed to keep the flames going was a horrible death as sacrifice to the offended tree god.

Among the strictest rulings was that no part of the trees, living or dead, on the ground or in the canopy, could be removed from the tree or taken from the grove. Nor could anyone but the priests enter groves, as the gods would maim offenders' hands and feet. Even more brutal was the punishment for picking a leaf or twig from the tree: Druid priests flayed the offender, using his skin to heal the tree scar.

Apparently, shepherds were terrified of sacred groves and took care to keep their livestock from wandering into them, for collecting a wayward animal could be a life-threatening experience! In contrast, Roman shepherds had some protection; the celebration of the festival of Parilia ensured the welfare of their flocks, but more importantly, it brought forgiveness if they accidently entered a holy grove or if the sheep fed upon the sacred leaves. A fifteenth-century manuscript includes a herdsman's charm to be intoned in hopes that his animals would not wander into the sacred groves. In its words is found the remarkable mingling of old and new faiths, pagan incantations combined with the saints of Christianity, in a plea that the magical beasts that guarded the Druids' groves would not attack the herdsman and punish him for entering to collect the animal:

To day my herd I drove Into Our Lady's grove, Into Abraham's garden; be good St. Martin This day, my cattle's Warden, May good St. Wolfgang, good St. Peter, Throat of wolf and vixen block, Blood from shedding bone from crunching! Help me, the holy one, Who ill hath never done, and his V [five] holy wounds Keep my herd from all wood-hounds!

JACOB GRIM, *Teutonic Mythology*

Druid priests also worshipped individual trees, particularly those that grew on or near springs. These were the oracle oaks which spoke to the priests, answering their queries about life, leadership, and religion. The priests interpreted answers given in the rustling of branches and the murmuring of the spring waters. This questioning, or querying, is so legendary it became the Latin root word of the oak tree genus, *Quercus*.

Eventually, Christianity proved stronger than the Old World tree gods, and this is best seen in the events at Fatima, Portugal, in 1917. In that tiny peasant village, the Virgin Mary appeared to three children tending their family's flocks out in the countryside. On a rocky hill they witnessed many apparitions of the Virgin standing on a young holm oak, *Quercus ilex*, one of the most common oaks of pagan Europe.

She could have appeared in a grotto, as she did to Bernadette in France, but here the symbolism is quite clear. During these apparitions she warned of the growing Russian power and the danger of its atheistic government. Her presence upon the holm oak's branches symbolically indicated that the pagan rites of the oak paralleled the atheism of the growing Russian revolution, and that both were a threat to the church. Standing upon the oak and not beside it showed that the danger could be overcome if enough people prayed for conversion.

Sorbus acuparia, known as rowan, witchwood, and quickbane, was once thought to be imbued with magical powers that protected against the spells of witches.

The Ash and the Rowan

Both the ash tree and the mountain ash, from entirely different genera, are frequently confused in religious folklore because both have interesting legends surrounding them. The true ash, genus *Fraxinus*, became an important part of Norse mythology as the giant named Yggdrasil, known as the Tree of the World. The ash was important because it grew large in the northern lands, where the evergreen forests were stunted by heavy snowfall and persistent cold. Ash wood is also very strong, and the Vikings used it as handles of their battle axes.

The rowan tree, or European mountain ash, genus *Sorbus*, is more often encountered in witchcraft and Druid lore, which inspired a host of common names, such as witchwood, quickbane, wicken tree, and witchen. It bears an annual crop of bright red berries, which were the most sacred part of the tree; if eaten, they imbued the person with special powers or guaranteed protection from evil. The color red is a potent talisman, which no doubt made the berries important by virtue of nothing more than their carmine hue.

This tree was the nemesis of witches, who believed that if touched by even a single leaf, they would be returned to the devil and suffer his punishments. Ship masts in old England were sometimes made of rowan to ward off evil on board.

For this same reason it was planted in almost every churchyard to discourage evil spirits and keep the dead in their graves until Judgment Day. Pallbearers carrying coffins into the churchyard for burial paused beneath the branches of rowans to drive away any evil lingering with the dead. Branches of rowan which grew in the shape of a cross were thought to be the most powerful means of preventing witches from causing dairy products to sour and milk cows to dry up. Rowan was hung above every cow's stall to ensure the milk would continue flowing. Sprigs of rowan were kept in beds of peasants to protect them while they slept, and even smaller sprigs were carried in pockets. The lyrics of this ancient song, "Laidley Worm of Spindleton's Heuglis," show just how pervasive this belief truly was:

> Their spells were vain, the boys returned
> To the Queen in sorrowful mood;
> Crying that 'Witches have no power
> Where there is Rowan-tree wood.

THE ADVENT OF CHRISTIANITY

The Romans built their religion with many links to Grecian gods, and in some instances the two mythological systems were nearly identical. When the Romans spread out to conquer Europe, Britain, and the Mediterranean, they encountered the ancient earth religions of the Celts and other northern tribes, who worshipped multiple deities as did the Romans.

When Christianity became the official religion of Rome, however, the monotheistic belief conflicted with the lingering pagan rites. Early church leaders were faced with the difficult task of converting peasants who clung to tree worship and the ensuing celebrations of seasonal changes. The social fabric of these tribal peoples included feasts and sacrifices of both animals and humans, practices that were not approved by the early church.

Christian priests, knowing that the oracle trees and the sacred groves were central to these pagan beliefs, set out to either destroy them or

Grottoes in the landscape find their roots in the Temptation of Christ in the desert where he fasted for forty days. Later natural and manmade grottoes in wild places became the homes of hermit monks and holy men who preferred to live separated from the rest of civilization. As a result, grottoes became sacred and a place for shrines. *Chateau de Nacqueville, Cherbourg, France.*

reclaim them in the name of Christ. In an effort to discourage such superstitions, the church had many of the most powerful groves cut down to prove they were no different from the rest of the forest. In some cases, though, the church utilized the supposed sacred nature of these places by erecting Christian altars and shrines near or beneath the trees. Where the pagan peoples hung their often grisly offerings on the branches of these trees, the Christians hung their crucifixes and images of the Virgin and saints, instead. This decoration of trees with offerings can be seen in the modern Christmas tree.

It is widely believed that many of the oldest Christian churches were also built in or around sacred groves, wells, and oracle trees. Signs of pagan holy ground, such as heel stones, monoliths, and earthworks, are also seen in the churchyards of rural Britain and France. This is not uncommon in history, for many conquerors

The towering walls and arches of early cathedrals were thought to have been inspired by the trunks and canopy branches of sacred groves. *Wells Cathedral, Wells, England.*

razed the towns of the vanquished and erected their own buildings and churches upon the rubble. This was done for practical reasons, but also to emphasize the victory and the submission of the conquered. Thus, a Christian church or shrine built in a place of pagan worship proved the church was the ultimate divine ruler and that the old gods had lost their power even when their sacred places had been desecrated.

Some suggest that the designs of early cathedrals may have been inspired by the sacred groves. Strong, upright masonry columns imitate the trunks, while the many arches are remarkably similar to the spreading branches of a tree. Perhaps lingering Druid preferences for praying in open air beneath the sacred groves made the early churches seek to imitate such conditions in order to ease the transition from pagan to Christian rites.

St. Patrick's Leaves

St. Patrick was the fifth-century saint who delivered Ireland out of the hands of Druid priests and into those of the Catholic church. Few know that Patrick was stolen into slavery as a boy and sought out his ordination only after escaping captivity many years later. This intimacy with the lowest people on the social ladder, the slaves and domestic workers, made him that much more cherished by the masses, and he retained a unique ability to communicate with them.

The true shamrock, *Oxalis acetosella*, was already part of Irish culture during pagan times. It was a lucky charm linked to the ancient Celtic sun wheel, and in their language it was called "little clover," *seamrog*, or shamrock. This is why a four-quadrant version of the shamrock leaf and its cousins the clovers are still recognized today as lucky, though few know it is linked to pagan rites in this old rhyme:

> One leaf for fame,
> And one for wealth,
> One for a faithful lover,
> And one to bring you glorious health,
> Are in a four-leaf clover.

The shamrock connection to St. Patrick

Oxalis Acetosella—the true shamrock used by St. Patrick to illustrate the mystery of the Holy Trinity.

arises from his early sermons, which attempted to educate the pagan Irish on the mystery of the Holy Trinity: God the Father, God the Son, and God the Holy Spirit. In his audience was a Druid priest who asked, "How can one be three?" Searching for an example in nature these earthy people would understand, he plucked a shamrock leaf from the turf at his feet. "Here is the one leaf," Patrick said. "There are three leaves in one, just as there are three Gods in one. The clover is the perfect symbol of my faith in the trinity." That was enough for that chief, for he promptly embraced the faith that would convert all of Ireland.

Isidore the Farmer

St. Isidore of Seville, a bishop scholar born in the year 560, became a celebrated doctor of the Church in honor of his writings on history and theology during the Middle Ages. Even though books sometimes list Isidore of Seville as patron of farmers, he lived over five hundred years before the poor and illiterate Isidore the Farmer, who was born in nearby Madrid and named for the great saint who preceded him.

Our farmer was a lowly laborer who worked on the estate of John de Vergas his entire life. He married, but after their first son died, both he and his wife devoted themselves to God. Each day Isidore attended mass before starting work in the fields. While guiding the plow, hoeing, irrigating, and performing every task, he kept up a dialogue with God, his guardian angel, selfless life that turned his endless work into an act of prayer. He became one of the most favored saints in Spain, and later the devotion to him took root in the New World. Wherever the Spanish, their descendants, and converted Indians tilled the soil, there would be a carved *santo* of Isidore in the home or church. Because the Southwest and Mexico share such a dry climate, survival of the crops was dubious and famine an ever-present specter. To invoke Isidore's aid, the image would be carried in procession through all the fields at planting time to bless the crops in hopes of a bountiful harvest. The feast day of St. Isidore the Farmer is celebrated on May 15.

REDISCOVERING A MAN NAMED FRANCIS

For a man who believes in and loves his Creator, with his whole heart must also dignify and love all of His creations.

PAUL GALLICO,
"St. Francis and the Animals"

The true miracle of St. Francis of Assisi is that he saw the divine in all of God's creations. He taught us that a simple life is filled with great discoveries, which would so often go unnoticed in our materialistic, fast-paced world.

Yet in the life of Francis, we find many of the same moral dilemmas that face us today. Francis was born in 1181 in Assisi, Italy, to a silk trader and lived as his station in life prescribed, with the freedom and wealth to become an international playboy. Francis was a bachelor with money and loved every minute of it. All that changed when he went to war against the Perugians in one of the many battles of the merchant guilds, who perpetually fought among themselves, just as entire nations do today. There he was captured, and he remained prisoner for over a year. Released and returning home in very bad condition, he then suffered a long illness.

His incarceration in the prison camp and the illness gave Francis much time to ponder. As with most people, the specter of death led to rev-

Jeanne Rose, San Francisco, California.

and saints. Isidore lived the model of Christ by sharing all he had with others and by many other acts of generosity.

We know that while he lived, the people of Madrid thought him a holy man who loved the earth and its plants and animals. One miraculous tale finds Isidore, on a cold winter day, carrying a sack of dry corn to be ground into meal, when he saw a flock of hungry birds perched sadly on the bare branches of a tree. Out of pity the man opened his sack of corn and poured out half of it onto the ground to feed them. His friends were shocked to see such valuable food wasted on birds, but Isidore ignored them and went on his way. When they arrived at the mill, the sack was full of corn once again, and when ground, it yielded twice the normal amount of flour.

Isidore the Farmer is the image of a man fully tuned to the natural world. He lived the elations about what is really important. The once-lighthearted boy became somber and reflective during the long road to regaining his health.

One day he passed the church of San Damiano, which had fallen into ruin. He stopped inside to pray, and there he saw a vision of Christ from a crucifix asking that he "repair my home which is falling into disrepair." Francis immediately began selling his father's silks for funds, but after a great argument he left his father, denied his inheritance, and promptly began begging for coins around town.

From that day Francis took on a life of poverty after coming to the realization that all evil in the world could be traced to material wealth. This inspired him to create a monastic order he called the Friars Minor, or "little brothers," who vowed a life of poverty, which was significant in this time when corruption was rife within the church. They would later become the Franciscans. During his lifetime Francis founded other orders, both ordained and lay, male and female, but all dedicated to helping the poor. Among these were the Franciscan nuns, known as the Poor Clairs.

St. Francis became most well known as a patron of nature because of his appreciation for all of God's creations. This was not limited to living things, either, because in his *Canticle of Brother Sun*, he respected the sun and moon, stones, and even the dark earth beneath his sandaled feet as miracles of the Creator.

It is the tales of his love of animals, for which he bore great compassion, which have come down to us in the twentieth century, however, and they are the reason why images of St. Francis, more than any other holy figure, are found in our gardens. He was a man of endless love and discipline, turning the other cheek to even the mice and bedbugs that infested his cold cell, in his prayers thanking God for their existence, no matter how much discomfort they caused him. On a frigid winter night during one of his many illnesses caused by his ascetic life, Francis struggled to remain conscious enough to say his office while kneeling on the stone floor. Despite his efforts, none of the monks came to

help him, for they were unwilling to leave the scant warmth of their beds. Just as he had nearly become unconscious, a grasshopper crawled through the snow and under the door to his cell. Its chirping sounds assisted Francis through the ordeal. In the morning it left tiny tracks in the snow outside, proving it indeed was there at midnight, and out of season, thus shaming the monks for their laziness.

At that time animals were routinely abused as beasts of burden, whipped until they fell, fed only enough to stay just barely alive, and cruelly hunted with snares, which left the wild things lingering in pain for days on end. Francis petitioned the government and nobility to pass laws against animal abuse and even requested that farm animals be given extra rations on Christmas Day. Though he was mostly ignored at the time,

Ryan Gainey Garden, Decatur, Georgia.

the people of Assisi still feed the birds in the marketplace in his honor.

St. Francis loved the birds—above all, the crested lark because its plumage was colored brown, just as was the habit and hood of the Franciscans. Once while Francis was traveling through the country, he came upon a large flock of birds perched upon trees and shrubs. As always, he saw them as equals in God's eyes, and he sought to enlighten them in how the Lord cared for them, as described in Luke's gospel. "You ought greatly to praise your Creator and always love him, who has given you feathers to clothe you and all else you need. God has made you the most noble of creatures; he has given you the air as a dwelling-place, and although you neither sow nor reap, he protects and guides you so you lack nothing." As Francis concluded his sermon, he found every bird fanning its wings as though cheering, with each tiny beak clicking in approval. It was then that he realized how even the birds were eager to hear his words and how much more valuable they must become to man.

Perhaps the most cherished tale is of Francis preaching to a crowd while the swallows flew acrobatics above his head, all the while rivaling his voice with their chatter. Annoyed at the competition, Francis looked up and rebuked them, saying "My brothers and sisters, the swallows, it's now my time to speak. You've said enough for now, so please let me be heard." History says that the swallows indeed quieted down and let him continue.

Another story tells of a fisherman who carried Francis as a passenger in his boat to the far shore of a lake. On the way he caught a huge carp, which he proudly offered to the monk. The saint marveled at the perfection of its glistening scales, and he took pity on the poor gasping creature and returned it to the waters. The carp, in thanks for such pity, followed Francis's boat across the lake and was waiting there in the shallows, staring up at its benefactor as he disembarked.

Despite these lighthearted animal tales, the life of an ascetic is one of pain, prayer, and passion. As he aged Francis became blind and faced the only known cure of the affliction with customary love and courage. Doctors believed that blindness could be relieved by cauterizing the temples with hot irons. Facing the glowing irons, Francis embraced them by name as Brother Fire and asked, "Haven't I always been good to you for the love of Him that created you? Now show me how gentle and courteous you can be and burn no more than I can stand." After his ordeal Francis said to his doctors, "If that was not enough burning, then burn it again, for I have not felt the least pain."

Upon his death not long after, the skies above his small cell were filled with the larks he loved, sadly mourning the loss in flight. Francis left the pain of this world and assumed the eternal peace of the next. We have much to learn from good St. Francis, for by his example we are shown the true way to spiritual happiness. It is not found in the mall, nor on Wall Street, nor even in our home. What Francis showed us is that material things may provide temporary comfort, leading our souls away from the true path to God. Perhaps most of all, Francis taught us that God gave us the world and all that is in it, and among these creations we may find the face of true spirituality. It lingers there, subtly carved upon a mossy stone, inscribed by the flight of the sparrow, glowing amidst the flames of autumn, and waiting deep inside the fragrant petals of the rose. To add Francis to our gardens or simply to read his canticles while basking in Brother Sun and appreciating each leaf and flower, we too may discover the greatest miracles of all right here beneath our noses in that miraculous place so deeply rooted in the spirit.

> All praise be yours, my Lord, through
>   Brother Fire,
> Through whom you brighten up the
>   night.
> How beautiful he is, how gay! Full of
>   power and strength.
> All praise be yours, my Lord, through
>   Sister Earth, our mother,
> Who feeds us in her sovereignty and
>   produces
> Various fruits and colored flowers and
>   herbs.
>
> "CANTICLE OF BROTHER SUN"

BIRDS AND BEES OF THE SPIRIT

When the dove returned to him in the evening, there in its beak was a freshly plucked olive leaf! Then Noah knew that the water had receded from the earth.

GENESIS 8:11

Perhaps the most famous bird in Western religions is the dove, and its first appearance in Judeo-Christian literature is in the story of Noah, where God made peace with man after the Flood. From very early in church history, the dove has come to represent peace, which was also extended to the olive tree, as both were linked in Genesis. In Mosaic law doves were considered suitable sacrifices at the Temple, particularly during the rite of purification of a child, and Joseph made the appropriate sacrifice of two turtledoves at the presentation of Jesus.

The dove became more important in the New Testament and the Christian church when it came to represent the Holy Spirit. Many people give Christian gifts that depict the dove, for it also represents the seven gifts of the Holy Spirit. The white dove is part of the lore of many saints, for it has been seen as a soul flying to heaven or the voice of God inspiring writers to greater truths.

Many years ago I built a sizable aviary beside my garden and was given a beautiful white

Aquilegia 'Music Box'. Columbine became a symbol of the seven gifts of the Holy Spirit because it so frequently bears seven flowers on each stem.

The Holy Spirit in the form of a dove, from an old English baptismal font.

dove. He first introduced me to the plaintive cry of doves at dawn and sunset, a sound which is more peaceful than any other I have heard. From him I discovered how well these birds take to captivity and bring us both symbolism and a love of wildlife by their passive nature. For anyone wishing to create a spiritual garden with an extra benefit, it is simple to keep doves, which ask only for water and seed and will quickly come to perch on your head or shoulder if offered bread scraps. Doves also breed easily.

Columbine flower profile showing its characteristic spurs.

The wild columbine, as are its domestic progeny, is a woodland flower. It came to be the floral symbol of the Holy Spirit because dove in Latin is *columba*. Columbine grows with small

A church birdhouse. *Thornton-Bailey Garden, California.*

tufts of delicate foliage and wiry stems, which rise up to bear the unique spurred flowers. Since there are often seven flowers per stem, they were likened to the seven gifts of the Holy Spirit as defined in the Vulgate. These are wisdom, understanding, counsel, fortitude, knowledge, fear of the Lord, and Love. A stalk of seven flowers is used to suggest the presence of the Holy Spirit in early Renaissance religious paintings, but if the flowers are blue, they represent the seven sorrows of the Virgin Mary.

Other birds, both wild and domestic, have important roles in Christian folklore and the lives of saints. Everyone knows the story of Peter's denial on the eve of Christ's death before the cock crowed three times. From this tale we find a new appreciation of the rooster, which served God with its timely reminder of Jesus' prophecy.

The crane is a Christian symbol of perpetual vigilance against sin. A legend describes that when a flock of cranes sleeps at night, some remain awake to stand guard for their leader. To do so, they stand on one foot, the other folded up and clutching a stone. If a crane should fall asleep, the stone would be released and drop upon the standing foot, thus awakening the bird to continue its nighttime vigilance. The Church adopted this symbol in its struggle against the lukewarm in their flock who would be more vulnerable to sin. The stone of the crane is likened to the sacraments and masses, a reminder that Satan is cunning and waits patiently for us to fall spiritually asleep.

The peacock is considered a bird of immortality because legends suggest it does not decay after death, much like the "uncorruptables," certain saints whose bodies failed to decay naturally, even hundreds of years after their deaths. The bird's tail, with its hundred "eyes," is the all-seeing church.

The blackbird, raven, and crow are often interchangeable, but in most cases they are associated with the devil and his works. St. Benedict, father of the Benedictine order, was perpetually tempted by the devil. Once while Benedict was at prayer, a raven flew in and attempted to distract him. With a sign of the cross, the saint banished the bird and its malevolent spirit. Noah sent out a raven from the ark before the dove.

Early apiaries, or skeps, used throughout the Middle Ages were made like inverted baskets and have recently reappeared as ornamental garden art. *Old Mill Dene, Mr. and Mrs. B. S. Dare, Blockley, Gloucestershire, England.*

ORNAMENTAL IDEAS

Some ancient peoples of Europe honored Green George, the "green man," a collective spirit of the forest. This pagan belief was transformed into a Christian festival honoring a like-named saint, St. George's day, the twenty-third of April. Recognizing the spirits of vegetation, processions draped in garlands headed through the streets, led by a village boy decked out in leafy branches to represent Green George. Garden art depicting the leafy face of this nature spirit is now among our ornamental options, with the leafy face of George cast in a concrete wall relief. Some sources offer four different versions of the green man, each representing a different seasons. You could hang the green man on walls, fences, trees, and any other vertical structure.

Legend says the bird was white until it failed to return to Noah, then was colored black for its disobedience.

The owl's preference for night hunting has made it another symbol of the devil, who lures Christians out of the light of Christ and into the dark wilderness. On the other hand, it also represents wisdom and can be found in tales of saints and in Scripture.

There are hundreds of examples of how God is manifest in his creations, and many of these relate to common fauna of the garden. Not all of these are ancient history, because the apparitions of the Virgin Mary at Betania, Venezuela, are occurring today, and pilgrimages are frequently made to this South American nation. Curiously, the name *Betania* means "Bethany," the town where Mary and Martha lived with their brother Lazarus. It was here that Lazarus lived, died, and lived again at the miraculous hands of Christ in the Gospels. What makes these apparitions most interesting is that the Virgin is believed to be manifested in the form of a blue butterfly, which flutters around the thousands of pilgrims, but Mary herself appears to only a chosen few. Those who have been to the shrine at Betania never again overlook blue butterflies, for rather than being just an insect, it is a creation of God and perhaps the fleeting spirit of his mother returned to earth.

The honeybee is the vector of pollen and is essential to the production of seed in gardens. The communal, industrious nature of the beehive provided an ideal image to express the church, with each Christian working to support the whole. The bee also provided an example to early monastic communities because of the spirit of cooperation in which the hive makes honey. Honey was the only source of sweetening until recent centuries and thus was precious; it would come to represent the benefits the church provided to the faithful.

Two saints are patrons of beekeepers, the first one being St. Bernard of Clairvaux, who lived from 1090 to 1153 and was a member of a Cistercian monastery. Though St. Bernard had no significant contact with bees, his ability to preach loving sermons on the Song of Songs, the most gardenesque book of the Bible, made his words sweet as honey, and thus the association was made.

St. Ambrose, a bishop of the early church during the fourth century, is well known for his efforts to stamp out the heresy of the Arians. His link to bees came from an event of his childhood, when a swarm of bees landed upon his mouth. Not one bee stung the boy, which was seen as a sign from God predicting his future as a great orator, with his words as sweet as the honey of bees.

THE ENCHANTED NEW WORLD

When Missionaries and explorers in the fifteenth and sixteenth centuries encountered the New World, they often called it an earthly paradise. The peoples who inhabited it were tied to the land and plants in fascinating ways.

Ancient Corn

Fifty times a year, the Mass interrupts work in the fields, the daily ceremony of communion with the earth. For the Indians, accompanying step by step the corn's cycle of death and resurrection is a way of praying; and the earth, that immense temple, is their day-to-day testimony to the miracle of life being reborn. For them all earth is a church, all woods a sacrament.

SPANISH MISSIONARY, GUATEMALA CITY, 1775

There are many biblical references to corn, but this is not corn as we know it. The word *corn* or *korn* was used to describe grains of every sort and was naturally applied to the new grain of the New World. Among the native peoples it was *maize*, which became the botanical name for the species. It was grown through much of North and Central America by hundreds of different tribes, but few held it in as high esteem as the ancient Maya, who saw it as a god and the rival of Christian saints.

Corn cultivation to the Maya, as well as so many other agricultural peoples, was the gauge of the passing seasons. The calendar of the Maya told when the seed was planted, when the tassels would appear, and when the green or milk corn was picked to eat fresh while soft and sweet. The remainder of the crop was left in the field until the harvest moon told it was time to pick and store the corn for the lean winter months.

The Maya worshipped a host of gods that watched over the cultivation of corn, which they used for ritual, as well as food purposes. It is believed that the Maya fertilized their cornfields with the blood of their vanquished enemies. Their Kings, considered maize gods in the flesh, willingly drew blood from their earlobes and penises to be sprinkled upon the fields.

To these people the symbol of corn was the equivalent of our Christian cross, both images representing the triumph of life over death. This can be seen in carvings among the ruins of Palenque in the Yucatan, where the Mayan Tree of Life is depicted with stems and leaves of corn bearing ears as human heads, from which sprout the silk. At the top rises the head of the maize god himself, perched upon the underworld, showing how the entire Maya universe was inextricably linked to corn.

Since the Conquest images of the crucifix and of the Maya Tree of Life have blended. The peoples of Chiapas, Yucatan, and Guatemala today observe dual images: saints become maize gods; Catholic priests become shamans. They still grow corn and inspect each ear for red kernels, because it is believed that these are colored by the blood of Christ, but perhaps earlier by the phallic blood of their kings.

Further north Spanish explorers found in the desert the corn of the Anasazi and their descendants the Zuni, who still cultivate the very same strains. These Pueblo tribes also followed a yearly cycle of planting and harvest, with their gods and calendars all linked to corn. So essential was this plant to the desert tribes that they counted it among the five elements of Pueblo life and legend: air, earth, water, fire, and corn.

These people collected corn pollen and considered it as sacred as Catholics believe their holy water today. Shamans and healers would christen virtually everyone and everything with the pollen or finally ground meal, known as *hoddentin*. An early ethnologist quotes an Apache holy man, who attests to this veneration of corn pollen: "When we Apache go on the warpath, hunt or plant, we always throw a pinch of *hoddentin* to the sun, saying, 'With the favor of the sun, or permission of the sun, I am going out to fight, hunt, or plant, and I want the sun to help me'" (John G. Bourke, *Medicine Men of the Apaches*, 1887–8).

Still farther north, discovered not by the Spanish missionaries but the Protestants, who came from the east, were the fertile river bottom gardens of the northern plains. There separate

CLOCKWISE FROM UPPER LEFT:

    In September the corn was planted using digging sticks.

    By February the corn has tassels and the ears nestle in the leaf axils. Women guard the fields from marauding wildlife and sing to the crops.

    Harvest falls around March, when birds threaten to damage the tips of the ears that emerge from their husks.

strains of corn were nurtured by the Hidatsa, Mandan, and Arickara, all of whom selectively bred the plant for centuries. Seed was carefully chosen to carry on the coming year's crop from block plantings, which were separated to avoid cross-pollination between varieties. From these, only the strongest plants were saved. Only kernels without a black heart, and from the center of the cob, carried on the lineage. The growers discarded kernels from the ends and ones either too small or overly large with starch. It was just these flint corn strains of the plains tribes that gave modern corn breeders the short-season genes that have allowed cultivation in the north.

    Hidden within the shriveled seed kernels is selective breeding practical long before Mendel and modern genetics. Buffalo Bird Woman, born in 1839 in the Hidatsa tribe of North Dakota, recorded her people's old ways of growing corn, which was planted by the women in unplowed ground and grew to maturity without irrigation. These women knew of the miracle of cross-pollination and marveled at their own ability to keep the strains pure. "We Indians knew that corn could travel," she recalled. "We did not know what power it was that causes this. We only knew that it was so" (*Agriculture of the Hidatsa Indians: An Indian Interpretation*, 1917).

Perhaps most charming of all was the belief that corn grew better if it was sung to often. Strangely, this practice links all Native American corn growers, from the Maya to the Hidatsa, and they poured out their respect for this living crop in song that ensured plentiful harvests. "We cared for our corn in those days as we would care for a child," Buffalo Bird Woman explained, "for we Indian people loved our gardens, just as a mother loves her children; and we thought that our growing corn liked to hear us sing, just as children like to hear their mother sing to them."

To grow the old strains called dent and flint and popcorn is to rediscover what was long forgotten in the American Corn Belt. Consider a patch of Yaqui Blue, Hopi Speckled, Apache Red, or Tarahumara Maize Caliente, because each one promises a surprise of color and the opportunity to share in plants of Native American spirituality. They are so simple to grow that even a novice gardener can join in the ritual and perhaps find peace in this age-old act. Like the Hidatsa and Anasazi, you too are likely to discover real beauty, the vibrant color and geometric forms hidden inside dried-out husks of the autumn fields.

> The sun, who is the Father of all.
> The earth, who is the Mother of men.
> The water, who is the Grandfather.
> The fire, who is the Grandmother.
> Our brothers and sisters the Corn, and
>   seeds of growing things.
> ZUNI PRIEST, 1884

Plants of the Shamans

One of the greatest excursions into Native American mysticism was recorded by Carlos Castaneda in his book *The Teachings of Don Juan: A Yaqui Way of Knowledge*, published in 1968. In this cult classic a young ethnologist made repeated visits to the desert outside Sonora, Mexico to visit a Yaqui Indian *brujo*, or sorcerer. Don Juan

shared with Carlos his view of life based upon experiences, or the "way of knowledge," learned while under the influence of very potent psychoactive plants.

According to Don Juan, the *brujo* typically selected one of these plants as his spirit world ally, depending on how the first few doses affected him. Such plants have been used by many other native cultures of the Americas, as well as those of the Old World, as vehicles for achieving dreamlike state, during which awareness of a separate reality expands the individual's supernatural view of the world around him. Often this is referred to as a "shamanistic trance," in which a holy man or witch doctor was able to enter the spirit world while under the influence of psychoactive plants.

The first plant given to Castaneda was a small cactus Don Juan called Mescalito in a very personal sense, as if this spirit fellow were a living part of the plant. He was referring to the peyote cactus, *Lophophora williamsii*, certainly well known to those who grew up in the counterculture. A small barrel cactus native to the southwestern deserts from Texas to central Mexico, it was well established in many cultures long before the Conquest. It is still used today by members of the Native American Church in their religious rituals. Peyote contains many alkaloids, which include mescaline, peyotline, anhaline, anhalamine, lophophorine, and others, which when ingested cause a strong hallucinogenic experience. Castaneda's detailed descriptions of his visions attests to this remarkable quality.

A second psychoactive plant, which Don Juan called "the devil's weed," is *Datura inoxia*, a native weedy perennial commonly known as jimsonweed. Castaneda consumed extracts from the root and applied a paste to his body, allowing the alkaloids to be absorbed into the skin. This is not uncommon; datura and its sisters of the deadly nightshade family (Solanaceae) figure largely in European witchcraft in much the same way. It was believed that witches applied "flying ointment" to their bodies, which allowed them to fly on broomsticks to their sabbats. Castaneda's hallucination of flying, as predicted by Don Juan,

LEFT: *Datura inoxia*. A toxic and psychedelic member of the night-shade family, datura is often called "thorn apple" because of its spiny seed capsules.

RIGHT: *Datura inoxia*. Datura is often overlooked when out of bloom, but its large, white, trumpet-shaped flowers are unmistakable.

attests to a specific effect of the devil's weed. In addition, datura can also lead the user to believe he or she is able to change into animals, and this is thought to have contributed to folktales of shapechangers, werewolves and vampire bats.

Datura is very dangerous because it contains toxic compounds which can easily cause death to sensitive individuals or if not administered properly. It is so potent that the alkaloids hyoscine, hyoscyamine, and atropine are still listed in today's materia medica as powerful stimulants. In addition to Castaneda's hallucinatory experience, he developed painful side effects typical of datura, which include extreme headache, high blood pressure, profuse sweating, and nausea. Indeed, with this plant there is a fine line between a ritual or medicinal dose and a deadly dose.

Use of datura by Native Americans originated in South America, where tree datura was part of rain forest cultures of the Amazon. It was used among the Zuni by rain priests as a divination plant, just as was described by Don Juan, and also as an anesthetic. Healers could perform mild surgery and set bones without the deeply drugged patient experiencing pain, and it is likely many other tribes of the Americas used it this way, as well.

Over time datura's religious use spread northward through Mexico and filtered into

other tribal rituals of the southern United States. After the missionaries spread their influence, particularly in the Spanish mission lands of California, the subtle aspects of other rituals were strongly discouraged by the church. In their place came cults of datura use known as *toloache* or *main-oph-weep*, which provided a much more powerful religious experience, capable of surviving despite the oppression of Anglo influence.

The more ornamental species of datura native to the tropics can grow to tree-like proportions. It has been reclassified into a new genus, *Brugmansia*.

Bridges and raised wooden boardwalks are frequently used to cross over marshy ground or to protect delicate plants from careless pedestrians. *Long Canyon, Selkirk Mountains, Idaho.*

INSPIRATION: NATURE AND THE GARDEN

Among garden designers there is often a struggle to define exactly what we are trying to do. Just where does our garden end and God's garden of nature begin? How does the hand of man enter the divine scheme of ecology and thus manipulate it into our own vision of the outdoor world? There are no easy answers here, and you will find widely differing opinions on the subject.

As we have seen, early people granted the natural environment spiritual powers, marveling at the seasonal changes and unexplained phenomena, such as lightning striking the oak. This was continued in St. Francis's view of nature, but the various spirits became manifestations of a Christian God. It is right to see nature as the most divine landscape, created by a mystical hand, each species of plant and animal fitting into an enormous puzzle. To walk in the woods, or wade through the tall grass of a wild meadow, we are awed at the majesty before us. One cannot help but realize that these landscapes are by far the most holy as they bear most distinctly the hand of divine creation.

No matter what your spiritual orientation, a native landscape has much to offer in terms of separation and inspiration. Monasteries are often located in rural areas and surrounded by field, fen, and forest. The monks find the solitude and beauty of such a place as inspirational as St. Francis did, and through their examples we may learn how to better find our higher power in the landscape.

The first way to discover the true magnificence of nature is to go out into it. That may sound obvious, but it is surprising how many people prefer to view such country from afar rather than experience it more intimately. Yet when I walk through the forests with others who do not know it well, I can share with them what I love and know about this vast community of organisms. This is why nature walks and ecotourism are growing much more popular—because people want to know these things but are too divorced from the natural world to discover them on their own.

For our purposes, we may call these the universal truths of nature, the fundamental principles that govern plants and animals on earth:

Christ Laid To Rest by Nicholas Fiddian-Green. Sculpture in the woodland garden is most natural when it blends with the surrounding colors and textures. *The Hannah Peschar Sculpture Garden designed by Anthony Paul Landscape Designer, Ockley, Surrey, England.*

Bridal Veil, Columbia Gorge, Oregon.

the unique relationships, the distribution of species, and the diversity that pulls it all together. Once the great picture becomes clear, many people find themselves in a spiritual awakening which leads them to both old and new faiths. We all need something to believe in, and the religion of nature is dogmatcally vague. Hence comes the rediscovery of Druidism and the quasireligious philosophies of the environmental movement, in which we find all earth a church and all woods a sacrament.

There are the things we see, and the things we don't see, and in between there are the doors.

JIM MORRISON

There are many universal truths of nature, which may be expressed as doorways connecting one realm to another. In seeking them we encounter one world that is visible and another buried beneath it, which may be seen only if we look very closely. True consciousness is the ability to see all the worlds of nature, for there is order to every aspect of the universe.

I first realized this many years ago, when I was fortunate to have a very good biology teacher. When our high school class studied microscopic life, she took us over to the edge of a small, somewhat brackish pond. There she made us get down on our knees with our faces nearly touching the water to discover in the shallows hundreds of minute hydras, which are like tiny squid, propelling themselves through their liquid environment. That day I discovered through the teacher a door between what I saw and what I had previously failed to see. My whole vision of stagnant ponds was forever changed.

If you are seeking greater meaning in your land or want to improve a wild site associated with a church or a community, there are some important things to consider. First, you must be ready to take on stewardship of the land and care for it properly. Many of the American ecosystems have been disturbed by any number of factors, from agriculture to the exclusion of natural fire. In some cases, it is important to apply some remedial measures to improve the health of the plants and animals which live there. A healthy ecosystem produces a much greater abundance of wildlife and makes all organisms easier to see and appreciate.

The restoration issues that follow are very general considerations that will vary, depending on the region and its current conditions. They represent, nevertheless, some of the ideas most critical to developing a healthy, useful, and spiritual natural site.

Help the land. Most of the dense forest we see today is not natural; it is the result of fire suppression. In an effort to save our most majestic trees, we have eliminated fire, which allows the forest to grow into a dense thicket. This shrubby growth shades and crowds out the tender herbs that once grew on the forest floor, which in some cases disappeared long ago without fire.

It's important to get a good picture of how the proposed restoration area looked a century ago under a normal fire regime, then begin a program of vegetation control. There are many examples of small plants reappearing on their own with such a program—from seed lying dormant until correct conditions returned. For large sites consult a local forester or environmental professional, who will help you get started and ensure you do the right things. There will be different approaches depending on the kind of land you are working with, be it marsh, fen, meadow, prairie, chaparral, or forest.

Assess the values. Every piece of land has its own set of good qualities and not-so-good qualities. To transform a wild piece of land into a place of spiritual experience, you must seek to enhance all the benefits to their greatest potential. A creek flowing underneath a canopy of prickly wild blackberry vines is of no benefit to humans, but if you clean up the area and expose its banks, you may enjoy it year round. Sites with fine views should enhance that quality. One with beautiful, smooth granite outcroppings should focus on them. A grove of buckeyes needs to be appreciated, as does the quiet beneath a dense grove of pines. The act of discovering these values is a spiritual excursion into nature which helps you become more intimate with all the

land has to offer.

Make moving around convenient. Monasteries and convents frequently have outdoor stations of the cross where those Christian truths may be appreciated in nature, the great cathedral. We gain from this the value of not only sitting but walking through the land on a designated pathway, which also keeps the surrounding plants untrampled. In addition, a path makes it easier for those with wheelchairs, or canes, or without suitable footwear, to still get around and enjoy all the site has to offer.

Some friends have a home in the redwood forests of California's north coast. Amidst the dense stands of trees, they created a pathway system, not paved or graveled, but simply a trail that takes you all over the site and immerses you in nature. A singular linear path guides you, eliminating the need to pay attention to where you are, and this frees up the mind to ponder other mysteries. The creation of access ways, steps, trails, and bridges allows anyone, familiar with the site or not, to see it in its entirety. This is the key to getting out into nature, rather than just observing it from indoors or far away, and making the site a spiritual and recreational experience everyone can enjoy.

Sit down and rest yourself. When was the last time you stopped everything and remained that way for a minute, maybe a quarter of an hour or more? If you're like most folks, it was a long time ago. The biblical passage, "'Be still, and know that I am God'"(Psalm 46:10), is so appropriate today when we feel guilty for not keeping busy all the time. In nature stillness is the rule, and there we may rediscover the small voice inside, the sound of God whispering answers to our prayers.

A natural site is suitable for meditation if it provides you the ability to stop and rest a while. It is in the quiet stillness that wildlife is likely to come out of hiding, for most animals know we are there by our scent and movement. If we eliminate movement, animals will continue their activities, the squirrels coming down from the treetops, the deer resuming their browsing, and the jackrabbits loping along in search of grass. A place to rest may be essential to those who walk with difficulty. Benches of natural wood or even flat-topped boulders make seating that does not smack of the hand of man but blends in with the surroundings. Subtlety in design ensures that we remain the visitors and do not overwhelm our hosts with a demanding presence.

URBAN FLORA AND FAUNA

We in the gardening world tend to be preoccupied with aesthetics, and many end up with unnatural gardens for the sake of style. In a way this is a one-dimensional treatment of a three-dimensional world. To find visions of Genesis in the suburbs or even in the city, you must turn to what can be created in your own backyard. In doing so, you may be surprised at just how much wildlife there is around you. Grow plants that bring birds, insects, and small mammals up close and personal. But first throw out your parterres, topiary, manicured lawn, and formal gardening notions, because what other creatures appreciate in plants does not always match our highly structured ideas of paradise.

Many books about wildlife gardening can guide you through the steps required to create a place where birds and other creatures come to feed. Above all, it is food and water they are after, particularly in winter, when food plants are

Pieces of broken concrete or flagstone may be pieced together to form an inviting walkway that naturally blends with the surrounding plants. *Roger Raiche Garden, Berkeley, California.*

barren, and late summer, when water holes are few and far between.

Most animals spend the bulk of their time feeding. Wildlife gardens must be planted with species that provide food in order to lure mammals, insects, and birds in to stay. Most natural food sources are plants that produce nectar, seeds, and foliage for grazing. The most valuable plants to songbirds are those with berries, fruit trees, grapevines, and significant seed-bearing annuals like the sunflower. Nectar feeders are essential to hummingbirds and are a marvel to watch up close. Artificial feeders can also enhance the supply of birdseed and are critical to migratory species or those who remain during winter.

Water is as important as food to birds and mammals. Birdbaths, always a part of gardens, are making a comeback today. Newer, more attractive designs are better than ever, and even a decorative fountain can double as bird water if it is shal-

The garden in winter. *Wayside Garden, Creston, British Columbia, Canada.*

Spacious walkways on well-drained ground may be created with a layer of decomposed granite, gravel, or even ground bark, packed and rolled smooth. *Idencroft Herbs, Kent, England.*

low and has a suitable landing place. In the dry summer months, they will lure butterflies and dragonflies, and at night you may find opossums and raccoons drinking there, too.

ENCHANTING THE LANDSCAPE GARDEN DESIGN

The unseen forces in the wild have always beckoned us to return and observe the subtle acts of both plant and animal life. When we cannot get away, a garden can provide a convenient alternative. The naturalized garden is soothing to spend time in and also offers a diversity of visual opportunities. A garden designed to lure wildlife into a suburban or urban space functions as more than just an aesthetic experience, because it offers the three critical needs of wildlife: food, cover, and water.

This plan contains the components of many different ecosystems. Forest trees were chosen for their association with woodland spirits and the old religions of Europe. The holm oak, revered by the Druids, was the ancient tree of thunder and the haunt of Thor and Zeus; the ash represents the tree of life, a mythological species of Nordic tribes; and the rowan, a powerful talisman against witches, and the moody yew, a churchyard tree of Britain, each offer their own legends and lore.

The plan includes a small pool of water, the most critical element to all living things. The pool attracts birds, insects, and small mammals during the dry season and may even contain fish or other aquatic plants and animals. Clumps of Japanese iris and horsetail reeds provide protective cover around the pool margins. The living spaces around the pool are paved with slabs of slate, flagstone, or sandstone, combined with natural boulders at the water's edge.

At the center of the garden is a broad meadow of perennial grasses, clovers, and wildflowers. It is irrigated and may be allowed to grow tall and flower naturally or be mowed to a more manageable height. A portion of the garden is devoted to plants that attract both butterflies and hummingbirds with their brightly colored flowers.

This enchanted landscape, created by a human hand, is one of harmony and peace and offers us a soothing place to relax. Here we may spend time quietly observing the subtle industry of nature, which helps us to better understand our connection to the natural world.

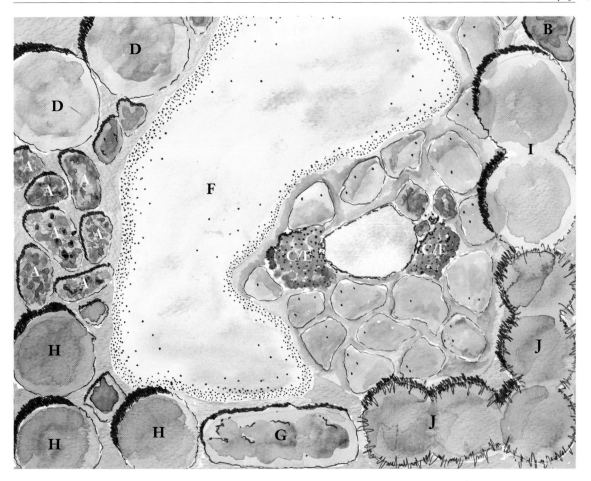

Earth's Garden

    A.   Butterfly and Hummingbird Plants
    B.   *Cotoneaster parneyi*—Cotoneaster
    C.   *Equisetum hyemale*—Horsetail
    D.   *Fraxinus excelsior*—Ash
    E.   *Iris* 'Kaempferi Hybrids'
    F.   Meadow Lawn—Irrigated
    G.   *Pyracantha coccinea*—Firethorn
    H.   *Quercus ilex*—Holm Oak
    I.   *Sorbus acuparia*—Rowan
    J.   *Taxus baccata*—Yew

Five

MONASTERIES AND MISSIONARIES

VITA CONTEMPLATIVA

FOR WE ARE NOT THE CAUSE WHY SUMMER AND WINTER RETURN IN REGULAR SUCCESSION; THESE SEASONS HAVE THEIR OWN LAWS, AND HAVE THEIR ORDER ARRANGED BY HEAVEN.

Seneca

he story of gardens is deeply rooted in classical civilizations, the destruction of order during the Dark Ages, the rediscovery of the Renaissance, and the further growth into new lands of the missions. Through these gardens we discover the roots of ancient peoples who lived and prospered in the Near East, northern Africa, and throughout the Mediterranean regions. Their relatively warm climates influenced how the gardens took shape. By understanding more than just design but the subtle relationships of the garden to medicine, religion, war, and, most of all, daily life, we see humanity and the landscape in a single continuous stream, which deeply influenced the aesthetic of the Americas.

The earliest garden makers, the ancient Egyptians, protected their gardens from the hot, dry winds by buildings and thick mud walls. Turning inward, such a garden became like a small oasis of water, shade, and soothing greenery, an arrangement that gave birth to the ornamental garden in the West. Like Near and Middle Eastern art and architecture, rigid geometry appealed to the ancients because it created order in the universe, and we have found similar organization in points of the compass, seasons, and both lunar and solar calendars.

Nepeta × Faasseni 'Six Hills Giant'. *Beryl Bed and Breakfast Garden, Wells, England.*

Parc de Canon, Mezidon, France.

By the end of the first century after Christ, the Roman Empire reached from Spain eastward to the Caspian Sea, and from Britain south to the Sahara. Soon the toll of heavy taxation and bloated government, combined with a splitting of the empire into two capitals, Rome in the west and Constantinople in the east, all weakened the provinces. In addition, dwindling slave labor and the transition from pagan to Christian helped put the once great empire into a state of disarray by the fifth century.

At the same time the tribes of Europe and Asia began encroaching into Roman territory. Among the first were the Vandals, Goths, Franks, Saxons, and Angles. They raided towns and villages, disrupting every aspect of daily life. Landowners built fortified castles, which provided refuge while the barbarians repeatedly pillaged Europe. The once fertile fields and orchards were abandoned because it was too dangerous to work far from the safety of castles. The roses and fruits, flowers, and medicinal plants so valued during classical times were no longer as important, because the most basic survival became the chief concern. With the threat of death so near at hand, it is not difficult to see why the medieval period was called "the age of faith." Continental Europe, Britain, and the Mediterranean countries in some ways slipped

Heavy wood doors and thick walls were designed for protection during the perpetual wars of the Middle Ages. *Rosa* 'Iceberg' frames this door at Broughton Castle in England. *Lord Saye and Sele, Oxfordshire, England.*

back in time to the kinds of conditions that prevailed before Roman influence. Feudal life and war among tribes became the daily focus rather than arts, letters, science, and agriculture.

During this time another influence appeared, the Arabs, or Moors, and their religion, Islam. Accustomed to living in the inhospitable deserts, the Moors invaded southern Spain and occupied that land for hundreds of years. They built homes and palaces much like those of the Egyptians, with protected gardens within high walls. In the Islamic garden there was a great deal of symbolism which related to their religious faith and the rules set down by Mohammed.

The Moors and their religion retained a close link between nature and art. To them the garden was a vision of heaven, and it was laid out with attention to religious symbolism. Spaces were typically divided into eight parts, representing the eight pearl pavilions of the Islamic paradise. They used water to further suggest a desert oasis, and their efforts built upon Roman techniques, maximizing the sight and sounds of water with ingenious fountains, pools, and channels. Though only a few of these Moorish gardens still exist, their themes live on through patterns in Persian carpets today. There with knotted wool are depicted the main schemes of Islamic paradise and the Persian heritage of both Mohammed and the earlier Zoroastrian religion that came before him.

At the same time the early Christians developed monastic communities of men, who often took up residence in the abandoned Roman homes. St. Benedict and his Rule of Monastic Order in the West initiated the first of many Benedictine communities. Benedict claimed the ruin of Nero's infamous palace in Rome, where the saint planted the *Roseto*, a medicinal rose garden of the church dedicated to the Virgin Mary, which still grows there today. More importantly, each monastery had to be entirely self-supporting. Naturally, they became the most productive examples of early agricultural communities.

The architecture of old Roman and Islamic homes were ideal protection from the raiding tribes, with open courtyards surrounded by a pillared, covered portico or cloister which linked all the rooms. As Christianity spread and various orders were organized, the need for new monasteries arose. Church architects began to develop a plan that would serve as the standard for new construction of monastic compounds. Based upon the successful, fortresslike Roman-Islamic house, the St. Gall Plan presented a cloister

Arches, colored tile, a central fountain, and basket-weave paving are all legacies of the Moors, who would indirectly influence the images of mission church compounds of the New World. *Medora Bass Garden, Santa Barbara, California.*

This fifteenth-century woodcut, from the old text *Fiore di Virtu*, depicts a friar in the viridarium of a cloister garden, gathering flowers in his habit for physic or church decoration.

divided into four quadrants, all meeting at the center in either a well, fountain, or holy water font. This layout symbolized the four quarters of the universe, with the central well being the water of life.

The St. Gall Plan shows more than one garden in the ideal monastery it depicted. There was, of course, a *hortus*, or kitchen garden, and the *herbularius*, or medicinal garden, surrounded by high walls to prevent thieves from stealing the precious apothecary herbs. The third type is a small meditation garden designed for *vita contemplativa*, the contemplative life. Most often located in a cloister setting after Roman home design, such a garden was set deep inside the monastic community to avoid undue outside influence. Sometimes the contemplative garden was surrounded by just a high wall. It contained a *viridarium*, or turf lawn, which was bisected or quartered by paths of gravel or sand. In most cases the water supply of older Roman homes or wells of newer sites could be found in the center of these gardens. It became the *fons vitae*, or fountain of life, supplying much of the community's needs.

A unique legacy of the Romans is the cloister, a covered extension of a building supported by a series of arched pillars that allows one to be both outside and inside at the same time. *The Cloisters, New York, New York.*

Another type of garden associated with every medieval Christian church was directly inspired by the little courtyard shrines of the Roman household gods. These pagan shrines so critical to our modern spiritual imagery were long rejected by the church due to their association with other gods. After this association had waned with the passage of centuries, the *paridaeza* garden evolved. It was in part tied to the perpetual medieval attempt to regain paradise on earth with walled gardens, such as those described in the Song of Songs. These places were filled with biblical imagery, using the apple as the Tree of Life in Genesis but also as the symbol of the true cross of Christ. Grapevines suggested the growing church, and the rose the Virgin Mary.

The *paridaeza* gardens were found beside early churches and cathedrals in the Middle Ages. At first their purpose was to provide a place where individuals would wait outside the house of God while in a state of sin until it was time to have confession heard. Today we find this very old tradition of paradise gardens exhibited in the outdoor shrines present at most Catholic churches, schools, monasteries, and convent grounds.

Originally, flowers inside the church were prohibited due to their close association with pagan mythology and the debauchery of Rome. Later this ban was also relaxed, so wreaths and garlands became important parts of Christian processions. Clergy were draped with them much the same way the caesars and their minions were clothed for various Roman festivals.

During the Middle Ages all plants were renamed and rededicated, this time to Christ, the Virgin Mary, the Apostles, and various early saints. Decoration with flowers refocused the role of these little paradise gardens, making them the ideal places to grow such decorations for feast days. They then became popular with clergy and lay people as a place of quiet contemplation.

The priests and brothers of monasteries were responsible for salvaging all that was left of the knowledge of the great classical civilizations of the Mediterranean, which included books on agriculture. Monasteries contained extensive libraries, of volumes in both Greek and Latin, which were rescued from destruction by war.

While the outside world disintegrated, the monastic communities preserved the important books and plants for many purposes. The chief task was the copying of texts into the great illuminated manuscripts. The monks had to create their own colored paints, and these were frequently derived plant materials grown in their gardens. The purple petals of Florentine iris was mixed with alum to create a green pigment. Purple and red came from elderberry and mulberry. Blue was derived from the petals of centaury, that familiar annual flower known as bachelor's button.

During these early times, healing, or physic, was closely tied to religion. As a result medical knowledge was concentrated inside the

Monasteries built according to the St. Gall plan provided places for the monks to say their prayers as they walked the cloisters. Here we find the vital elements: a central water feature, shade provided by fruit-bearing trees, and woven wattle fencing to frame the view. *The Cloisters, New York, New York.*

The ultimate garden, a *paridaeza*, or vision of paradise, was surrounded by walls and often located beside the church. At first they were places for those "in sin" to await their confessions, but later they evolved into a place to grow flowers for the altar and processions. Here, plantings of *Allium*, byzantine gladiolus (*Gladiolus byzantina*), and *Campanula Portenschaliana* evoke the same spirit. *Kiftsgate Court, Gloucestershire, England.*

Monasteries housed precious botanical and medicinal texts while Europe was in strife during the Middle Ages. Their gardens became a vital source of healing herbs for both monks and local peasants. Here, boxwood frames rosemary, lemon balm, and other herbs. *Chateau de Brecy, Saint-Gabriel-Brecy, France.*

Along the pillars of the cloisters, monks grew aromatic herbs, sheared into patterns that closely resembled Roman home gardens. Such patterns are beautiful in contemporary formal gardens. *Mrs. Dulaney Garden, Savannah, Georgia.*

monastic world, where the brothers practiced the healing arts. This combination of medicine and religion can be seen in a prescription for "elf disease," as described in the medieval *Leech Book of Bald*, one of the most famous herbals. This cure required collecting a small yellow daisy popular with the Romans called *potio Paulina*, or "drink of Paul," which is today known as elecampane, *Inula helenium.*

To collect elecampane in its most potent form, one was to go to the place where the plant grew after sunset and there sing the Benedicite, the Pater Noster, and a litany, then stick a knife into the plant and go home. At the same time the following day, he was to go to church, make the sign of the cross, and ask for God's blessing. Then in complete silence he was to return to the plant, sing the various litanies, dig up the plant, take it to the church, and leave it beneath the altar for the night. In the morning a drink was to be made of the plant combined with other common herbs, all the while singing the Pater Noster, the Credo, and the Gloria in Excelsis Deo, plus another litany. After all this the prescription could finally be consumed.

While medicine was still very primitive, the cures could be more debilitating than the diseases. The secular doctor's methods were primarily bleeding, purging, and the unsavory practice of applying leeches. The monastic methods of healing more clearly mirrored those of Greece and Rome, by using preparations made of herbs in the form of poultices, teas, tinctures, and essential oils.

The cultivation and use of medicinal plants is proven today by remnants of these gardens, the odd non-native plants naturalized at isolated monastic ruins. Wild peony still grows on the island of Steep Holm off the coast of Britain, where in the twelfth century Augustinian monks once staffed an abbey. The plant is native to the Mediterranean and was once valued for its power to cure epilepsy, and it was no doubt planted there for just such use.

In fact, church leaders feared that the monks might learn too much, which would lead them to the sin of pride. An old tale tells of a monk who sought virtue everywhere, but when offered a ladder to heaven, he could not help but look back one last time at his beloved garden. In seeing its flowery mead, he was filled with such yearning, he fell from the ladder into the flower beds, which had become the earthly temptation that denied him a place in heaven.

With such strong emphasis upon healing, there arose medieval legends surrounding many common plants, and most involved a change from pagan mythologies to stories appropriate the expanding realm of Christianity. Plants of Greek mythology became dedicated to saints, the Virgin Mary, and various mysteries of the faith. Herbs once part of tribal earth religions of Europe and Britain became familiar symbols of the new religion.

St. Fiacre, Patron of Gardeners and Florists

St. Fiacre was born in seventh-century Ireland and there became a monk. He chose a voluntary exile to France, where he was welcomed by the bishop of Meaux, St. Faro. The bishop knew of Fiacre's natural talent for horticulture and offered him a piece of land for a hermitage at Breuil. "I will give you all the land you can plow up in a single day," the bishop said. Come evening, the bishop checked up on Fiacre and found that he did not use a conventional plow, just a pointed stick, which he had dragged back and forth over a huge area. Fiacre explained to the bishop that he had not stipulated how deep he should plow, and for his ingenuity the entire "plowed" piece of land was given to the saint.

At the hermitage Fiacre cultivated his vegetables and lived in a tiny, austere cell, while visitors to the hermitage stayed in relative comfort. It is said that after Fiacre cleared all the briars and weeds off his land, a fence suddenly appeared around the perimeter. It was partly to enclose the garden but also to keep out women, whom the saint forbade to enter his hermitage. When a church was built on the site to hold the relics of the saint, women superstitiously refused to enter for fear of being struck blind. St. Fiacre's feast day is August 30.

The herb garden at the Washington Cathedral in Washington, D.C. makes the important connection between the church and the art of apothecary.

THE ROSES, FROM PAGAN TO VIRGIN

The rose is one of the oldest flowering plants known, and its cultivation can be traced back as far as five thousand years. This plant, which grew wild throughout the East, contained such potent oils it was naturally a favorite of early civilizations. We find its presence in Greece on the island of Rhodes, where it was named "Rhoden" and so loved it was imprinted on coins. In mythology, where the Greek civilization attempted to define the origin of all things through the gods of Mount Olympus, the flower was dedicated to Aphrodite, goddess of love.

Naturally, the Romans, with their reverence for all things Greek, also found the rose immensely appealing, dedicating it to their own goddess of love, Venus. Through their trading arteries dozens of wild rose species were scattered about Europe and grew in every Roman

The remains of a great hall from a manor house becomes a garden for 'Lady Hillington' climbers to snake across the ancient stonework. *Sudeley Castle, Gloucestershire, England.*

home. It was the petals of the rose that the Romans lusted after, because they provided bedding for the nobility. It was reported that the despotic Nero, infamous for banquets and orgies, spent three million sesterces ($160,000 today) to buy an immense number of roses for just one event. The floor of the hall would be covered with the petals in order to allow guests to recline on a wall-to-wall bed of roses. The rose was also considered a potent medicinal, and Pliny the Elder attributed thirty-two remedies to the plant.

With the fall of the Roman Empire in the fifth century, widespread cultivation of roses ceased, as barbarian tribes sacked Europe and Roman roads fell into ruin. Many of the roses so loved in classical times were lost, along with much agricultural knowledge.

The monastic communities did much to preserve the roses, for it was mandated by the church that at least one member of each monastery be knowledgeable in the botanical healing arts. With Pliny's rose prescriptions plus many new preparations, the rose retained its importance inside the monastic sanctuaries.

Over time the rose lost its connection with Roman orgies and was accepted by the Christian Church as a symbol of triumph over pagan oppressors. The Roman preference for wearing rose garlands during festivals had been stopped, but it was later revived during medieval times when priests donned them for feast day processions. These rose garlands, called *coronae sacerdotales*, were worn until the Reformation. Christian emperors were later crowned by the pope with wreaths of roses. A mosaic in the Church of St. Susan in Rome depicts the coronation of Charlemagne by St. Peter and the presentation of a staff of roses.

The rose is found in much Christian symbolism. Red roses became *Rosae martyres, rubore sanguinis,* or the blood of the martyrs. White roses were dedicated to purity and thus became the flower of Mary's virginity—canceling out previous associations with Venus and Aphrodite. The white rose also represented the martyrdom of celibacy embraced by the Catholic clergy. Pink roses mean first love, and the red rose pure love as well as the loss of life through martyrdom. A thornless rose, probably either *Rosa banksiae* or *Rosa multiflora,* was dedicated to the purity of the Virgin as a second Eve. This was in part because the roses generally were believed to have been thornless in the Garden of Eden until Eve's betrayal, and from then on they bore thorns as a reminder of her guilt.

The rose was also a symbol of secrecy, based upon a Greco-Roman myth involving Venus and the god of silence, Harpocrates. A rose hung from a doorway of a room

The most famous of all the monastic roses, *Rosa gallica*, the apothecary rose, thought to be in cultivation for over three thousand years.

Rosa banksiae—Lady Banks' rose. *Bourton House, Mr. and Mrs. R. Paice, Bourton-on-the-Hill, Gloucestershire, England.*

where a meeting was held announced to all that the subject matter under discussion was to remain confidential. Thus the term *sub rosa*, or "under the rose," indicated the secrecy of a conversation.

The rose became forever tied to the rosary, that litany of prayers dedicated to the Virgin Mary. This flower is found depicted in religious art and gothic architecture, most visibly the rose stained glass window of Notre Dame Cathedral in Paris. It is dedicated to saints Elizabeth of Hungary, Dorothea of Cappadocia, and Benedict of Nursia.

PADRES, PLANTS, AND NEOPHYTES

The world of plants and the kingdom of heaven were deeply linked centuries ago when Catholic priests made their way northward out of Mexico into the wilderness of Alta California, accompanied by Spanish soldiers and small herds of sheep to provide food. The seeds of the Old World—those in the stomachs and wool of the animals—were first introduced into the California countryside. Along the chain of missions began the first

regional formal agriculture, although Native Californians had already been practicing horticulture among wild plants for centuries by pruning, distributing, and burning. In the religious communities of the missions we find some of the most unique uses of plants, not for sustenance but as tools of conversion.

From the seed scattered in the footsteps of the mission padres, we see the very first California missionary tale, one of magical plants that grew quickly into treelike proportions in the mild climate of the south. They were mustard plants, so familiar in Gospel parables, which came to brilliantly mark El Camino Real, the road that linked the entire mission chain, with a trail of bright yellow flowers. These provided the first tangible learning experience for the Indians, who related far better to plants than anything else, since they knew almost every species of California flora by name.

A remarkable flower used by missionaries to teach and convert New World natives is that of the passionflower vine, native to South America. The name originated in the New World missions, derived from the deep religious symbolism

The passionflower with its fruit, clinging tendrils, and leaves.

seen in the complex architecture of the blooms.

Every part of the passionflower's exotic and intricate bloom was importantly related to aspects of the Crucifixion. The vine's supporting tendrils symbolized the whips of the scourging. The bloom's purple coloring reflected that of the robe placed on Jesus' shoulders during his mockery, and the corolla is the crown of thorns or halo. The central receptacle was the pillar of the cross; the five anthers were the hammers of the Crucifixion; and the three stigmas were the nails that pierced Jesus' flesh. The small seed vessel

This turn-of-the-century view of Mission Santa Barbara shows the true character of California missions and their extensive agricultural holdings.

became the vinegar-infused sponge. Last, the five red spots on each of the passionflower's leaves represented the slain Christ's five wounds: the four nail holes and the spear wound made in his side to verify his death.

The California missions were considered the far reaches of the Spanish Empire. Isolated in a barren, dry land, the padres had to provide for all their needs by farming and developed an extensive trading network of seeds and roots along the King's Road, El Camino Real, which linked all twenty-one mission sites. To supply water to land that saw no rain for well over six months at a time, systems of ditches and aqueducts were constructed. The same techniques used in early California were inspired by those developed in Spain during the Moorish occupation, a legacy of early Persian and Egyptian engineering.

The mission compounds were laid out much the same way as the early Roman and Arab homes, with courtyards bounded by high adobe walls. Here a fountain or pool was located at the center of the same four-quarter layout promoted in the St. Gall Plan. In these sheltered enclosures the padres could meditate in peace and walk along the pathways as they said their daily prayers.

Among the plants found in these sites are those that provided food for man or livestock,

such as fruit trees, grapevines, corn, and wheat. Other plants, both native and introduced species brought from the Old World, offered medicinal value, notably the opium poppy and the musk rose. Some were integrated into religious observances: palms for Palm Sunday, the flowers associated with saints, such as hollyhock for St. Joseph and pot marigold for the Virgin Mary.

There is little doubt that the native plants so well known to the peoples of California became vital to the missions as food, fiber, and medicine. Perhaps some good did evolve from this often maligned relationship, the remnants of which we see throughout California in many species, including the golden mustard and the passionflower vine.

Jesuit's Powder

The Jesuits and other orders of Catholic missionaries that traveled with the Spanish were highly educated in the sciences. Many were fascinated by the New World flora and its use as medicinals by native peoples. Among these Jesuit

Mission San Diego (*Courtesy California Department of Water Resources*).

missionary explorers was Father Antonio de la Calancha, who in 1638 resided in Peru. He stood by helplessly as the second wife of the viceroy suffered from malaria in Lima, which at that time was the number-one killer of human beings in warm climates. At that time none knew that malaria was spread by the bite of the mosquito, and even today it acts as a population control mechanism in many Third World countries.

In the seventeenth century neither the priest nor the viceroy's physician had anything to give the woman, dying of the fever and chills that continually racked her body. In desperation the viceroy sent messengers out into the country and mountains to find a botanical cure among the Indians. In the Andean town of Canizares, now in Equador, they found a tribe which used the bark of a tree, *Chinchona succirubra*, to suppress the devastating effects of this incurable disease. The bark contained quinine, the active chemical which stopped the recurring fevers.

The messenger ran back to the capital with the bark, which was administered to the woman, who miraculously recovered. She showed her gratitude by giving her discovery to the Catholic Church, specifically the Jesuits. Father Calancha documented the cure and presented the new drug, quinine, in a paper written for his order's chronicle in 1633.

With so many "wonder drug" claims flowing out of the Americas, however, Calancha's testament was not widely accepted, probably because he was not a physician. Only when Jesuits carried quinine to Rome did it finally receive attention. It was called "Jesuit's bark" and its use extolled "against quartan and tertian fevers accompanied by shivers." Malaria was common in Rome, as well, since there were once extensive marshes outside the city, which kept the people perpetually suffering what was then called the ague. The turning point was the cure of the aging Cardinal de Lugo, who promptly packaged the bark and distributed it throughout Europe.

As was often the case in the medical world at the time—such as it was, with its practices of purging and bleeding—physicians remained reluctant to accept such a simple cure as powdered quinine, since it would prevent their collecting high fees for extended treatments. In fact, they further rejected quinine because of ill will felt against the church and its clergy in the era of the Reformation.

It was later discovered that Jesuit powder varied in its effectiveness, because there were different species of *Chinchona* tree, and only one contained sufficient amounts of quinine. Yet the discovery of one of the world's most important medical treasures can still be traced back to Jesuit missionaries, whose work in botanical medicine was so deeply rooted in the spirit.

FATHER GREGOR MENDEL AND HIS PEAS

The valuable role of monasteries as centers for learning and science did not cease with the end of the Middle Ages. The Catholic Church, with its many universities and schools, proved that even into the nineteenth century there were still great discoveries to be made in the field of science. Whereas many Christians were struggling to reconcile modern science with their religious beliefs, the great minds of the Catholic institutions were not only embracing science but furthering it in profound ways.

This is proven most poignantly in the life and work of Gregor Mendel. Born in what is now the Czech Republic to a family of peasant farmers, Mendel was gifted with great intelligence. His childhood of tending the crops and orchards on his father's land, however, left him little hope for the future. Although he was not given a burning passion for his faith, Mendel entered the rich Augustinian Monastery of St. Thomas at Burenn in 1843, where he was assured a good education and was ordained a priest in 1847. This monastery, founded in 1350, had a long history of both science and culture. Among its members were mathematicians, mineralogists, and botanists engaged in scientific research and teaching. The atmosphere of this great monastery, Mendel once wrote, with its mineral collections, botanical garden, and exten-

ORNAMENTAL IDEAS

The famous Notre Dame gargoyles.

Perched high upon the facade of the twelfth-century Cathedral of Notre Dame in Paris are a flock of gargoyles carved out of stone. These fantasy figures are depicted as grotesque angels, dragons, dwarfs, and a host of other mythological beings—all sharing a devilish countenance. It is thought that the purpose of gargoyles was to show that the interior of the cathedral was so sacred that the demons were quickly departing. Many of them cantilever outward beyond the walls as part of the downspout system, designed to direct water away from the masonry walls.

Such cantilevered gargoyle spouts are well suited for fountain spouts, as well. Gargoyles have become very popular ornaments both indoors and out, offering us a unique tool with which to lend that medieval character to a garden. You can buy the very best outdoor gargoyles from the color Design Toscano catalog, listed in the resource section of this book.

Angels, too, are familiar spiritual figures with roots in biblical creation myths. These winged creatures reflect all that is good and pure in heaven. Guardian angels protect us, messenger angels are links between heaven and earth, and hosts of angels glorify God. To bring angels into our gardens is far more inspiring than bringing in gargoyles. A stone representation becomes a physical reminder that perhaps an angel is there among the flowers awaiting our return.

---

sive herbarium, fueled his interest in the natural sciences.

Once his studies were concluded, Mendel became a teacher but failed his examinations for a credential, so his Abbot sent him to the University of Vienna, where he studied natural sciences from 1851 to 1853. After his return to the monastery from Vienna, his work in the garden really began.

Until this time scientists hoping to discover the secrets of heredity used many different plants in an attempt to find the consistencies in inherited traits. This approach was far too broad to obtain any usable results, so Mendel narrowed the field to the common pea. Using thirty-four different kinds of peas, which had been tested for their genetic purity, he tried to determine whether it was possible to obtain new variants by crossbreeding. Over a period of eight years, from 1857 to 1865, he focused on specific traits, such as seed size or flower color. This type of research was most tedious, and during those years he inspected over 10,000 pea specimens.

The results of the experiments proved there were indeed mathematical laws governing the inheritance of certain traits when two individual plants cross-pollinated. These were, in essence, the process of hybridization and the prediction of characteristics of subsequent generations.

Much of Mendel's work is complex, and

A stone angel lends its special message of love to this garden seat. *Chalice Well, Glastonbury, England.*

This stone angel bears the unmistakable medieval Celtic influence. *Anne McIntyre Garden, Church Westcote, Oxfordshire, England.*

selectively change God's creations to better serve man, would later feed the world by enabling the breeding of better, stronger, and more prolific strains of the plant kingdom he so intimately loved.

The monastic traditions created over many centuries among those who gather together in the name of God have contributed much to today's gardens. The cloisters, the apothecary arts, science, scholarship, meditation, seclusion, and prayer summarize the greatest benefits of a Christian community. Medieval motifs, gothic styles, and haunting chants are as poignant today as they were so long ago, proving that the monastery and its members will be just as important at the end of the third millenia. Spirituality transcends time and space—it is a constant. We may share it by reintroducing the fruits of monastic life into our own holy garden.

without a botany or genetics background, it is difficult to know just how profound his results really were. He basically developed three fundamental laws of inheritance: the Law of Dominance, the Law of Segregation, and the Law of Independent Assortments. Unfortunately for Mendel, the top scientists of his day failed to understand his discoveries. Carl Naeglei of Munich, a well-known biologist, corresponded with the monk but never in his extensive writings even mentioned any of Mendel's theories or discoveries. It was not until after his death on January 6, 1884, that the magnitude of Mendel's work was finally discovered by the great fathers of modern genetics, Hugo de Vries, Carl Correns, and E. von Tschermack.

The beauty of Gregor Mendel's life and work lies in his genius and the fact that the church provided him an education and the environment in which to carry out his important horticultural experiments. This humble Catholic priest who devoted his life to God was clearly rewarded for his faith, which was never distorted in the face of modern science. What he discovered there in the monastery garden, the ability to

Architecture inspired by the monasteries of Europe is reflected in this stone gazebo and pathway at the Washington Cathedral, Washington, D.C.

MONASTERIES AND MISSIONARIES GARDEN DESIGN

Catholic missions of Mexico, California, and the American Southwest share many of the same elements found in medieval monasteries. Many mission churches sat beside a courtyard such as this, where the monks could say their office while strolling along the tile walkways. These spaces were later dotted with the monuments and tombs of the priests and brothers who spent their lives there in service. It is a style that combines elements of Rome, the Middle East, Old Spain, and Mexico, and it is still popular today where there are warm, dry climates.

This courtyard garden contains a green turf called a *viridarium*, which is broken into four quadrants and has a central tiered fountain. The fountain sits two steps above the walkways on a

A Mission Garden

A. *Alcea rosea*—Hollyhock
B. *Arecastrum romanzoffianum*—Queen Palm
C. *Citrus* 'Improved Meyer'—Meyer Lemon
D. *Passiflora alatocaerulea*—Passionvine
E. *Rosa banksiae*—Lady Bank's Rose
F. *Rosa gallica*—Apothecary Rose
G. *Rosa* 'Hybrid Tea Climber'
H. *Rosa moschata*—Musk Rose
I. *Rosmarinus officinalis*—Rosemary
J. Turf Grass Viridarium
K. *Verbena peruviana*—Verbena
L. *Vitis vinifera*—Grapevine

raised patio, depicting the square-upon-square design often found in the tile patterns of Islamic mosques. The open space is surrounded by an abundance of plants suited to warm climates. The cloisters, covered walks that typically surrounded a monastery courtyard, are suggested by two long arbors cloaked in climbing roses and grapevines.

At the far end of the symmetrical garden is a crucifix surrounded by hollyhocks and framed by two arbors bearing passionflower vines. This establishes the Christian portion of the design by linking the Passion with the cross. In the corners are groups of Meyer lemon trees, naturally dwarfed in size, but these may be replaced by any other kind of citrus.

Four queen palms, a substitute for messier date palms, frame and shade the paved living space and enhance the sense of symmetry. Beneath them is a floral carpet of annual bedding plants honoring the Moorish tendency to plant expanses of low-growing flowers that became the inspiration for Persian carpet designs. Behind the bedding plants rise mounds of old roses typical of mission landscapes, as well as rosemary and verbena, both drought tolerant and once popular in Spain.

The monastic garden may be easily adapted to virtually any space. The vital elements are the central water feature and the space divided into four quadrants. Terra cotta pavers, pots, and brilliantly colored glazed tiles all help create the character of Old Spain.

Gothic stone windows and *Phlomis fruticosa. Sudeley Castle, Gloucestershire, England.*

Six

MARY'S GARDEN

SALVE REGINA

The once small cluster of people who love and venerate Christ's mother, Mary, has grown into an enormous, far-flung following. She has been the inspiration of great leaders, but most of all she is a woman—a common woman, pregnant out of wedlock—who would forever become the patron of the lowly and the special comfort for mothers, grandmothers, and daughters. Should there be one person who best expresses the power and compassion of Mary, it is Mother Teresa, who does not preach but simply tends to the poorest of the earth's people. Through her example many are drawn to God.

In the nearly two thousand years since her son's birth, there has grown an entire Marian culture, sustained by a series of miracles and apparitions. Many attribute this to the fact that she replaced a number of old pagan goddesses and therefore became the primary female entity of the Christian era. Her influence upon Latin America in the form of Our Lady of Guadalupe is well known, as detailed in chapter six. She also appeared to Bernadette at Lourdes and to three shepherd children at Fatima, Portugal. The most recent appearance was at war-torn Mejugori, Bosnia, where faith has grown despite war and adversity, fueled by an apparition again visible only to a handful of children. Oddly, these apparitions occur mostly in countries and times of great strife.

A statue of Mary placed in a niche high on the wall of a French monastery. Beside her is the white rose symbolizing her purity. *Nathalie Becq Garden, Grisy, France.*

Mary, high up on a rooftop shrine to protect the house. *Snowshill Manor, Gloucestershire, England.*

This outdoor space arched by climbing roses 'Clair Matin' resembles old monastery and church gardens, which used the flower to honor the mother of Christ. The roses here resemble the garlands used by the church during feast days. *Pat Henry Garden, Laurens, South Carolina.*

Today we find images of Mary in many gardens, in tile, sculptured marble, cast concrete, and bronze. Her name and legend cross over much of our plant literature time and time again. Often a plant or garden once associated with earth goddesses or classical mythology's many female deities was rededicated to Mary, usually during the Middle Ages, in an effort to discourage the old beliefs.

OUR LADY OF THE ROSES

Poor men and women who are sinners, I, a greater sinner than you, wish to give to you this rose—a crimson one, because the Precious Blood of Our Lord has fallen upon it. Please God that it will bring true fragrance into your lives.

ST. LOUIS DE MONTFORT,
The Secret of the Rosary

In her litany, Mary's many names are said, and among these is her most beautiful title, Mystical Rose. It is not easy tracing back the relationship of roses to the Rosary and the Virgin, but we do know that prayer beads have been used by many religions to count their mantras in the East. Early monks began counting their prayers, too, by passing stones from one hand to another until all were done. It was later discovered that beads worked much better because they could be strung together—and the word *bede* in old English means "prayer."

A thirteenth-century tale explains the origins of the Rosary. A young man each day offered the Virgin

The red rose symbolizes the shedding of Christ's blood for the sins of the world. *Jeanne Rose Garden, San Francisco, California.*

one hundred and fifty roses (the number of "ave" beads on the older, larger Rosary), which he wove into a garland to place upon her altar. Later, when he had become a monk, he lamented to his abbot that he lacked time to show such devotions.

"Say one hundred and fifty aves to Our Lady, which I'm sure she will find just as acceptable as the roses."

At certain times each day the monk knelt at her altar and said every one of the Hail

When we pray the rosary we offer Mary a gift of roses.

Marys. One day he was on a journey, and his time to pray came while traveling through a dark wood. True to his devotion, the monk had knelt down to say his prayers, when robbers beset him. At the same moment a beautiful, shining lady appeared amidst the robbers. Reaching down, she pulled from the monk's still-praying lips one hundred fifty roses and wove them together. As the garland grew longer, the roses decreased in size, until they were no larger than rosary beads, which she then placed around the neck of the monk. This vision was so miraculous, the robbers renounced their sins and eventually became monks themselves. It is said that they each said their rosaries, with each bead carved into the shape of a rose.

This beautiful tale differs from the official story of the Rosary. In the year 1206 St. Dominic Guzman was struggling to teach the illiterate of Europe about the prayers of the church. The Virgin appeared to him and sent a means of helping the ignorant to pray and meditate on the life of Christ.

It became called the rosary because this common plant so perfectly symbolized the various mysteries that are part of church teaching. The beauty of the flower represents the Joyous Mysteries, or the positive times in the lives of

both Mary and Jesus. Its sharp thorns, with their painful pricks, are the Sorrowful Mysteries, and the fragrance of the rose in both flower and foliage becomes the Glorious Mysteries. To say the Rosary was likened to planting a garden of roses within one's own soul. To say it daily means to tend the garden and keep it beautiful.

The word *rosary* means "crown of roses," which suggests that every time it is said, the words become a crown of fifty-three red roses and six white roses upon the Blessed Mother's head. When each prayer is completed, it is likened to placing a rose before Mary, and just as the rose is the queen of flowers, so it is fitting for it to honor the Queen of Heaven.

Victorian women often created their own beads for the rosary out of real rose petals. Since the rosary is held in the hands for quite a while, the body heat causes them to release their fragrance. This would please the senses while pray-

Rosa 'Alister Stella Grey' and *R.* 'Fellembers'. *Huntington Gardens, San Marino, California.*

ℛOSE PETAL ROSARY BEADS

Rose flowers should be collected in dry weather. Promptly remove the petals and chop them up finely by hand, in a blender, or by food processor. Place the pulp in an old iron saucepan, preferably a rusty one, with water to cover. Heat slowly but do not boil, and simmer for one hour. Allow the mixture to cool and sit until the following day, then repeat the heating process. Add small amounts of water, if needed.

Do this again the third day, until you are left with a thick, black mass that can be worked with the fingers into balls the size of a hazelnut. When drier but still pliable, impale each bead on a stout needle or hat pin, then allow them to dry on waxed paper. Dried beads are brittle, so take care when stringing them.

ing and leave behind residual fragrance on the fingers afterwards. The above, just one of the many recipes for creating rose beads, is far from precise, and amounts may require some experimenting.

The Rosary is not always represented by beads. One of the most beautiful Catholic customs is the outdoor Rosary walk, a circular path punctuated by markers, which represent each bead. As you travel down the walk, you pause by each marker, say your prayer, then move on to the next one. These walks are sometimes found in convents, where the sisters say a regular Rosary. The rosary is adapted to the walk, where we may pray outdoors and take in all God's natural beauty. Some monasteries create very long Rosary walks that meander through forests, where the environment is quiet and contemplative. The markers

The Virgin in a Rose Arbour, by Stephan Lochner. (*Wallraf-Richartz Museum, Cologne, Germany/Bridgeman Art Library, London/Superstock*)

themselves are simple to make out of materials at hand, from stubs of fence posts to painted rocks.

There has been much created over the ages tying in the symbolism of the rose to Mary. This may be best seen in the painting *The Virgin in a Rose Arbour,* by Stephan Lochner (d. 1451), in which Mary sits with the infant Christ in her arms before an arbor draped in red and white roses. The red ones represent acceptance of God's will, the white flowers her purity.

Like most religious icons, there are elements in this composition have other specific meanings, and in this case we find four different plants. Mary sits upon a field of violets, one of the smallest woodland flowers, which grows hidden beneath the canopies of trees. They represent humility and the beauty of our souls, hidden within us. Mixed in are English daisies, *Bellis perennis,* the sign of innocence. There are also strawberries to suggest righteousness. At the base of the arbor grow white lilies, representing strength of purity and Mary's acceptance of God's will. They suggest one of her other names, the Lily Without Stain. Even more intriguing, however, is the apple in the infant's hand. It is a sign that Christ offers us salvation in the form of the fruit of the Tree of Life, reconciling himself to us after Adam and Eve's fall from grace.

Folktales have also blended Mary with roses over the ages. One tale tells of a woman condemned to death for a crime she did not commit. She was taken to an open field and bound to a stake, and branches were piled all around. As the flames were lit and grew tall, she cried out to the Virgin. At that moment the flames vanished, the glowing embers turned into red roses, and the still-unburned wood became white roses.

Bellis perennis, the small English daisy, also known as Mary's flower, became a symbol of innocence in Christian art.

ST. THERESA, THE LITTLE FLOWER

To strew flowers is the only means of proving my love, and these flowers will be each word and look, each daily sacrifice.

St. Theresa is not a saint of ancient times, for she was born in 1873 in a small French town. All five of her sisters entered the convent, and at the early age of fifteen, she dedicated herself to the Carmelite Order; she would die among her sisters at twenty-four. In this one woman was a deep love of simplicity, which was ideal for the often austere conditions of the convent. She called herself Theresa of the Child Jesus and often called her life the "little way," an approach remarkably similar to that of St. Francis of Assisi, who founded the order of the Friars Minor, or "little monks," seven centuries earlier.

At the urging of her sister, Theresa wrote down her spiritual biography, which was published after her death under the title *The Story of a Soul*. Among its pages lay the essence of humility. The passage most well known: *After my death, I will let fall a shower of roses. I will spend my heaven doing good on earth*. After her death the rain of roses began, not as flowers but as a series of miracles, which led to her canonization in 1925.

Among her surviving relics at the National Shrine of the Little Flower in Chicago is a golden branch of five rose blossoms, with each flower containing a separate relic. There is also a crucifix carved from the trunk of a rosebush that grew in her convent, from which the saint had plucked flowers to set before the statue of the Christ Child. There is even a lily woven from the cascade of her hair shorn upon entering the Carmelite Order. So great was her following that Theresa became the patron saint of florists worldwide, and Pope St. Pius X declared her the "greatest saint of modern times."

St. Theresa painted by her sister, Celine. (*Courtesy of the Society of the Little Flower*)

Pink rose 'First Kiss' and borage.

In another story, St. Francis of Assisi, the saint who embodies poverty and self-denial, found himself shivering in his cold stone cell one frosty winter day. Forever subject to Satanic visions of comfort, he was sorely tempted this day, and lest he give in, Francis ran outside to a snow-covered briar and rolled upon its thorns. As each thorn pricked his flesh and drew blood, the crimson drops turned to perfect red roses. Encouraged by this miraculous reward for his continued faith, Francis gathered up the roses and brought them to the monastery chapel, where he laid them at the altar of the Virgin Mary with the Christ Child in her arms.

COATLAXOPEUH

"She Who Crushes the Serpent"

The dahlia is a flower of birth and death, of war, and of the thirst for blood which was so much a part of the Aztec religion. The earth goddess, the Serpent Woman Tonantzin, was one of the most important deities of this last great civilization of Mexico, and around her the legend of the dahlia flower begins. This is not the dinner-plate dahlia we know today, but a little red wildflower of the Valley of Mexico with a daisylike bloom bearing only eight petals.

According to the myth the Serpent Woman lived at the foot of Tepeyac Hill, or Serpent Mountain, the first of many hills enclosing the basin of Mexico City. This barren, rocky place supported only the most lowly of weeds. The Serpent Woman climbed to the top of the hill each day to hold conversation with the eagle, the symbol of the Aztec empire. Through the bird the sky gods communicated to her.

One day a mature maguey plant suddenly appeared on the hilltop and was discovered by the Serpent Woman. Maguey is the common name for *Agave pacifica*, from which the Aztec drink *pulque* is fermented, and it was drunk during most Aztec rituals. From beneath its leaves came a rabbit, which sat holding a small red flower stem in its mouth. When the eagle

This medieval woodcut shows Mary in a walled garden. The two trees allude to those of Eden in the Old Testament.

Agave ferax. This agave shows the viciously spiked leaves responsible for the creation of the Aztec war god—it is also the plant from which mescal is harvested and *pulque* is fermented. This plant's characteristic blue coloring is typical of many species of agave native to Mexico.

swooped down to bring his message to the woman, the rabbit hopped out into the open and laid the flower at her feet.

The eagle's message was that the sky gods instructed her to tear off a maguey leaf and upon its sharp tip impale the red flower. Then she was to hold the leaf and the flower to her breast all night long. This she did, and the next morning her son, the war god, was born. He was Huitzilopochtli (hummingbird of the left"), born fully grown, armed with a weapon as sharp as the maguey leaf, and immediately thirsty for blood, the carnal inheritance from the red dahlia flower.

The Aztec built a temple of Tonantzin upon Tepeyac Hill and there celebrated this birth event every eight years at a sacrificial stone, around which they arranged red dahlias and maguey plants. In these brutal rites they cut out the hearts of their hundreds of prisoners and offered them to Serpent Woman and her son, the war god. Tepeyac had become a place of death and honor among Aztec priests and their helpless victims.

One of the greatest Christian events in the New World occurred in early-sixteenth-century Mexico City, shortly after the conquest that would change the face of Latin America forever. In the wake of Cortez and the devastation of the Aztec empire, there arose great confusion due to the decentralization of that government. In an effort to quell the difficulties, Charles V, king of Spain, appointed the First Audience as a loose government over all the people. Unfortunately, this body was rife with corruption and likened to the reign of the brutal Roman emperor Diocletian, which naturally discouraged the Indians from accepting the Catholic faith. Reports of torture and other heinous acts caused Charles to appoint a bishop to the New World, hoping that a single honorable man could help reduce strife.

His name was Juan Zumarraga, and upon arrival in Mexico he knew immediately that the First Audience had wrought such disorder, a major revolt was at hand. With so few Spaniards and hundreds of thousands of Indians, this could boil into a massacre capable of wiping out all traces of European conquerors. In desperation the bishop prayed to the Virgin Mary, requesting she send him Castilian roses, the old species of arid Spain, to prove she had heard his prayer.

Many miles away a 57-year-old Indian, Juan Diego, had taken over the care of his

beloved, aged uncle in the typical mud and thatch hut. He frequently walked the nine miles to the church of Tlaltelolco, located near Tepeyac Hill, to hear the padres give instruction on Catholic religion. One cold winter morning, December 9, 1531, he approached Tepeyac Hill and heard faint music and smelled a strange perfume in the air. Then a soft voice came calling, "Juanito," from high atop the hill. Juan was compelled to find the source. In the ruins of the war god's temple stood a shining woman, her skin dark as an Indian's, her clothing in the royal colors of the Aztec priests, and

Our Lady of Guadelupe. (*Superstock*)

surrounded by a shining aura. She asked Juan to tell the bishop that a church dedicated to her should be built on that once-bloody hill. "Here I will hear [the Indians'] weeping and their sorrows, and will remedy and alleviate their sufferings, necessities and misfortunes." Juan agreed to bring the bishop her message.

Although he was granted an audience, the bishop did not believe the lowly Indian. So Juan, after much teasing by the household servants, sadly returned to the shining lady with his failure. She said to go back a second time and make the same request, but again the bishop remained unconvinced, although he asked Juan many questions about the vision. He still did not believe Juan, but requested he ask her for a sign, for if she was indeed the Virgin, then a sign would appear.

Once more Juan returned to the lady and cried out his unworthiness. "Come back here tomorrow and I will give you a sign," she said. Juan went home and found his uncle very ill, so

he remained at home the following day and failed to make his date with the Virgin. Finally, in the predawn hours of the third day, Juan set out to find a priest who would offer the uncle last rites, but when he passed by Tepeyac on a different route in order to avoid the Virgin, that beautiful voice called to him from the hilltop. He looked up to see the Virgin coming down to him. After hearing about his uncle's illness, she comforted Juan and promised the uncle would be well.

Then she told Juan to climb the hill, and at the top he would find beautiful flowers growing. "Pick them and gather them in your *tilma* [cloak], and bring them back to me." Flowers were absent in that high-altitude climate during winter, and nothing but thistles and cactus grew there. After his hike, however, Juan found growing there bushes of brilliant Castilian roses speckled with crystal prisms of dew. (In every version of this story, they are called "Castilian" roses, which are the highly fragrant damask, *Rosa damascena*. There were other flowers, which no doubt included the blood-red dahlia of Huitzilopochtli, the Aztec god of war, but it was the

A spray of Castilian roses like those which filled Juan Diego's cloak. (*Maureen Gilmer*)

roses that are most deeply tied to the story.)

Juan laid out his *tilma* and filled it with roses, then scrambled back down the hill to the waiting apparition. The Virgin rearranged the roses in Juan's cloak, then sent him off to the bishop with his sign. After a long wait he finally got in to see the bishop, who was meeting with important dignitaries. "I have brought the sign," Juan said as he opened the cloak to let all the flowers fall at the bishop's feet. The bishop seemed to hardly notice the flowers, though, and Juan found him staring at the *tilma*, one end still tied around the Indian's neck. Then the bishop and many others fell to their knees, for there on the *tilma* was a brilliantly colored image of the Virgin. The bishop knew it was related to his secret request for Castilian roses, which came to fruition at the hands of this poor uneducated Indian from the countryside whom he had already turned away twice before.

This same *tilma* bearing the image still hangs in the new cathedral of Our Lady of Guadalupe at the foot of Tepeyac Hill in Mexico City today. But there is far more to this story than meets the eye. First, the Virgin appeared to an Indian, the lowest of the social order, and her image was dark skinned, not with the light coloring of the Spanish Europeans. She also appeared to Juan on a former site of pagan slaughter in the form of a woman similar to the Serpent Woman of Aztec mythology. The image of the Virgin shows the tassel of a special girdle or waistband that meant she was pregnant with Christ, just as Tonantzin had been soon to give birth to the war god. The *tilma* was woven of agave fiber, which corresponds to the maguey plant in the Aztec tale. Strangely, this short-lived fiber, with an estimated typical life span of just a few years, has managed to survive over four centuries without disintegrating.

A great and wondrous sign appeared in the heaven: a woman clothed with the sun, with the moon under her feet and a crown of twelve stars on her head. She was pregnant and cried out in pain as she was about to give birth.

REVELATION 12:1–2

This passage in the book of Revelation further explains the meaning of the Virgin of Guadalupe's image. She was originally named *Coatlaxopeuh*, which in Nahutal, the language of Mexico prior to Spanish, means "she who crushes the serpent." Not only did Mary supplant the Serpent Woman, but the snake was also the symbol of the bloody Aztec empire, and the Virgin seemed to come in order to crush out brutal rites and replace them with her image and deep love of the Indian. The Guadalupe Mary also stands on a crescent moon, which connects her to this apocalyptic literature, as does the girdle of a pregnant Indian woman. The Franciscans then in Mexico had taught their neophytes about the Mother of God by calling her "she who crushes the serpent," as well. Only later on did the name *Guadalupe* appear. The Nahutal language was so difficult for Europeans to pronounce, they substituted a word phonetically similar and indeed already familiar to them and linked to the Virgin, there being a shrine to Our Lady of Guadalupe in Spain.

The Aztec plumed serpent god, Quetzalcoatl. (*Codex Borgia*)

There is yet is another Mexican tale connecting serpents and flowers, one about the benevolent feathered serpent god Quetzalcoatl. He first taught the Indians of Mexico City the art of agriculture, which was no small feat, considering the saturated conditions of the marshy lake bottom upon which they lived. The other gods were always jealous of Quetzalcoatl because he was so well loved, and they chased him all over Mexico.

Tired of running, Quetzalcoatl finally built

Viola tricolor, also known as Johnny-jump-up, St. Mary's herb, or Lady's flower, was avidly cultivated in medieval gardens.

himself a funeral pyre and lay down upon it to die and burn. The god retreated through death to the underworld for four days. Then a wind came up and blew his ashes into the sky, where they turned into birds and flew away. The soul of Quetzalcoatl remained in the earth and after eight days emerged as the dahlia flower. The red petals were his body, and the golden center, now representing the morning star, was his heart.

MARY GARDENS

The story of Mary gardens is one of plant nomenclature and world history. It begins before the Christian era, when every plant was given to the care of pagan gods of many cultures, and some were surrounded with deep mythology explaining this dedication or the origins of the plant on Earth. When the Roman Empire became Christian, the old pagan names were no longer appropriate, so the church fathers sought to make these plants honor the one true God by their names. For example, in Iceland the plant known as "Freyje's heir," in reference to a goddess, became Our Lady's hair. During the Middle Ages, or the "age of faith," plants were all renamed to commemorate Jesus Christ, Mary, the saints, and apostles. By far the most common dedications were to Mary in all her names and

forms, for she replaced a host of goddesses. This era of nomenclature lasted until the sixteenth-century Reformation, which dropped part or all of the Marian names.

During medieval times there were special gardens at various places dedicated exclusively to the Virgin Mary and planted only with flowers that bore her name. In the twelfth-century St. Bernard praised her with flowers as "the rose of charity, the lily of chastity, the violet of humility, and the golden gillyflower of heaven." The first real mention of gardens of Mary is in the fifteenth-century accounting record of the purchase of plants "for S. Mary's garden" by the sacristan of Norwich Priory in England.

It was not until the twentieth century, hundreds of years after the Reformation and birth of Protestantism, that the idea of a Mary garden reappears. In 1932 the first modern Mary garden was created around a figure of Our Lady of the Annunciation beside the angelus tower of St. Joseph's Church in Woods Hole, on Cape Cod, Massachusetts, by Frances Crane Lillie. She was a summer resident of this beach town and a generous benefactor to the parish. The

These golden chain trees (*Laburnum anagyroides*) trained over the walkway were once known as Lady's fingers. *Barnsley House Garden, Rosemary Verey, Barnsley, Gloucestershire, England.*

MARY GARDENS AS FUND RAISERS

One of the greatest benefits of most garden flower seed is that it is plentiful and inexpensive if purchased in bulk. This provides an opportunity for church communities to spread the word about Mary gardens and raise money for worthy causes at the same time. With gardening now America's favorite pastime, it makes sense to follow the lead of Stokes and McTague by creating a Mary garden seed packet.

For best results the seeds should be of the easiest to grow varieties of annual flowers. Attached to the packet should be a sheet explaining the role of Mary gardens and plant names in medieval history, some information on the various seed varieties enclosed, and basic how-to planting instructions. What costs just pennies to prepare becomes a fine item to sell at church functions, particularly in time for spring planting. Here are five of the most common Mary seed plants available today, which make a good starter packet:

Religious name	Popular name	Botanical name
Lady's mantle	Morning glory	*Ipomaea purpurea*
Mary bud	Pot marigold	*Calendula*
Mary's gold	French and African marigolds	*Tagetes erecta*
St. Mary's herb	Pansy	*Viola*
Virgin Mary's candle	Giant mullein	*Verbascum thapsis*

garden still exists and was restored to its original planting plan for its golden jubilee in 1982. The second most famous Mary garden was laid out by horticulturist Tony Dove at Annapolis, Marylnd, and dedicated to Mary on the Vigil of the Assumption in 1988.

There is a movement afoot to reinstate devotion to Mary by bringing back the old plant names and using these species to create beautiful gardens as a form of worship and honor. The role of such gardens is not merely to call public notice to the Lady-names of flowers but to restore the prayerful, religious sense and true dignity to gardening that was so widely practiced in medieval monastic communities. Robert Ostermann said it so well in his article "Mary's Gardens," published in the *Irish Ecclesiastical Record*, February 1953:

There is much more to the religious tradition on gardening than the existence of symbolical names for flowers. In the garden we participate in the fundamental relationship between God, Man and nature, as set forth in God's command to Adam to 'subdue the earth'. We deal with essences, the seeds; and with substances, the grown plants. We see the effects of original sin in the disease and death which enter our gardens each season. We also witness the promise of our resurrection following spring:… *but if the grain of wheat dies it brings forth much fruit.* And we learn again to trust in God's Providence: *consider the lilies….*

Inspired by the garden at Woods Hole, two Americans, John Stokes and Edward McTague, decided to further the tradition of Mary gardens as a new form of worship among Christians. In 1951 they put together a seed packet called "Our Lady's Garden," which contained seeds for ten easy-to-grow varieties of Mary flowers. The men felt that the gardens would help us better understand the need for our stewardship of the land as a gift from God. They also believed that through this seed packet gardeners could begin their own Mary gardens at home, and it also helped non-gardeners become familiar with this new devotional hobby.

It was not long until Stokes and McTague had distributed over 750 Mary garden seed packets to clergy, religious schools and societies, home gardeners, and children. This first offering proved so popular, they went on to develop twelve-seed and twenty-five-seed Mary flower packets. The drive to spread this garden idea continues, and now that gardening is so popular, it makes sense that the Mary garden tradition continue.

Over the years Mary garden aficionados have done a great deal of research into ancient manuscripts to find the lost Marian names of plants. Not only were the names discovered, but many of the unique associations link every aspect of Mary's being with plants. Extensive study of the Virgin and her plants has yielded an enormous palette to choose from when creating such a garden. This list also shows which plants were in cultivation during medieval times, so it presents a good palette for a monastery garden, as well.

(For more inspiration, there's a Mary garden site on the Internet: www.mgardens.org is the address.)

Plants Named for Our Lady and the Mary Garden

Religious name	Popular name	Botanical name
Annunciation lily	Madonna lily	*Lilium candidum*
Assumption lily	Funkia	*Hosta plantaginea*
Blue-eyed Mary	Blue-eyed grass	*Sisyrinchium*
Candlemas bells	Snowdrops	*Galanthus nivalis*
Joseph and Mary	Lungwort	*Pulmonoria officinalis*
Lady apple	Apple	*Malus* spp.
Lady bell	Bellflower	*Adenophera*
Lady bracken	Bracken fern	*Pteris aquilina*
Lady by the gate	Soapwort	*Saponario officinalis*
Lady eleven o'clock	Star of Bethlehem	*Ornithogalum umbel*
Lady fern	Lady fern	*Anthyrium felix*
Lady laurel	Laurel	*Daphne mezereum*
Lady of the snow	Alpine anemone	*Anemone vernalis*
Lady o' the meadow	Meadow sweet	*Spiraea ulmaria*
Lady's bower	Traveler's joy	*Clematis vitalba*
Lady's clover	Wood sorrel	*Oxalis acetosella*
Lady's comb	Venus comb	*Scandix pecten*
Lady's delight	Pansy	*Viola tricolor*
Lady's eardrop	Fuchsia	*Fuchsia* spp.
Lady's earrings	Balsam	*Impatiens capensis*
Lady's fingers	Golden chain	*Laburnum anagyroides*
Lady's fingers	Everlasting pea	*Lathyrus praetensis*
Lady's fingers	Cowslip	*Primula veris*
Lady's flower	Viola	*Viola tricolor*
Lady's frills	Primrose	*Primula vulgaris*
Lady's garters	Blackberry	*Rubus fruitcosus*

Religious name	Popular name	Botanical name
Lady's looking glass	Venus' looking glass	*Campanula speculatum*
Lady's mantle	Lady's mantle	*Achillea vulgaris*
Lady's mantle	Morning glory	*Ipomaea purpurea*
Lady's meat	Hawthorne	*Crataegus oxayacanthus*
Lady's milk	Milk thistle	*Carduus marianus*
Lady's nightcap	Wood anemone	*Anemone nemorosa*
Lady's nightcap	Canterbury bells	*Campanula medium*
Lady's pincushion	Sweet scabious	*Scabiosa purpurea*
Lady's pouches	Shepherd's purse	*Capsella bursa*
Lady's signet	Black bryony	*Tamus communis*
Lady's slipper	Ladyslipper orchid	*Cypripedium*
Lady's smock	Marsh marigold	*Caltha palustris*
Madonna's lily	Madonna lily	*Lilium candidum*
Madonna's milk	Nettle	*Lamicum purpureum*
Madonna's pins	Wild geranium	*Geranium maculatum*
Madonna's rose	Hybrid tea rose	*Rosa odorata*
Mary bud	Pot marigold	*Calendula officinalis*
Marygold	Marigold	*Tagetes* spp.
Mary's flower	Daisy	*Bellis perennis*
Mary's heart	Bleeding heart	*Dicentra spectabilis*
Mary's plant	Catnip	*Nepeta cataria*
Mary's root	Tansy	*Tanacetum balsamea*
Mary's rose	Peony	*Paeonia officinalis*
Mary's rose	Dog rose	*Rosa canina*
Mary's slipper	Monkshood	*Acontium mepellus*
Our Lady's balsam	Costmary	*Chrysanthemum*
Our Lady's beds	Yellow bedstraw	*Galium verum*
Our Lady's belt	Meadow sweet	*Filipendula ulmar*
Our Lady's birthday flower	Italian aster	*Aster amellus*
Our Lady's candles	Evening candles	*Lychnis alba*
Our Lady's candlestick	Cowslip	*Primula elatior*
Our Lady's cushion	Rock cress	*Arabis albida*
Our Lady's cushion	Thrift	*Armeria maritima*
Our Lady's cushion	Mossy saxifrage	*Saxifraga hypnoid*
Our Lady's eyes	Forget-me-not	*Myosotis scorpioid*
Our Lady's fingers	Honeysuckle	*Lonicera* spp.
Our Lady's flannel	Bugloss	*Echium fastuosum*
Our Lady's glove	Foxglove	*Digitalis purpureus*
Our Lady's hair	Maidenhair fern	*Adiantum* spp.
Our Lady's hair	Quaking grass	*Briza media*
Our Lady's hand	Spotted orchid	*Orchis maculata*
Our Lady's lace	Dodder	*Cuscuta gronovii*
Our Lady's mint	Pennyroyal	*Mentha pulegium*
Our Lady's modesty	English violet	*Viola odorata*
Our Lady's needle	Wormwood	*Artemisia* spp.
Our Lady's resting place	Germander	*Veronica* spp.

Religious name	Popular name	Botanical name
Our Lady's rose	Rose of Jericho	*Anastatica*
Our Lady's tears	Lily of the valley	*Convallaria majal*
Our Lady's thistle	Blessed thistle	*Carduus mariana*
Rose of Sharon	Rose of Sharon	*Hybiscus syriacus*
St. Mary's herb	Mint geranium	*Chrysanthemum balsam*
St. Mary's seeds	Sow thistle	*Sonchus oleraceus*
St. Mary's tree	Rosemary	*Rosmarinus officinalis*
Santa Maria	Feverfew	*Parthenium* spp.
Sweet Mary	Jupiter's beard	*Centranthus ruber*
Sweet Mary	Lemon balm	*Melissa officinalis*
Virgin flower	Periwinkle	*Vinca rosea*
Virgin oil	Olive	*Olea europea*
Virgin pink	Garden pink	*Dianthus pulmarius*
Virgin stock	Virginian stock	*Malcomia maritima*
Virgin's bower	Clematis	*Clematis virginiana*
Virgin's bower	Wisteria	*Wisteria frutescens*
Virgin's nipple	Spurge	*Euphorbia lathyrus*
Virgin's tears	Spiderwort	*Tradescantia virginiana*

Mary's Gold

Mary's name was woven into that of the pot marigold, the calendula of Europe. This is not to be confused with the marigolds of the New World, genus *Tagetes*. The pot marigold, an ancient flower, was often found in the earliest gardens. Its other name is calendula, meaning "little first day of the month," because its everblooming nature provided flowers during any month on the calendar. Originally known as "gold flower," it was changed to "Mary's gold" because it was used as a powerful charm against the devil. Legend says it was first born of the Virgin's tears (a familiar story), its gay color had cheered her during the hurried journey into Egypt, it had sprung up in her footsteps, or it had provided a soft carpet upon which she could rest.

Calendula is one of the easiest annual plants to grow, and it will indeed bloom throughout the winter months in milder climates, despite a light frost. It is available in flower colors yellow and orange. Dwarf bedding varieties of calendula are bred for their short, compact growth habit. They remain popular as edging for seas of spring bulbs or by themselves in a mass. Tall calendulas, closer to the medieval strains, can become rangy but provide excellent cool-season cutting flowers. Fast to grow, they should be purchased young in six-packs and planted out in spring or fall.

The Lily of the Valleys

The white lily was dedicated to Mary, but as with the "lilies of the field" in the Gospels, many lily-like plants are interchanged with true lilies. The lily of the valley was often the plant mentioned, due to the phrase in Song of Solomon, "I am a rose of Sharon, the lily of the valleys" (Song of Songs 2:1). No matter what the species, the lily represents chastity and purity. In fact, the often prudish notions of the past caused the sexual organs of the flower, the pistil and stigma, to be plucked out before they could be brought to the altar.

One story tells that St. Thomas, the doubting one, was absent when the Virgin Mary died, and when he returned, refused to believe reports that she had been assumed into heaven. "Open the tomb and show me," he demanded. When the tomb was opened by the other apostles, it contained nothing but fresh flowers: lilies and

Calendula officinalis, also known as pot marigold, is a flower grown since ancient times in Europe. The petals were eaten in salads, used to color cheddar cheeses, and also proved ideal for packing fresh wounds to staunch the flow of blood.

roses. One Madonna lily fell at Thomas's feet, and when he raised his eyes again, he found the Virgin floating before him.

In the year 1048 King Garcia of Navarre, Spain, was ill and nearly dead. Finally, after the doctors had done all they could, a priest came with a vase of Madonna lilies to place beside his bed. The king then opened his eyes and saw the image of the Virgin rising from the lilies. He recovered miraculously and in gratitude instituted the Order of Knights of St. Mary of the Lily. Each knight in full armor wore on his breast a lily made of silver and hung upon a gold chain. The lily bore the letter M for "Mary." Later Louis IX adopted the same order in France, but its emblem was the flower of broom combined with the lily.

Some stories explain the colors of lilies. Legends state that at first lilies were yellow, but as the Virgin was walking to the temple, she picked some of the flowers, which turned white at her touch. St. Joseph, who walked beside her, found his staff suddenly sprouting white lilies at its top. In eastern Europe a tale surrounds the drooping red lily native to the Caucasus. Originally it was pure white. When Christ prayed in the garden the night before his death, all the flowers bowed humbly as he passed—all but the lily, which kept her head up high so he would notice and admire her beauty. He paused at the proud flower, which under his direct gaze realized her sin of conceit and blushed red, then hung her head in shame.

Candlemas Flower

This tiny, pure white flower, snowdrop, which blooms early in spring, is also called Candlemas flower because it blooms around February 2 in England, which is Candlemas Day. It was dedicated to the Virgin from the first years of the church, said to have sprung up in her footsteps along the road from Bethlehem to Jerusalem when she carried baby Jesus to the temple for presentation. When the picture of the Virgin is removed from church altars on this holiday, the empty place is strewn with hundreds of fresh-cut snowdrops, grown by nuns in their convent gardens.

A snowdrop legend begins with Eve after she was driven out of Eden. She found only a vast, snow-covered wasteland in which to live. Weeping at the prospect of life in that place, she was heard by the angels, one of whom came to earth to console her. "Take heart," the angel said. "The snow falls, and the winter is bleak, but I shall give you a token, and whenever you see it, know that spring will soon come." As he spoke he caught a falling snowflake, then dropped it to the ground, where it turned into the flower. In the angel's footprints in the snow as he left were patches of snowdrops.

Blessing of the Herbs

In pre-Christian Europe, the period from the middle of August to the

Salvia officinalis.

middle of September was considered the time to give thanks to the spirits of nature for a plentiful harvest. Over the centuries these days were rededicated to the Virgin and called Our Lady's Thirty Days, during which falls the feast of the Assumption.

On the feast of the Assumption, many countries carry on the old Catholic tradition of blessing the herbs, which is a continuation of an ancient pagan rite where magical herbs were dedicated to the spirits of the woods in order to increase their potency. In medieval times it became Our Lady's Herb Day, and the official Roman Catholic prayers ask that "God may bless the medicinal powers of these herbs and make them mercifully efficient against diseases and poisons in humans and domestic animals."

Legend says that during Our Lady's Thirty Days, all animals and plants lose their harmful traits. Snakes will not strike, plants contain no poisons or spines, and wild animals, notably the nearly extinct wolves of Europe, will not attack. Much food preservation was done, as all believed that the food would not spoil and would contain

special nutritional value. During this time there is also the feast of Mary's Nativity, September 8. Also called the feast of Our Lady of the Grape Harvest, winter planting of wheat is blessed, and in the vineyards of France great festivals are held. Clusters of the most beautiful, perfect grapes were tied to the hands of her statue in the church.

In Sicily people abstain from eating fruit for two weeks prior to this feast day, known as *La Quindiciana*, in honor of the Virgin. Before the Reformation all Christian countries had the clergy bless the countryside, its farms, orchards, fields, and gardens. In Austria priests still bless the land and people of the Alps. The priest would ride through the entire parish sprinkling holy water everywhere.

A MARY'S GARDEN DESIGN

This simple garden is designed to create drama in a very small space. The planting scheme includes the most basic Mary plants, which are chosen not necessarily for their names but for their deeper religious associations and blue flowers. The garden provides space to add more Mary plants but functions just as well in this basic form.

The central focus of this cross-shaped layout is a broad walkway leading up to a statue of Mary. The statue is framed by an arch covered with morning glories in front of a background of green laurel. Arches of roses like those at Giverny and rows of mounding shrub roses provide a framework for the approach, since these plants are most deeply connected to Mary. The shrub rose of Sharon suggests Mary's biblical name. The most popular Mary flowers are planted around the base of the statue: marigold, madonna lily, viola, and two large patches of delphinium.

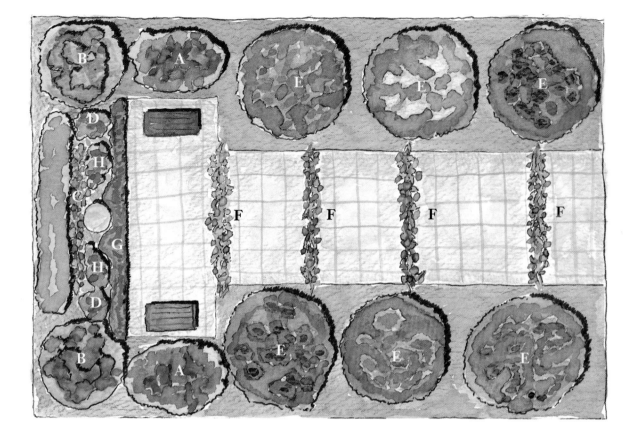

A. *Delphinium* Hybrids—Delphinium

B. *Hibiscus syriacus*—Rose of Sharon

C. *Ipomaea purpurea*—Morning Glory

D. *Lilium candidum*—Madonna Lily

E. *Rosa* spp.—Assorted Shrub Roses

F. *Rosa* Hybrid Climber—Climbing
Roses

G. *Tagetes erecta*—African or French
Marigold

H. *Viola* spp.—Blue Viola

THE MEMORY GARDEN

Non OMNIS MORIAR. (*I shall not wholly perish.*)

Horace

A colonial sampler stitched over months, sometimes years, with muted colors of vegetable dyes and handwoven linen, speaks to us of lives long forgotten. It tells of candlelight and home births, of autumn harvests and cold winters by the hearth. This little piece of fabric and threads speaks more loudly about the hands that made them and a point in time than all the history books in the Library of Congress.

The art of remembrance needn't be embodied only in objects. A landscape may serve as a special, living, reminder. There, plants and sometimes entire gardens are used to mark and cherish vital points in time. In California during the 1920s, Florence Bixby was creating gardens around her family ranch house, which was situated on an old Spanish land grant. Bixby was an avid gardener who took great personal interest in the evolution of her landscape, which would eventually be one of the most extensive in southern California. She hired the famed landscape architecture firm Olmstead Brothers to help her expand her gardens.

Forever exchanging seeds, cuttings, and plants with others who shared her passion, Bixby wasn't

A gravestone can become a work of art. *Box Parish Cemetery, Box, England.*

always able to fit every plant into her garden. Yet she treasured her gift plants and knew where each one had come from. When a friend suggested she create a garden just for the gifts, she agreed and had the Olmsteads create a small, rectangular "Friendly Garden" on a scale that reflected the intimacy of friendship. The plant beds surrounded an hour-glass-shaped lawn, at the center of which was a shallow pool. Her husband later gave her a bronze sculpture, "Playdays" by Harried Frismuth, for their anniversary. It is not difficult to imagine what Florence Bixby felt when she strolled through her little garden, with every plant recalling a generous friend from near or far.

Remembering was also important to Vita Sackville-West, the famous novelist and garden writer in Kent, England. She grew up amidst a rambling castle manor house that covered a full four acres of ground, with parts dating back to the time of Elizabeth I. Forever the romantic, Vita was at home in this often drafty old house, whose ambience of age and moody atmosphere helped inspire her to pen many poems and stories. For those who can feel old houses and hear their whisperings, there grows a special bond, a deep sense of place, that opens the avenues for the creative mind.

When she reached adulthood, Vita, who always saw herself residing here at Knole, was devastated to discover she would not inherit the ancient ancestral estate, due to illegitimacy in her family tree. Many years later she purchased a run-down medieval tower and surrounding outbuildings called Sissinghurst, which in some ways was similar to Knole. Sissinghurst was in ruins, and she set out upon a monumental restoration task, driven by her deep-seated need to recapture Knole, even if it was vicariously through the transformation of her hew home. Sissinghurst became Vita's memory garden.

This tale of longing for the comfort and familiar things of childhood is of universal appeal. Perhaps this is exactly the point of all old gardens or those created with historic or period themes, for they reach back in time, linking the past to the present with plants and space. They also allow us to step into a separate reality in which our perception of time is temporarily altered by living things suggesting memories of deep significance.

PLANTING POINTS IN TIME

In our culture some Americans are gradually losing many rites of passage once deeply ingrained. These vital points mark when we experience the great changes common to most every man and woman. Perhaps this is due to a waning of religious tradition, because often these rites are an intrinsic aspect of faith. Coming of age rites among African tribes is in many ways similar to those of the Jewish faith or Christian confirmation, for example. Transitions from child to adult are surrounded with great festivity and ritual to underscore their importance. Similarly, marriage and the birth of the first child are powerful rites of passage, milestones that change our lives forever. Death is sometimes marked by a wake, a monument, and a memory.

During the counterculture 1960s, when natural childbirth and the back-to-nature movement came together, there arose a unique means of forever commemorating the birth of a child. The placenta remaining after the birth was not discarded but instead promptly buried beneath the roots of a young tree selected for just this occasion. The little tree's roots would be enriched by this human organic matter, so that the tree and the remnants of the birth would merge into a single symbolic living memorial.

Although planting the placenta was a rather novel idea, the planting of trees at the birth of a child is not at all new. Peoples the world over have done this. In the past, when families remained in the same home, town, or farm, the tree and the child grew up together, and the mature tree would always be dedicated to that child *cum* adult. Watching the tree grow throughout his or her whole life, a young one developed an intimacy with plants and a respect for nature. No doubt it also provided the parents a memory of this wonderful point in time.

We can find many examples of historic plantings in public places, where civic groups seek to leave lasting memorials to difficult times. In 1897 the Ladies of the Grand Army of the Republic of California and Nevada obtained a number of sapling trees, ferns, and flowers transplanted from the famous battlefields of the Civil War. They were planted in the city of Sacramento as a memorial to those who died in the most devastating of all our wars. Here we find plantings to commemorate a point in time, underscored by the fact that the trees had originated upon the actual bloody fields.

The idea of commemorating by planting trees or memorial groves is an important part of our remembering. For we all know that history repeats itself, and if we fail to learn from the mistakes of the past, we are doomed to suffer the pains of war and death again in the future. What this woman's group did was not only honor those who died, but point out the past in a way that would educate future generations on the value of our union of states and how much we sacrificed to keep it intact.

The Famous and Historic Trees project has its roots in this concept. This project is an educational program of American Forests, which was founded in 1875, making it our nation's oldest conservation organization. With many of America's historic trees aging and vulnerable to encroaching development, many felt that the trees' preservation through their offspring was an ideal way to remember the past and at the same time encourage more tree planting. The project grows seeds of historically significant trees, providing a link that encourages remembrance with people, places, and events of the past.

The program allows us to touch history in a very personal way. Contributions of African-Americans may be honored with the offspring of the George Washington Carver Persimmon from the Tuskegee Institute or the Martin Luther King, Jr. Water Oak, the tree that shaded his address at the Brown Chapel AME in Selma, Alabama. The struggles of Native Americans may be honored with the Trail of Tears Redbud, taken from the original tree that stood in New Echota, Georgia, where that fateful winter march to the reservation began. Our Hispanic roots may be recognized by the Mission de Nombre de Dios Live Oak, taken from a tree at the 1565 landing site of the Spanish in St. Augustine, Florida.

The Famous and Historic tree catalog offers and describes hundreds of trees from famous sources. Each sapling is shipped with planting instructions, a photo-degradable tree-shelter, fertilizer, stake, bird safety net, and personalized certificate of authenticity giving the story of that individual tree.

For those designing gardens of meaning to recognize people, events, or our many great struggles, trees and plants should be chosen with great care. The connections, those vital links of species or origin, make the planting plan far more important than simply environmental considerations. The Famous and Historic Trees program is the first to establish these relationships, which are so crucial to the integrity of memorial sites, whatever their focus or purpose. Never forget that there must be a tangible reason for each and every plant we select for a garden. When the goal is to reach beyond aesthetics and into the realm of symbolism, meaning, and remembrance, we must draw from a new well of awareness. There we find a plant's origins and its relationship to people in order to raise the value of the garden well beyond that of simple beauty.

REMEMBERING THE DEAD

Death is one of the few aspects of the natural world that we still do not truly understand. In many respects little has changed since those primitive cave burials of the Ice Ages, to the elaborate ceremonial interments of the Egyptians, and to the modern funerals of today. Death has not changed, and we still don't really know all that may be on the other side. Yet it is a fully human quest to want to know and to soothe the pain of our losses. To these ends every culture has developed religions which attempt to explain death, the greatest of all mysteries.

Some cultures were much more comfortable with death than we are today. The Druids celebrated their memorials around the first of November, the same date as All Saints. Their

Lochcarron Graveyard is so old most tombstones are illegible, yet they remain standing in mute testimony to loved ones. *Lochcarron, Scotland.*

day was the eve of their festival of thanksgiving to the sun, when their god Samhain, the Lord of Death, was supposed to call together and pass judgment upon those who had died the previous year. Druids believed that the dead who had died unnaturally inhabited the bodies of animals, so the priests thought their offerings would soften this punishment by the sun god and release the spirits. This in some ways is similar to the Catholic All Souls Day, November 2, when people pray for the souls of the dead doing penance in purgatory.

The Greeks performed rites called *Zoai* at every new grave by placing upon it offerings of olives and flowers. Romans had an even greater regard for their ancestors and honored them each year in a festival called Parentalia, celebrated from February 13 to 21. During this period all temples were closed, and on the last day, Feralia, they honored their dead as did the Greeks, with wine, milk, honey, oil, and fruit. Each grave was decorated with wreaths of greens and flowers, particularly roses (the favorite flower of the Romans), lilies, and tiny scented violets. Although Romans typically cremated their dead, the ashes were often placed in catacombs or family tombs, where parties were held in the name of the dead.

It was not until the sixth century that the Benedictine monasteries began to hold a memorial service for all their dead brothers at Pentecost or Whitsuntide. In 988 this celebration was officially recognized as the Feast of All Saints. The Feast of All Saints is known as *La Toussaint* in France, where it is celebrated on the same day as *Le Jour des Morts*, which is probably a remnant of the old Druid thanksgiving. In honor of this day, people gather in the cemeteries to lay wreaths and flowers upon the graves of their loved ones. It was widely believed that an undecorated grave offended the soul of the forgotten relative, who would come back to haunt the living. Therefore every grave was decorated to ensure no souls would have reason for haunting.

In America there is a different day to remember the dead, first instituted after the Civil War. Since the battles were waged on home soil, graveyards of dead soldiers were scattered about most of the southern states. There was a great desire to honor the sacrifices of both Union and Confederate armies, so the states designated May 30 as Decoration Day. It was a day when people gathered in the graveyards, cut and trimmed the grass, then decorated the graves with flowers in remembrance, just as the Europeans had done for many centuries.

A cloister walk of trees leads to the doorway of St. James Church. *Chipping Camden, Gloucestershire, England.*

MONUMENTS: HOW THE ANCIENTS REMEMBERED

Some of the greatest monuments to death, built with great belief in the afterlife, still stand after thousands of years. From these early builders we gain a greater understanding of the role of the monument and the various forms it can take. Gardens with such themes may reach back in time to obtain a piece of such a design, using stone, or brick, or simply the good earth.

Perhaps the least recognized are the neolithic tombs of England and France, which were built with great effort by people who had not yet discovered the wheel. The simplest can be seen upon the rolling hilltops of Britain, where they stand out starkly amidst the natural topography. Little more than giant mounds of earth, they represent years of work with primitive digging tools and earth carried in wicker baskets.

In some old churchyards in rural Britain, we see occasional standing stones that rise far above traditional gravestones, unhewn and clearly out of place. These markers of very ancient burials bear an almost mysterious quality, as they have neither images nor letters etched in their surfaces, but they still command our attention. From this we learn that any large stone can become a memorial, whether or not it bears the

St. PHOCAS, PATRON SAINT OF GARDENERS

We know St. Phocas lived in the third-century, a time when Christians suffered great persecution under brutal Roman emperors. He was an accomplished market gardener who resided just outside the city of Pontus, on the Black Sea. A farmer by nature, Phocas sold his vegetables to the markets and cultivated herbs as medicine for the poor who could not afford such luxuries.

Eventually word spread of his generosity which pointed to the fact that he was a Christian and two soldiers were sent to arrest him. They reached town just as night was falling and decided to stop for shelter at a nearby cottage surrounded by a large garden. Phocas welcomed them with a place to sleep and food from the garden, and while dining they confided in him their reason for being in Pontus. He did not betray himself but said he knew the man they sought and would bring him around in the morning.

Realizing that he would soon die, Phocas went out late that night while the soldiers slept and dug himself a grave in the garden. This was because he loved his garden so much he preferred that his remains lie among the plants and flowers. He also knew that as his remains decomposed, they would improve the soil and be taken up by plant roots to create new life. So beside the grave he prayed through the night, and upon greeting the soldiers in the morning, the saint announced who he was.

Although the soldiers were reluctant to put such a generous man to death, like true Romans they executed the saint as ordered, and buried him as requested in the garden. Many years later when Phocas was honored as saint and martyr, a church was built upon the very spot where he lay at rest in the earth he so loved. Officially recognized as the gardener's patron, Phocas' feast day is celebrated on September 22.

Some of the earliest European tombs were rock cairns to mark an underground tomb. Many still exist. *Nether Largie South Cairn, Temple Wood Stone Circle, Kilmartin Valley, Scotland.*

prominent plant in graveyard art. It represents a very romantic sentiment of tears and mourning, on stones hundreds of years old, and is the most universal symbol. The willow also has the unique ability to sprout from the driest cutting, which illustrates a promise of resurrection on the last day.

Grapevines, a symbol of the Christian church, can be found in many places, symbolizing the freedom as nature with networks of leafy runners. Laborers threshing wheat in the fields persist to this day in graveyard imagery, representing the harvest of souls in the name of Christ. Flower images abound, as well. Those with a noticeably broken stem show the irreversible termination of earthly life. To find a pansy on the tombstone means that the survivors sought a reminder of humility, for even the

name of the lost one, and in the garden this provides a focus for the design.

Stoneworkers who today make the granite headstones for modern cemeteries are ideal resources for memory gardens. We tend to think of them just as part of the burial process, but they are perfect artisans to carve our special names or favored phrases upon weatherproof stone for gardens.

Gravestones through the ages have borne the universal symbols of death. These aren't the skull and crossbones, but the emotional images that represent sadness, grief, and tears, at the same time ones that spring eternal with a vision of life after death and resurrection. They may be of vastly different faiths, from the lotus flower of Egypt to the white lily of the Church.

Some of the most accessible early American Catholic grave art can be found in the old graveyards of New Orleans, because the high water table there necessitated aboveground crypts that left more surface for art. This and many other graveyards, including the Roman catacombs, contain a wealth of memorial symbolism related to plants. The weeping willow is by far the most

Gravestones from the last few centuries are still quite legible. This cross is cloaked in a carved passionvine, suggesting the loss of a lover. *Box Parish Cemetery, Box, England.*

wealthiest and most beautiful people are reduced to the level of the common man after death.

The language of flowers so popular during the Victorian era explains the sentiment behind much graveyard flower art, for each flower has a specific meaning. Those most suitable for memorial garden art, be they inscribed in stone, painted on a rock, or expressed in the landscape, are listed here in the language of flowers, with meanings linked to death, loss, the afterlife, love, and sadness.

Pink-flowering *Hyacinthus* 'Amethyst'.

Flower or Plant	Meaning
Almond	Hope
Amaranth	Faith, immortality, unfading love
Arborvitae	Unchanging friendship
Asphodel	My regrets follow you to the grave
Carnation	Admiration
Cypress	Mourning
Forget-me-not	Remembrance
Heather	Solitude
Iris	Hope
Ivy	Fidelity
Laburnun	Forsaken
Marigold	Sorrow
Myrtle	Love
Olive	Peace
Palm	Immortality
Parsley	Death
Poplar	Time
Poppy	Sleep
Rose	Love
Rosemary	Remembrance
Snowdrop	Hope, consolation
Sunflower	Devotion
Sweet pea	Departure
Tulip	Eternal separation
Veronica	Fidelity
Violet	Steadfastness
Wallflower	Faithful in adversity
Yew	Resurrection
Zinnia	Thoughts of absent friends

PLANTS OF GREEK MYTHOLOGY

There are hundreds of myths which explain the presence of flowers and trees, but none are as complex and convoluted as those of the Greeks and Romans. Many plants have more than one myth, and in some cases the tales contradict each other. Nevertheless, the naming of plants and their resulting symbolism can often be traced back to these myths, which provide a unique means of relating memory garden sentiment to plant selection. Here are just a few stories which illustrate how the gods and goddesses were linked to virtually all types of vegetation.

The Greeks believed that the god Jove and his wife, Juno, lay together on the slopes of Mount Ida. There in the place warmed by their bodies sprang the crocus. In Jason's quest for the Golden Fleece, a tale sug-

Myrtus communis, the myrtle sacred to the goddess Venus.

Narcissus, the flower of an ill-fated youth.

gests that the enchantress Medea planned to restore old Aeson, Jason's father, to his youth. She prepared a love potion, and where drops were scattered upon the ground, the crocus sprang up and bloomed.

In classical mythology Hyacinthus was a handsome boy loved by both Apollo and the wind god Zephyrus. When Hyacinthus showed greater affection for Apollo, the wind god became jealous. In a game of quoits between Apollo and Hyacinthus, Zephyrus deflected one of the missiles, which struck and killed the boy. Apollo at once turned the boy into a blue hyacinth, which would forever honor his memory with great beauty and fragrance.

The Greek nymph Minthe attracted the attention of Pluto, the god of the underworld. His jealous wife, Persephone, retaliated by turning Minthe into a plant, although the attractiveness of Minthe persisted as the refreshing mint. Myrtle plants have always been a symbol of sensual love and passion sacred to the goddess Venus. The name first appeared in mythology as Myrtilus, the son of Hermes. Myrtilus betrayed his master and was cast into the sea. The ocean refused his body, so the gods transformed it into a myrtle tree.

One of the most well-known classical myths shows the relationship between a plant and the term *narcissistic*, which describes excessive personal vanity. In the Greek tale Narcissus was the son of Cephisus, god of the rivers, and a water nymph, Liriope. He was so handsome, all the maidens longed to become his beloved. The water nymph Echo, who was particularly enamored of the young man, followed him into the forest, where he found a still, spring-fed pool, where he stopped to rest and take a drink.

There he heard a strange voice—that of Nemesis, a goddess of justice—bid him to look into the pool. As he bent down to drink, he was startled to see a clear reflection of himself for the very first time, but he thought it another man who was irresistible. He found the face so very beautiful, he could not interrupt his study of the reflected image. So enraptured was he that Narcissus did not hear Echo's calls to return home, so the little nymph left without him. Years later Echo came back to the pool to find Narcissus, but all she found was a single flower. It would forever be the symbol of vanity, for the gods had transformed the vain boy into the narcissus flower there beside the pool, where he could peer at his own reflection for eternity.

REMEMBRANCE FOR HEALING, "LEST WE FORGET"

Today we seek healing on many different levels. Burdens of past wounds, both physical and spiritual, can linger to inhibit our lives. Healing is the process of letting go of those wounds, be they childhood abuse or the death of a loved one. The Vietnam War Memorial is one of the most profound expressions of grief ever created in the landscape. The black granite wedge that bears the names of the dead rises up ominously out of the surrounding turf. It does not lend the sense of triumph that we see in memorials of other wars, because this sad struggle divided our nation, leaving the servicemen in a never-never land of obscurity. The dark wall, with its thousands of names, is an expression recognizing their sacrifice, finally paying tribute to these fathers, sons, and brothers.

The friends and families of those stricken with AIDS and other fatal diseases seek a way to

ORNAMENTAL IDEAS

Classical art has come down to us from cultures long vanished, yet whose mythology remains eternal. The images of gods and goddesses each have their own relationship to humanity and nature. To bring the ancient classics into the garden is to rekindle the same philosophies or to underscore the god's connection to our own lifestyle or that of the one we've lost. Bacchus, god of wine, honors vintage aficionados, Mercury taking flight remembers athletes or runners, Venus recalls a woman we have loved, or Apollo for the men we cherish. Angels, though not part of Greco-Roman mythology, became powerful images in Christian Rome, and sculptures of these winged beings are becoming very popular as we reach for the mystical realm of life. Common in graveyard art, angels belong in memory gardens, for once we have lost loved ones, it is comforting to imagine them like angels residing in that infinite peace we call heaven.

A cherub suggesting the young Bacchus, god of the grape. *Anne Carr Garden, Atlanta, Georgia.*

Angels assure us there is heaven. *Pat and Ron Van den Berghe Garden, Danville, California.*

soothe the pain of their grief over the premature deaths of so many. Such dedication was expressed in the great quilt spread out upon the turf of Washington during a massive demonstration. Each square is a glimpse of a human life, now gone but not forgotten.

Remembrance need not be expressed on such a grand level. For women who are now haunted by past abortions, the need to heal is critical to emotional comfort late in life. Among the suggestions is to create a memorial to that little life, just as you would if the child had been stillborn. The memory garden gives us an opportunity to do so, with a shrine, marker, or favorite plants that come to life each spring. These memorials do resurrect the notion of hallowed ground, for there we remember a child who lives no more. In the process of creating such a place,

our souls shed the burden, and there we find healing.

Animals can be as close to us as family members, and anyone who has loved a dog or cat knows just how deep this bond is. After a pet dies there is always the dilemma of what to do with the body, and it is often too painful to allow the veterinarian to dispose of it. A memorial garden provides a place where we may bury our animal companions and later evoke fond memories of their lives. Where children are concerned, the burial of a cherished pet in the garden helps to teach them about the passing on of life and the ultimate return to the earth.

A few years ago I purchased two Rottweiler dogs from a local breeder, Diane, a young woman whose main sire, Ninja, was her pride and joy. Though he was an enormous one hundred forty-five pounds, Ninja proved to be a gentle, loving partner. At a relatively young age, Ninja developed lymphoma and died, leaving Diane with a deep sense of loss. Soon after, as we drove by her house, there appeared a little enclosure surrounded by white pickets beneath the branches of a tree. Inside there were flowers of every color laid upon Ninja's grave. Even now, so many years later, the splashes of brilliant flowers appear there, along with a miniature Christmas tree in December or little flags for the Fourth of July.

Although we cannot bury human remains in our gardens any more, we may incorporate their ashes into a memory garden. A Japanese farming family in California's most fertile central valley lost an elderly aunt who wished to be cremated. She asked that her ashes be scattered over the orchard land that had supported her ancestors and offspring. Today her niece, now with children of her own, says that the greatest comfort of their loss is the ability to go out into that very same orchard and know the remains of their loved one is there among the good earth and plum trees that supported them all. Death and the scattering of ashes represented the rite of passage, the orchard itself became the memorial.

If you choose to keep the ashes in an urn, this too may be made part of the garden by creating a shrine. The act of making a shrine as described in chapter one is particularly important to healing after loss for it gives tangible form and meaning to all that is left of that life. Perhaps the most poignant aspect of this is that you may still visit the ashes, just as you would a grave, to rest awhile and know that the spirit they once contained is close by.

> They shall not grow old, as we that are left
> grow old,
> Age shall not weary them, nor the years
> condemn
> At the going down of the sun, and in the
> morning
> We will remember them.
>
> LAWRENCE BINYON,
> "For the Fallen"

PLANTING THE CITIES OF SILENCE

There are many plants that have traditionally been part of funerals and the landscaping at graveyards and cemeteries. In many cases, we no longer know their original purposes in these places of eternal repose. There were also practicalities of the day, which we no longer must contend with, that influenced planting. Their stories are still essential to the memorial garden, though.

The custom of planting on top of graves originated in the countryside because there was rarely enough space or soil to grow much in urban cemeteries. There the tending of graves went on periodically all year around, allowing these burial places to take on a gardenesque character.

Some of the old ways of planting were strictly kept. Only sweetly scented flowers, usually perennials, had a place with the dead. Among the few flowering perennials allowed for planting in consecrated churchyards were pinks, primroses, sweet William, wallflowers, carnations, thyme, hyssop, chamomile, and rosemary.

We find remnants of the Roman preference for roses in some customs of allowing the planting of rose trees only by the hands of survivors upon the graves of their relatives. A white-flowering rose was preferred for the grave of a virgin, while a red rose grew upon the grave of those who were known to be of good character.

There are other plants that have appeared in graveyards or are associated with death by superstition and folklore. A quick study of old English churchyards proves that yew trees held special significance, since they exist at practically every one. Some of the original yews were over a thousand years old at the time of the Norman Conquest of 1066, and therefore part of a much earlier religion. This is supported by the belief that the yew was a tree of death and dedicated to its goddess, Hecate, who also oversaw ghosts.

Early Christian missionaries found little

Top LEFT AND RIGHT: Ivy is a symbol of fidelity and planting such upon the grave of a loved one suggests devotion even after death. *Box Parish Cemetery, Box, England.*

Roses are common in many graveyards as a sign of the martyrs and often naturalize into lovely briars. *Blockley Church Graveyard, Blockley, Gloucestershire, England.*

ABOVE AND RIGHT: The small circular planting at the center of this garden contains tiger lilies and a rose tree like those the Romans planted upon graves of their family members. *Mr. and Mrs. Joel Brink Garden, Vancouver, British Columbia, Canada.*

The yew, *Taxus baccata*, was dedicated to the goddess of death, Hecate, and was later made a Christian symbol of everlasting life, due to the tree's longevity. *Blockley Church Graveyard, Blockley, Gloucestershire, England.*

shelter in the countryside and often camped beneath these old yews. They naturally built their chapels nearby, showing that the church-yard often grew up around the yew, rather than the yew being planted in the churchyard. To explain its presence in Christian terms, their natural longevity inspired preachers to consider them a symbol of everlasting life. This is furthered by the fact that it is one of the few evergreens in that northern climate, making it an ideal sheltering tree for church grounds.

The shade trees most frequently found in graveyards are cypress or cedars, there for a variety of symbolic reasons, of both biblical and pagan origins. Greek myth tells us that the young man Cyparissus was transformed by the gods into the cypress tree, whose wood was prized by both the Greeks and Egyptians for coffins, since it was so resistant to decay. It and its relative the cedar are reluctant to grow again once cut back, thus becoming symbols of the finality of death. Wands of cypress were carried by mourners in funeral processions, as were those of palm, the symbol of life.

Among the smaller plants found in graveyards are the myrtle and boxwood, whose placement there stems from very ancient Mediterranean myths. American graveyards of the nineteenth century are often choked with *Vinca major*, known as dwarf periwinkle or creeping myrtle. History tells us that during the Middle Ages, this plant was woven into a wreath and placed around each condemned man's neck as he was led to the gallows, which forever associated it with death.

The Chapel of St. Anne on Kew Green

The Royal Botanic Gardens at Kew is probably the most well-known botanical establishment in the world. Here the great glasshouses enclose exotica brought back from the far corners of the British Empire when it was at its peak. On the grounds is Kew Palace, where members of the Georgian Royal family lived (George IV was born there). Behind the palace today is the famous Queen's Garden, which was created in seventeenth-century design and plants.

Members of the royal family who lived in

A rustic arbor at St. Anne's.

Kew Palace and other residences on the royal estate worshipped in their own little chapel on Kew Green called St. Anne's. The original building existed as early as I 522 and was the haunt of Tudor and Stuart courtiers. Nearly two hundred years later, the old church was demolished and a new one built. Records show it was consecrated in I714. St. Anne's lies just across the lane from the palace and outside the gates to Kew. Always cherished by the royal family, its members enlarged and improved it in I770, then again in I837 and I884.

What brings us to St. Anne's is its churchyard, which is filled with roses and foxgloves, rustic arbors, and the dense and seemingly disorganized assortment of headstones and tombs so typical of urban English cemeteries. Here at St. Anne's many of the great gardeners, horticulturists, botanists, and plant hunters for Kew Gardens chose to be buried, not beneath somber sod but amidst the beauty and color of a garden.

Some headstones have no names, others are long gone, scoured away by time's ravages, but many of the inscriptions still exist, though they are hundreds of years old. They tell of gardeners and Kew in a mute testimony to those who wished to lie eternally in earth close to the gardens they loved. Though we know of a few famous botanists and gardens, most of these graves are of the minions who served there, with names never famous nor their resting places noted.

Inside the church in wall crypts lies the body of William Aiton. In 1759 he assisted Augusta, Dowager Princess of Wales and mother of George III, in her efforts to develop 3.5 acres of her estate into an educational botanic garden, which would later become Kew.

The Hooker family lies in a tomb at St. Anne's. Both father and son were the most influential men behind the development of the gardens during the nineteenth century. They were responsible for most of the garden improvements, a number of glass conservatories, monuments, plant collections, and follies. Sir William Jackson Hooker (1785–1865) was the first director of Kew and a professor of botany for twenty years in Glasgow. His great love for ferns encouraged the erection of the original coal-heated fern house. Sir William was also responsible for the construction of the great Palm House, which would become the most well-recognized symbol of the gardens and a monument to Queen Victoria's Jubilee. He also felt strongly that the once-private Royal Botanical Gardens should be opened to the public as a national treasure.

His son and successor, Sir Joseph Dalton Hooker (1817–1911), is buried there as well. He was not only director of Kew for a time, but he ventured to China on one of the great Victorian botanical expeditions. There in the Himalayas he found rhododendrons that still grace the gardens today.

For anyone fortunate enough to visit Kew Gardens, do take a moment to see St. Anne's, particularly in May, when all is in bloom. It is such a unique horticultural monument, and shows so perfectly how graveyards need not be dark and brooding. Instead, they too should become gardens where the living plants mingle with memorials to the dead in a fascinating celebration of life.

HALLOWEEN, ALL SAINTS', ALL SOULS': THE DAYS OF THE LIVING DEAD

A number of celebrations that fall on or around the first day of November are often collectively celebrated as Halloween. The reality is that many cultures shared this date as one which marked the changing of the seasons, from the harvest to the darkest season winter, when evil was nigh and the spirits grew powerful. Halloween—or All Hallows' Even, the eve of the Christian feast of All Hallows'—is celebrated on the night of October 31. The feast day of All-Hallows', or All Saints', extends from midnight to midnight of November 1. All Souls' Day extends from midnight to midnight of November 2.

Halloween is a remnant of Druid beliefs that on the night of November 1, demons, witches, and evil spirits roam the earth to greet the arrival of "their season," a night of joyous romping when frightening tricks were played upon mortals. To avoid trouble, people either left sweet treats, in hopes of pacifying these night marauders, or dressed as the ghouls did, in order to blend in.

This was also a time when bonfires were lit to drive away the spirits of darkness. The carving of the pumpkin is not just an American tradition but is a practiced shared with Europeans. The candle within is a remnant of these bonfires, placed outside the house to keep it sufficiently lighted as to be unsuitable for the evil spirits.

November 1 is also the feast of Pomona, the Roman goddess of orchards. Her name was taken from the Latin word for fruit, *pome*, and

The goddess Pomona.

today the study of fruit crops is called pomology. On this day the Romans feasted, eating and exchanging fruit, most often the apple, since it ripens much later in the season than other fruits. This popular practice spread throughout the empire and remained after the Romans had lost their hold on Europe. The game bobbing for apples, which we enjoy at Halloween celebrations, is a living remnant of the Roman rites.

All Souls' Day is the date when the Christian world celebrates their dead, who rise and walk for this single night. Throughout Europe on the night of November 1, people go to the cemeteries and restore the graves of their ancestors, picking the weeds, mowing the grass, and then decorating them with flowers. They light candles, place them in little glass lanterns called "lights of the holy souls," and leave them on the graves to burn through the night and light the way of the rising dead.

Also connected with both pagan and Christian beliefs is the preparation of All Souls' bread, which are little cakes left upon the graves to feed the dead. Meals of lentils, called "soul food," are also distributed in bowls upon the graves. In northern Spain the people make a special pastry called *Huesos de Santo,* or "Bones of the Holy." Evidence suggests that this practice was originally intended to appease the dead so they would not wander too far in search of food or light and become lost.

El Día de los Muertos

In recent years the Mexican celebration of All Souls' has become popular in the United States, filling a special need of those who mourn the loss of lovers and friends to AIDS. Where the Mexican influence is strongest, primarily in the West, the Mexican *El Día de los Muertos* has found a great following here.

It is important to understand the religion of Mesoamerica as it was before the arrival of the Spanish. A great series of ruins flanking a broad promenade stands just outside Mexico City. It is called the "Avenue of the Dead," for upon all the temples that line its edges, including two outstanding pyramids, the pre-Aztec priests sacrificed hundreds of thousands of people to their bloodthirsty gods. Their skulls were fastened to great walls and partitions, which the Spanish found to be a gruesome pagan practice. Death was indeed quite familiar to this great civilization of Mexico.

Aztec mythology is filled with the afterlife, expressed in up to eleven different heavens, as complex as the cosmos of ancient Egypt (it is interesting to note that both cultures share the practice of building pyramids). Such great belief in the netherworld and the long journey of the dead to reach it created a separate reality in which death took on multiple dimensions. As many as eighteen days throughout the year were dedicated to helping the dead reach their destination, with offerings of sustenance laid upon their graves.

As is often the case when Catholic doctrine is presented to people of vastly different perspectives, the Church sought to replace the pagan celebrations with those of the true faith. As a result they combined all of the old Aztec days dedicated to the dead into a festival called *El Día de los Muertos,* which falls upon the days of All Saints' and All Souls', November 1 and 2, respectively. On these days, the Mexicans believe, the dead rise and walk, returning to share the time with their loved ones. Just as they clothed their gods in flowers, so do the celebrants cloak the entire festival in fresh flowers, beeswax candles, ritual foods, and the pervasive scent of copal, the Mesoamerican incense. Most visible of all are the masks and folk art skeletons and skulls known as *calaveras,* the hallmark of this celebration. They bear images remarkably similar to those on Aztec frescoes and carved stone blocks depicting collections of sacrificial skulls adorning temples on the Avenue of the Dead.

Even the poorest of Mexicans gather in their graveyards on the Day of the Dead and erect altars and shrines, upon which they place their ceremonial food and drink. There is much music and dancing, for this is not a day of mourning but one of celebration at the communion of the souls of the dead with those of the living.

The most important of all flowers associat-

Dwarf French marigolds.

Celosia cristata 'Apricot Beauty'.

ed with the festival is *cempasuchil*, or flower of the dead. This is the African or French marigold, genus *Tagetes*, which is entirely native to the New World. Bright orange and yellow pompons are strung into great garlands emitting the marigold scent, which is potent enough to distill into pesticide. The flowers are also strewn upon the ground into a flower path which begins at the family home, then trails down the street in the direction of the nearest graveyard. It is believed that wandering souls need such a trail to find their way back to the grave, lest they become lost and haunt the home or village. Marigolds and their petals are everywhere in Mexico during this celebration and have become the botanical hallmark of the dead.

A second flower is the odd cockscomb, an ornamental strain of the grain amaranth, introduced into the Americas with the Spanish. In the original, pre-Hispanic Aztec rites of the dead, little cakes were made of the seeds of the native amaranth, *Amaranthus retroflexus*, to represent a bevy of gods. These were eaten during the rituals as an Aztec communion. The Catholic missionaries found the practice uncomfortably similar to the consecration of the mass. To discourage this old way, the padres encouraged the use of the ornamental red cockscomb, *Celosia*, locally known as the lion's paw.

Celosia cristata 'Centary Yellow', also known as cockscomb, replaces the amaranth used in Aztec communion with the dead.

Gladiolus and carnations are also commonly added to the altars and shop displays. All these flowers are used in the church with petitions, typically asking for good health and a plentiful harvest. The favors are written on circular pieces of cotton cloth and tied to a spray of fresh flowers brought to the church. These are set before statues of the saints and upon special coffin-shaped altars set up for the two-day festival.

There are reports of the use of hallucinogenic peyote cactus during the feast, as well, a practice among those of pure Indian blood that

Gladiolus byzantius.

continues today in Mexican witchcraft. Those partaking in the peyote rituals claim to have seen and spoken with the dead souls walking among them while under the influence.

TO SLEEP, PERCHANCE TO DREAM

> Taken in too large quantities it is productive of sleep unto death even.
>
> PLINY

Papaver somniferum is perhaps one of the most powerful, deadly plants on the face of the earth. It has the power to relieve pain, bring sleep, and provoke dreaming. Its species name is derived from the Roman god of sleep, Somnus; from the latex that flows through the plant, the drug morphine is made. Greeks so valued this narcotic for its pain-relieving properties that they crowned all their nocturnal gods with wreaths of poppy blossoms. Among these were Nix, goddess of the night; Thanatos, god of death; his twin brother, Hypnos, god of sleep; and Morpheus, god of dreams. Represented by

such an array of less-than-pleasant gods, it's easy to see how the opium poppy obtained such an infamous reputation.

The Romans often laid poppies upon the biers of their dead before they were cremated, praying that the body be protected from evil spirits, the poppies no doubt suggesting a peaceful sleep. In medieval monasteries the monks surely knew of the power of opium, and the Capuchines made a sleeping "dwale" containing the drug called "baume tranquille," which was jealously guarded as the only real pain reliever of that time.

Perhaps the most well-known poppies are those in *The Wizard of Oz*, which in the movie are shown paving the way to the Emerald City. Once among these flowers Dorothy and her companions find themselves uncontrollably sleepy, which is directly linked to the narcotic quality of the opium latex.

Another species, the red corn poppy, *Papaver rhoeas*, native to Europe, is considered the emblem of eternal sleep and oblivion. As a wildflower of open spaces and meadows, it grows on many of the old battlefields. Legend has it

Papaver somniferum, the opium poppy, showing buds, open flowers, and the characteristic seed pods which are tapped for their latex.

Papaver rhoeas, the corn poppy, with its hairy flower stems, is a wildflower of Europe which sprang up in seas of red flowers on the bloody battlefields of France.

that the fields of Waterloo, where Napoleon was defeated by the English army, came up thick with this red flower in the ground enriched by human blood. Thence it became the symbol of fallen warriors and soldiers.

It also became the official U.S. flower of Armistice Day, also known as Poppy Day, after its flowering at the sites of horrible trench warfare in the Flanders region of France during World War I. In his famous poem, "In Flanders Fields," John McCrae has forever linked the battlefield with the red corn poppy:

In Flanders fields the poppies blow
Between the crosses, row on row,
That mark our place; and in the sky,
The larks, still bravely singing, fly
Scarce heard among the guns below.
We are the Dead. Short days ago

We lived, felt dawn, saw sunset glow,
Loved and were loved, and now we lie
In Flanders fields.
Take up our quarrel with the foe:
To you from failing hands we throw
The torch: be yours to hold it high.
If ye break faith with us who die
We shall not sleep, though poppies
    grow
In Flanders fields.

MEMORY GARDEN DESIGNS

The death of a beloved pet can be a devastating experience. We grieve for a pet in much the same way that we do a human, with the same need for closure through the process of burial. Backyard pet graves have always been a ritual among children—the hamster or parakeet buried in a cigar box with great reverence—but adults can also benefit from the burial of a pet.

This small garden is designed to grow beneath the branches of a shade tree. The garden is planted with species that have connections to animals and centers on the headstone monument and (if applicable) a grave covered with a fragrant lawn of chamomile. Surrounding this is a sea of low-growing annual bedding plants in a mix of colors that may be changed from season to season. Dogs are represented by the dog rose, hound's-tongue, and red twig dogwood; catnip is for our feline friends; bird's-foot clover and columbine is for those with wings; and pennyroyal offers protection from fleas.

A War Memorial Poppy Garden

I once had a client who had retired from the US military and in his front yard created a beautiful memorial centered around a stately flag pole. He created it to honor all soldiers who had died in combat and as an act of thanksgiving that he had been spared. Behind the central flag pole was a simple white cross similar to the thousands that stand in Arlington National Cemetery and the graveyards of Europe.

The plants are mostly poppies, like the wild corn poppies with red flowers that grew on

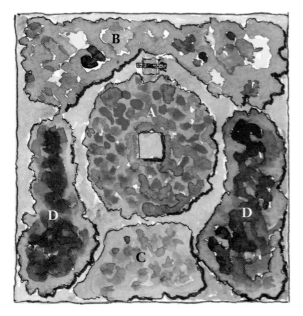

A War Memorial Poppy Garden

A. *Eschscholzia californica*—California
    Poppy
B. *Iris* Hybrids—Bearded Iris
C. *Papaver nudicale*—Iceland Poppy
D. *Papaver rhoeas*—Corn Poppy

the battlefields of France in soil. Many colors of
iris represent the hope that there will be no
more great wars in the future. For those who
have lost a loved one to war, creation of a memorial becomes a healing act, particularly if their
grave lies in foreign soil.

Day of the Dead Garden Shrine

This small garden draws its inspiration from the
warm colors so popular in Latin American folk
art. The walkway is paved in the buff tones of
Arizona flagstone, a sandstone mined in the
Desert Southwest. The altar may be constructed
of stone masonry—avoid wood or other flamma-
ble materials. It will be decorated for the holiday
with *calaveras*, pictures of the dead, and masses of
cut flowers. Beeswax candles and copal incense
are burned there as well.

Hardy Mediterranean fan palms flank the
altar as background foliage and provide plenty of
small fronds for cutting material as well. The
lion's paw celosia are grown in two matching
terra cotta pots on each end of the altar. Behind
is a rustic arch upon which grows the passionflower that suggests the underlying Christian
feast days, All Saints' and All Souls'. The brilliant color is derived from clumps of mixed gladiolus. Flanking the flagstones are linear masses of
dwarf French marigolds, and behind these are

the taller African marigolds, the true *cempasuchil*
which guides the wandering souls.

An AIDS Memorial

For those who have lost friends and lovers to this
devastating illness, a garden provides a beautiful
way to help deal with the loss. Just as quilts were
sown for the dead, this garden can be laid out
and planted as a means of healing and remembrance. The design is formal and is based upon
Greek and Roman courtyards. At the center is a
standing sculpture, perhaps of an angel, winged
Mercury, Apollo, or another timeless image.

The planting is primarily green foliage, a
soothing color that makes the space more
somber and contemplative. The statue is surrounded by a sea of variegated Hahn's ivy, which
represents fidelity and has always been linked to
the ties that bind us with its creeping, sinuous
runners. Around that is a low hedge of rosemary,
for remembrance, which may be clipped frequently for a neater appearance and to release its
aromatic scent. Drifts of flowering bulbs, with
calla lilies for purity, are mixed with hyacinth and
narcissus, two plants named after youths in
Greek mythology. At the corners are four Italian
cypress, chosen for their association with mourning and named after another young man of
mythology, Cyparissos.

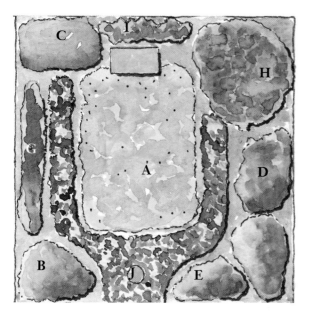

A Backyard Pet Memorial

A. *Anthemis nobilis*—Perennial Chamomile
B. *Aquilegia* Hybrids—Columbine
C. *Cornus stolonifera*—Red Twig Dogwood
D. *Cynoglossum officinale*—Hound's-Tongue
E. *Dicentra spectabilis*—Bleeding Heart
F. *Lotus corniculatus*—Bird's-Foot Trefoil Clover
G. *Mentha pulegium*—Pennyroyal, Flea Bain
H. *Rosa canina*—Dog Rose
I. *Nepeta cataria*—Catnip
J. Annual Flowers

Day of the Dead Garden Shrine

A. *Celosia* 'Cristata'—Lion's Paw Celosia
B. *Chamerops humilis*—Mediterranean Fan Palm
C. *Gladiolus* Hybrids—Gladiolus
D. *Passiflora* Hybrid—Passionflower Vine
E. *Tagetes erecta*—African Marigold
F. *Tagetes erecta*—Dwarf French Marigold

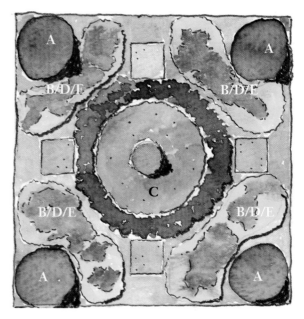

An AIDS Memorial

A. *Cupressus sempervirens*—Italian Cypress
B. *Calla* Hybrid—Calla Lily
C. *Hedera hahnsi* 'Variegata'—Variegated Hahn's Ivy
D. *Hyacinth* Bulbs
E. *Narcissus* Hybrids—Narcissus Bulbs
F. *Rosmarinus* 'Prostratus'—Rosemary

Eight

THE CELESTIAL GARDEN

*I*T IS WELL TO REMEMBER THAT EVERY LIVING THING NEEDS THE LIGHT OF THE MOON AND THE LIGHT OF THE SUN. THE RAYS, VIBRATIONS, AND POWER OF THESE TWO BODIES DIFFER BUT BOTH ARE NEEDED IN THEIR OWN WAY.

John Carroll

*G*OD HAS MADE MEN, SPRINGING FROM THE GROUND, TALL AND UPRIGHT, THAT, WITH EYES LOOKING TO HEAVEN, THEY MIGHT ACQUIRE A KNOWLEDGE OF THE DIVINE BEING. FOR MEN ARE NOT TO CONSIDER THEMSELVES AS MERE DWELLERS ON EARTH, BUT AS IT WERE PLACED THERE TO GAZE ON THE HEAVENS AND HEAVENLY BODIES, WHICH IS THE PRIVILEGE OF NO OTHER ANIMATED CREATURE.

Cicero

eaven is the haunt of celestial bodies which change position from minute to minute, all day and all night long. It is the realm of the earth, sun, moon, planets, and solar systems *ad infinitum*. These movements are so regular and predictable, they set the pattern of the days, weeks, and months by which all peoples organize the passing of time.

It is just this heavenly order that drives the plant kingdom, for all plant life is phototropic. This means that more than any other kinds of organisms, plants respond to the patterns created by the sun and moon. For those who are new to gardening, the first discoveries of such relationships can be profound and deeply moving. Perhaps this is why

Rare white tulips combined with the pompons of snowball viburnum. *Mrs. Hendricks Garden, Atlanta, Georgia.*

gardeners enjoy sitting in their landscapes during the early morning, the period when the influence of the moon gives way to the rising sun, and at the end of the day, when the sun wanes into darkness.

This subtle relationship is most apparent with the sunflower, a plant which turns its head to follow the sun throughout the entire day. In the morning, even before the sun breaks over the horizon, the flower heads droop to the east, waiting for the first rays of light. At high noon they stand straight up, heads aimed at the glowing orb in the sky, only to follow it through the western sky until dusk. Such movement ceases once the flower buds open; then the blossom remains in the same position of its opening to mature and set seed. A garden of sunflowers demands we notice these changes, which leads us to a deeper awareness of how celestial bodies influence plants and ultimately our perception.

Many of us want to become closer to the great mystery that is the night sky. People go to mountaintops everywhere to discover that awesome sight of millions of stars glittering across a big sky unobscured by pollution or city lights. In Yosemite National Park a new project is underway on one of the mountaintops overlooking the Yosemite Valley and Half Dome. The plan is to create a star-viewing site with comfortable seating that is oriented for the best view of the skies during the meteorite season in late summer.

Wing Haven Garden, Charlotte, North Carolina.

Perhaps we've come full circle now and are returning to the roots that early nomads knew so well, for they studied the skies for every purpose, both spiritual and scientific. Although we individual gardeners cannot build such magnificent viewing platforms as the park, our gardens may become places to sit comfortably and watch the skies, just as our more primitive ancestors did.

As we cluster under our protective roofs at night, it's easy to forget just how profoundly the heavens influenced the lives of early nomadic hunters. Although their villages or camps may have had huts or hide tents, those out on the hunt spent their nights under open skies, observing the subtle changes with each passing sun. After millenniums beneath this canopy of twinkling stars, they began to see patterns in the configurations of the brightest bodies, to which they gave names linked to their expanding mythologies. These constellations moved gradually across the sky, and as a person aged he learned how to find them all, in what season they appeared, and when they were absent. From these observations came the North Star and the Southern Cross, which established the very first continuum of celestial navigation.

They also saw the more obvious changes in the moon, the monthly cycle of waxing and waning, the increasing light followed by growing darkness of no moon at all. This moon, the bright glowing orb of the hunter and harvester, exacted other changes as well: it defined the nights as no planet can and presented a force so powerful it created ocean tides. From its mysterious, pocked face came a host of superstitious beliefs in the light and dark virgins and the odd female cycle of fertility, which has forever linked the moon to women and the garden.

Finally, the sun, the bringer of warmth, the solar fire that is born each morning in the east and dies to the west at sunset, is the greatest celestial element of all, for without it there would be no life. It was worshipped as a god, for its benefits were great, and its triumph over darkness became the basis for the greatest observances of early religions, the celebration of both winter and summer solstices and the in-between points, the equinoxes.

Today we have lost touch with the magnificence of the heavens, because our lives are no longer focused on the changes in the sky, but ordered by squares on a paper calendar. This loss of focus is perhaps a poignant sign of our struggle to reclaim our place on earth and with nature, trying to find a sense of belonging, rather than separation. New space telescopes are renewing our awareness of the majesty of an endless universe as they report no limits to this infinite heavenly realm.

Though much of our celestial history is rooted in pagan beliefs, we find that St. Francis of Assisi realized in the thirteenth century that heavenly bodies were creations of the Almighty for the greater benefit of our human existence.

> All praise be yours, my Lord, through
>   all that you have made,
> And first my lord Brother Sun,
> Who brings the day; and light you
>   give us through him.
> All praise be yours, my Lord, through
> Sister Moon and Stars;
> In the heavens you have made them,
>   bright
> And precious and fair.
>
> ST. FRANCIS OF ASSISI,
> "Canticle of Brother Sun"

SOL INVICTUS

In ancient times gatherers discovered that wild grass sprouted in great quantity near their camps where gathered seed had fallen, an observance which marked the advent of farming. The ability to grow food eliminated the need for constant travel, and with the settlement of villages, celestial changes took on a new relevance. These people found their lives ruled by the movement of the sun, which regulated the length of daylight. In order to organize their agricultural tasks, the length of the day became the ideal means of establishing dates of planting and harvest.

This logical source is the founda-

The Celtic cross combines the symbol of Christianity with the circle representing the ancient sun gods. It is a prime example of how the church took up imagery from pagan beliefs. *Sharon Abroms Garden, Atlanta, Georgia.*

tion upon which many cultures developed a complex series of religious customs. One of the most consistent beliefs is that the sun dies at dusk, abandoning the earth and her people to the hours of the night. Among the primitives there was always a fear that the sun would not return, dooming them all to perpetual darkness. But rise it did, and the first day after the winter solstice was a time for great rejoicing. Such is the part of the origins of the Celtic cross, which is a Christian cross superimposed upon a circle, which married ancient European sun worship with the new religion focused upon the Son of God.

The four cardinal points, north, south, east and west, were established in response to the points at which the sun rose and set. The four-sided Egyptian pyramids were aligned with these four primary points. In fact, if we reach back far enough, we find that most religions have some sense of the four directions, as we see in the biblical Paradise, where "a river watering the garden flowed from Eden, and from there it divided; it had four headstreams" (Genesis 2:10).

It's important to understand that the foundation of these beliefs lie securely in science. The four seasons established the four basic phases of solar orientation on earth. The seasons officially change on certain dates that split the 365-day year into four roughly equal parts. The chart below shows how the year is divided and the approximate dates upon which the official changes takes place.

Imagine the people who sought evidence of the sun's location in order to accurately predict these turning-point dates. A shadow cast by trees or rocks would not only indicate the sun's location during the passing of the day, much like a sundial, but also by its length show the point in its cyclical journey from solstice to solstice. The earliest cultures to develop the more technical astronomical skills in the West were the ancient Egyptians, who called their empire Heliopolis, or "City of the Sun," in 2900 B.C.

> You rise glorious at the heavens' edge, O
> living Aten!
> You in whom all life began.
> When you shone from the eastern
> horizon
> You filled every land with your beauty.
> You are lovely, great and glittering,
> You go high above the lands you have
> made
> Embracing them with your rays
> Holding them fast for your beloved
> son Akhenaten.
> PHARAOH AKHENATEN,
> "Hymn to the Sun"

The Pharaoh's "Hymn to the Sun" illustrates how many—Persians, Egyptians, Romans, and Greeks—revered the sun as god and life giver. Great cults arose surrounding some of these gods, and their rituals gradually blended into those of the conquering Romans, and later the Christians. In the New World there were the equivalent sun gods of the Aztec, Maya, and Inca civilizations, which each built temples, many oriented exactly to the rise and set of the sun.

In a way the stone circles and solitary standing stones of the old Europe were gardens of the heavens. Though they lacked plants, except for the carpets of wild grasses, they created a sense of place within the larger landscape of the countryside. One of the most important aspects of design is to create a specialized environment where none existed before, and even today modern landscape architects would be hard pressed to create such dramatic public places as neolithic peoples did with their monoliths.

The most well-known monument to the sun is Stonehenge, on the Salisbury Plain of England. Stonehenge took many phases to build, spanning 1900 to 1600 B.C. During this time it is clear that Egypt had already risen into a great nation, with the Hebrews still in bondage. The Greeks were emerging at that time as well, and neither culture, Greek nor Egyptian, knew the arch. Their architecture consisted of post and beam technology, clearly seen in temples and ruins, and most importantly, Stonehenge.

Despite conflicting folklore surrounding the standing stones of megalithic Brittany on the continent and the henges of Britain, they are

The Annual Cycle of Solstice and Equinox

Winter solstice	Spring equinox	Summer solstice	Autumn equinox
December 21	March 21	June 21	Sept. 21
Shortest day	Equal day	Longest day	Equal day
Longest night	and night	Shortest night	and night

Note: The dates here are approximate, as they can change a day or two in either direction in some years.

Avebury stone circle, Avebury, Wiltshire, England.

Stonehenge.

above all stones placed to record the passing of the sun. Stonehenge is the most famous because it bears many unique features. Its architecture is based upon trilithons, arches composed of three rectangular stones: two uprights with a beam laid across the top. The stones are of a blue rock quarried far away and dragged by ship and skid for many miles to the site. It is far more sophisticated than the other henges scattered about those islands; the stones are hewn, while the other henges are naturally shaped stone. Finally, the trilithons are connected with mortise and tenon joinery, a feature unparalleled anywhere in Bronze Age Britain.

Contrary to popular belief, these monuments were not erected by the Druids, although modern-day Druids have chosen such places to hold their seasonal celebrations. The Druids were priests of the Celts, worshippers of nature whose true temples were tree groves, pools of water, and mountains, not in the open amidst standing stones. Their rise to power occurred long after these megaliths and henges were erected. Evidence suggests that people of the Iron Age built them, perhaps the Beaker People, who left tombs nearby, their name denoting the

Stonehenge trilithons.

practice of burying clay vessels or beakers with the dead.

The great question of Stonehenge is where the Bronze Age Britons obtained the technical knowledge to quarry, transport, and hew the bluestone. Incidentally, these people had been creating earthworks and placing natural stones at Stonehenge for hundreds, perhaps thousands, of years before the bluestones were erected.

The explanation for the jump from fieldstone to hewn, imported bluestone lies with itinerant builders. Archaeologists now believe that these advanced masonry skills were likely to have been achieved under the supervision of a master builder. At that time master builders were itinerant, traveling from city to city in order to find enough construction to keep their families fed. Many of these builders came from the more advanced civilizations of the eastern Mediterranean and Egypt, where massive monuments, temples, and tombs were central to the cultures.

Many believe that one of these builders ventured well into Britain and there saw the need of local people, who were struggling to build

Callenish Standing Stones, Outer Hebrides, Scotland.

their massive outdoor timepieces and calendars. Perhaps the builder learned to move massive blocks of stones and create doorways with trilithon construction from Egyptian pyramids. He understood how to hew a mortise and tenon joint to hold the trilithon together. The signs are all over Stonehenge that one or more builders found their way across the English Channel, which was more shallow then, or perhaps dry all the way across at some point. This isn't unrealistic because the English coastline has changed considerably over the last few centuries, leaving ancient ports high and dry, while some old islands are now part of the mainland.

Modern astronomers have studied Stonehenge and other henges for their mathematical bases and relationships to solar movement. Calculations have proved that the henges were indeed astronomically correct, designed by people who knew the sun and wanted to accurately record its movements. In fact, the henges are so exact, their alignments can predict eclipses. Imagine the power such prophecy would have upon the people if their priest or holy man could indeed foretell this sudden dark-

ening of the sun! It's likely that most of the mysticism attributed to the henges began with such predictions.

Some believe the astronomical purposes of the maypole and Egyptian obelisk are similar, because both serve as vertical needles like that of a sundial. In addition to the henges, isolated standing stones dot the French and English countryside, and it is believed that these may have served the same role as the maypole and obelisk. Because they were each created out of a single piece of stone, they became immortal monuments still standing to this day.

In America the medicine wheel of Plains Indian tribes is of growing interest, for its geometry was used to create monuments out of stone. The greatest of these is the Big Horn Medicine Wheel, which is similar in design to a giant wagon wheel, with an outer circle and radiating spokes all meeting at the center. Like the henges, the twenty-eight spokes of the medicine wheel have been linked to solar and lunar cycles. Through such sacred forms these Native Americans organized time and space.

The stone objects used by early people to mark the passing of time are elements on the land that are not just dramatic, but have specific purposes as well. All designers are trained that form follows function, and the monoliths and henges embody just that principle. From the beauty of such creations we may be inspired to create gardens composed of similar dramatic elements in order to rekindle that ancient relationship between the heavens and the landscape.

MAGICAL PLANTS OF ST. JOHN THE BAPTIST AND THE SUMMER SOLSTICE

"He must increase, but I must decrease."
JOHN 3:30 (KJV)

The great saint of the summer solstice is the cousin of Jesus, St. John the Baptist, who was the last of the Hebrew prophets. His feast was set in the fifth century on June 24, which falls just

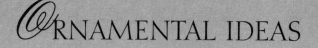

ORNAMENTAL IDEAS

The beauty of the sundial in all its myriad forms is that it is a precision instrument. Sundial time varies as much as sixteen minutes from official clock time through what is called "the equation of time." This tool that is half art and half science has grown into the most popular ornament in today's gardens. A sundial is affordable and natural as the focus of any garden, but it seems to blend best in a formal or semiformal setting.

The typical horizontal sundial is composed of two basic parts: the gnomon, the vertical spindle that actually casts the shadow, and the dial plate, the flat portion upon which the numerals are scribed. But as long as you are incorporating a dial into your garden, why not choose an armillary sundial, which is more like a piece of sculpture, for it is truly three-dimensional. An armillary sundial has three parts, which includes a gnomon, but here it is usually created in the form of an arrow. The two remaining parts, related to longitude and latitude, are the meridian ring and the equatorial ring. Armillary sundials are usually adjustable to make them more accurate for the location where they are to be used. Many of the catalogs in the back of this book sell all sorts of sundials, but the most elaborate can be found in Wind & Weather.

The buff tones of decomposed granite and sandstone lends a Mediterranean character when combined with suitable dryland plants such as rosemary and sages. *Genie White Garden, Charlotte, North Carolina.*

three days after the summer solstice and happens to be the oldest date on the Church's calendar. Most feast days were based upon the date of the saint's death, but with John it is his supposed birthday. Celebration of his feast has blended with the rites of the summer solstice and Midsummer's Day, which has placed him in dominance over the old pagan magical rites and plants.

In the fourth Gospel, John the Baptist, upon recognizing his heaven-ordained role as friend of the bridegroom, stated, "He must increase, but I must decrease" (John 3:30 KJV). This became the focus for the folkloric association of John with the summer solstice, suggesting that "he," the Lord, represents the increasing

darkness, while "I," John, represents the waning sun.

The feast of St. John is one of great significance, both pagan and Christian. In New Orleans this is the greatest feast of the Voodoo year. During the nineteenth century most of the black residents, both slave and free, left the city for the bayou on the Eve of St. John, holding mysterious nighttime dances with African drums, live chickens, and bonfires beneath the light of blazing torches.

Writing in sixteenth-century London, John Stow, author of *Survey of London and Westminster*, tells us that "on the Vigil of St. John the Baptist, every man's door being shadowed with green birch, long fennel, St. John's wort, orpine, white lilies, all lighted with candles." These are many of the most powerful plants of that day; St. John's wort (*Hypericum perforatum*) was a powerful charm used to protect home and barn. Its large, bright yellow flowers symbolized the sun; the red spots on its leaves were said to be the blood drops of John, appearing mysteriously on the leaves around the time of his beheading in August. The plant was believed to have special powers of fertility, and barren women used it in all sorts of secret rites in hopes it would bring a child. On the Eve of St. John, young women went out into the garden at midnight to gather flowers and bring them indoors. If the flower was still fresh in the morning, the coming winter would bring good fortune and a child, but if it was withered, it was a bad omen.

St. John the Baptist

So, too, orphine (*Sedum purpureum*), also known as witch's moneybags, was invoked upon this date as a charm to bring love. This is one of the few native succulents in northern Europe, and its ability to remain turgid for a long time after picking gave it yet another name, live-for-ever. On the Eve of St. John, the faithfulness of a lover could be tested by placing a leaf of this plant in a door or wall crevice, then spending the night with the lover. In the morning, if it had turned toward the right, the lover was true, but to the left, he was false.

In old England there was a fern amulet called St. John's hand, which could only be prepared on Midsummer's Eve. The root of the male fern, *Dryopteris filix-mas*, was dug up and all but five coiled fiddlehead stems removed. The root then looked much like a human hand, with the fiddleheads being the fingers. This was smoked and hardened in the midsummer bonfire, which preserved it indefinitely. The preserved charm was then hung in homes and barns as pro-

tection against evil.

There's more to this fern, a plant which represents fire and lightning. Its tiny spores, borne on the backs of the leaves, were considered very powerful magic. Many thought it "flowered" only on the Eve of St. John's Day, and the gatherer went out in the darkness to find the fern, then spread a white cloth on the ground beneath it, just as the Druid priests did to catch the falling mistletoe, lest it too touch the earth and lose its power.

Next, we find the Christian influence, for upon the cloth was placed a pewter dish and an opened Bible. The man or woman never touched the magical fern, but bent down a spore-laden frond with a hazel stick, the best wood for divining rods. With the rod the frond is tapped or shaken so the spores fall upon either the bowl or the book. This entire harvest process was wrought with fear because the demons and spirits were always trying to prevent mortals from obtaining the powerful spores, as was described by Richard Bovet, in his 1648 manuscript, *Pandaemonium*:

If one went to gather it, and the spirits whisk't by his ears like bullets, and sometimes struck his hat and other parts of his body. Although he apprehended he had gotten a quantity of it, and secured it in papers, and a box besides, when he came home he found all empty.

Whoever wore the spores on his or her person could theoretically become invisible. If a man held them in his hands, they directed him to hidden treasure or gold veins in the earth. The possession of just three grains gave him power to summon all living creatures that swam, walked, or flew in the skies to do his bidding.

GARDEN OF THE WINTER SOLSTICE

Worship not the sun, but him who made the sun.

ST. AUGUSTINE

The winter solstice is a day shrouded in the myth and mystery of plants that have been handed down to us over many centuries and figure largely in our modern holiday celebrations. It is also the time of the winter garden, when all sleeps except a few hardy evergreens, which seemed magical in the eyes of primitive peoples. They considered the solstice to be the date of the birth of the sun. St. Augustine, whose followers persisted in recognizing the pagan solstice rather than the birth of Christ, were encouraged to worship not the sun "but him who made the sun."

The poem *Inventor Rutilis*, written in 405 by Prudentius, a Roman official and Christian poet, further shows the role of the solstice in both the empire and the church:

A tree of berry-laden holly, *Ilex × altaclarensis* 'Balearica'.

Eternal God, O Lord of Light
Who has created day and night:
The sun has set, and shadows deep
Now over land and waters creep;
But darkness must not reign today:
Grant us the light of Christ, we pray.

Third- and fourth-century Christians originally set their date for Christmas on January 6, which today is the feast of the Epiphany. The similarity of the pagan solar rebirth and the Nativity, however, caused them to change the date at Antioch in 375 to December 25, four days after the winter solstice and one day after the end of Saturnalia. This also allowed the church to borrow the festival of lights, or midwinter fires, for its own celebration.

Saturnalia, an origin of our holiday feasting and merry-making, lasted from December 17 to 24, a period in which the benign god Saturn was honored with endless debauchery. In military Rome all war was suspended during Saturnalia, public places were decorated in flowers and greens, slaves were temporarily peers of their masters, and, most importantly, lavish gifts were given and received, hence the Christmas "goodwill."

The custom of hanging things from the branches of trees can be traced back to many civilizations, but the seeds of our modern Christmas tree traditions were in medieval Europe, where Christian beliefs were overshadowing past pagan nature worship. A legend of that time claimed that on the night Christ was born, all the trees in the forest, despite snow and ice, bloomed and bore fruit. A German folktale explains how on Christmas Eve in a cold storm, a woodcutter's family was snugly indoors around a warm fire. Just as they were about to go to bed, someone knocked on the door. The father opened it to find a child shivering from cold and hunger. He was invited indoors, and the woodcutter's son offered his bed to the lost child. The next morning they were awakened by a choir of angels singing in the heavens. They discovered the Christ child arrayed in all his glory and recognized him as the waif who had spent the night with them. Before the miraculous child disappeared, he took a twig from a fir tree, planted it in the ground and claimed, "I have gladly received your gifts, and here is mine to you. This tree will never fail to bear its fruit at Christmas."

In an effort to honor such legends of trees flowering in the dead of winter, medieval people cut boughs of hawthorn and cherry, then placed in water and kept them indoors, forcing early blooms. Sometimes entire trees were cut and brought indoors to intensify the false spring. This desire for blooming or fruiting trees initiated the practice of decorating trees, although many pagan religions hung offerings on their holy trees during important dates.

In medieval Europe there arose in the eleventh century the practice of holding religious plays, known as mystery plays. In them, basic stories of the church were acted out as educational and commemorative rituals for the largely illiterate masses. The most popular of these was the Paradise Play, which depicted God's creation of Adam and Eve and their inevitable fall from grace. The closing scene was one that promised the return of Christ in triumph, which made it a natural pageant for the Advent season.

The only prop in this play was the Tree of Life, or Paradise Tree, symbolized by a freshly cut fir tree hung with red apples. Later the plays were abandoned after difficulties with content arose, so the people created their own Paradise Trees at home instead. Our round glass ornaments may have evolved from these first apples or other fruit hung on the Paradise Tree. With candles such a tree became known as the Christmas Light, which represented the Light of the World (Jesus) or the Star of Bethlehem. In a Christmas Eve ceremony, the family would light the candle on the tree, which burned throughout the night, symbolizing the Savior's arrival, but also showing a lingering vestige of the fire festivals.

It was not until the Reformation that the evergreen Christmas tree as we know it was born. On one sixteenth-century Christmas Eve, Martin Luther was said to have seen fir trees outlined against a background of stars, which reminded him of the Star of Bethlehem.

Inspired, he cut a small tree and brought it home, where lighted candles were placed on its branches. Martin Luther's idea had roots in Germanic tradition. In the 1600s tree decorations were described as "roses cut out of many-colored paper, apples, wafers, gold foil, and sweets."

In North America, the traditions continued. Moravian settlers built wooden pyramids and covered them in evergreen boughs decorated with candles and apples, a very old European practice which was popular among the wealthy. One of the most famous colonial Christmas stories concerns Hessian soldiers, fighting as mercenaries for the British, who furthered the custom in America during the Revolutionary War. It is believed that they were celebrating around just such a "sugartree" when Washington and his troops surprised them at Trenton on Christmas night 1776.

THE GREENS

Templa exornantur

To understand the intimate relationship between indoor greens and Christmas, again we must go back to the earth religions of old Europe. Many believed a spirit resided in all things, and their entire consciousness was arranged around the elements of nature and their intrinsic spirits. Druid priests, inhabiting the ancient tree groves, believed that the oracle spirits of the trees spoke to them through the wind rustling in the leaves and branches. The priests became translators of such sounds as servants of their sacred trees.

With this in mind, it's not hard to see how early Europeans felt about their trees. During these dark months, those safe in the warmth of their houses thought the woodland spirits outside suffered from the wind, sleet, and cold. A custom evolved where branches of shrubs and trees were cut and brought indoors to provide the spirits a temporary comfortable abode. Surely a tree spirit ensconced in a home would bring good cheer to these dark winter days.

The pagan origin of the greens custom

Ilex × meservreae 'Blue Girl'.

I will have the maistry
In londes where we to."
Than spak Heivy "I am loud and
  proud;
And I will have the maistry
In londes where we go."
Than spak Holver, and set him downe
  on his knee,
"I pray thee, jentil Heivy,
Sey me no velendy
In londes where we go."

Over time holly did become a plant symbolic of this festive holiday, remaining part of church decorations today. Ivy, on the other hand, was too deeply rooted in bacchanalian symbolism and never did become a truly Christmas plant.

There are many Christian stories and legends based upon holly which probably evolved from efforts to stamp out any lingering pagan associations. In northern Europe the red berries were the symbol of the chaste maiden chosen to be the Mother of Christ, glowing with the sacred fire of the Holy Spirit. They were also the blood drops of the beautiful Norse god Balder, who was shot with an arrow of mistletoe wood, but this story was replaced by the belief that they were blood drops drawn from the crown of thorns on Christ's head at the Crucifixion.

Though it has fallen out of use in modern times, rosemary was once a central plant in the Christmas celebrations, primarily valued for its scent. As the scent of a fresh holiday tree permeates the home to recall memories of Christmas past, so did rosemary evoke such feelings before the Christmas tree came into use. Swags of rosemary hung beside the holly and ivy, scenting the air with its aromatic oils.

As always, the Christian church wove legends around its history. The scent of rosemary was attributed to Mary, who hung the swaddling cloths of the infant Jesus upon this bush to dry. The Spanish claimed the flowers were originally white until the Virgin, on her flight into Egypt, cast a purple robe over a rosemary bush; hence the lavender-colored flowers. Until the eighteenth century, choir boys of the Ripon Cathedral came into church on Christmas morn-

known as "bringing home Christmas" was not pleasing to the early Christian church. Later on, though, when the practice would not disappear, the church allowed the custom. The pagan origins were denied, and the practice justified by biblical scripture incorporated into the Protestant Advent offices: "'The glory of Lebanon will come to you, the pine, the fir, and the cypress together, to adorn the place of my sanctuary" (Isaiah 60:13).

This mingling of the pagan and Christian resulted in curious mixes of beliefs and symbolism. Among the most common plants were holly, ivy, mistletoe, and rosemary. The holly (rigid and prickly) was considered a man's plant by pagan estimates, and ivy (twining) the woman's. There was forever a battle as to which would rule the house. A fifteenth-century poem clearly shows the conflict between "Holver" (holly) and "Heivy" (ivy):

Holver and Heivy made a grete party,
Who schuld have the maistry
In londes where they go.
Than spak Holver "I am frece and
  joly;

The cutting of mistletoe, or golden bough, was a solemn Druid ceremony. This nineteenth-century illustration shows the chief priest cutting it with a golden blade, and it will be caught in a white cloth in order to retain all its magical powers.

ing bearing baskets of red apples all stuck with sprigs of rosemary.

Perhaps the most controversial of all the Christmas plants is mistletoe, due to its central role among the Druid rites. This plant is unique in that it is an evergreen parasite which grows on the branches of deciduous hardwoods, such as oak and ash, both sacred trees of the old religions. As mentioned before, the nature spirits of these trees were important oracles; it was believed that the heart of the spirit actually resided in the evergreen mistletoe while the remainder of the tree was barren in winter.

Mistletoe has long been known as the golden bough, all-heal, or *guidhel*, and cuttings were taken to hang over doorways as charms against the forces of darkness, witchcraft, and sorcery. It was also thought effective in enhancing fertility of people, their livestock, and crops of the field. Druid priests cut the mistletoe on Midsummer's Eve (summer solstice) or at the winter solstice with golden sickles, as it was taboo for iron to touch the plant. White cloth was laid out beneath the tree where the cuttings were taken so that none of the sprigs fell to touch the bare ground. It was believed that once in contact with the earth, the spirit of the tree immediately left the mistletoe.

Legend has it that Balder the Beautiful, the Scandinavian god of peace, was accidently killed with an arrow made of mistletoe, the only wood to which he was vulnerable. At the request of other gods, he was restored to life, and mistletoe was to be forever guarded by the goddess of love. Thus, anyone who passes beneath the mistletoe should receive a kiss to honor the goddess and show that mistletoe had become an emblem of love rather than hate.

This relationship of love, fertility, and protection provided by mistletoe caused it to be rejected by the early church as a pagan plant, but it later crept into Christian households, though never accepted for decoration inside the church. The practice of kissing under the mistletoe evolved from this story of Balder, and Nathaniel Hawthorne wrote of his shock to find such a pagan plant plentiful in the houses of the English during the holidays. "The maids of the house did their utmost to entrap the gentlemen boarders, old and young, under these privileged places, and there to kiss them, after which they were expected to pay a shilling."

Victorians on both sides of the Atlantic thought that any young woman who wasn't kissed under the mistletoe would not be married during the following year. A berry was always plucked off with each kiss, so the young ladies made sure that the sprigs were generously full of them. Families with numerous unmarried young women became obsessive about mistletoe and purchased huge quantities of the stuff. If young men were slow to propose, an enormous kissing bough in the maidens' home was thought to be a big encouragement.

Mistletoe grown in England was considered more potent than North American species. Since crossing the Atlantic took many weeks, imported mistletoe arrived dry and limp, unsuitable for decorations. Still, the superstitious gladly paid nearly twice the price, until over time the American species from the southern states replaced the import.

Mistletoe is a very toxic plant. It is spread from tree to tree by birds, which consume the berries and excrete them elsewhere. This parasite tends to take hold far better on trees which are stressed and will completely colonize very weak individuals. It has been known historically as a medicinal, but it should not be used, as its actual chemical nature is as yet unknown.

All Christmas greens were considered sacred and not to be taken down until the Epiphany, January 6. Even then they were to be disposed of carefully, not just thrown out like they are today. Holly was often burned or fed to cattle. Mistletoe was carefully preserved until the following year's holiday, obviously a remnant of the Druid belief that it was a charm. Perhaps this seventeenth-century lyric best points out the fear of careless handling:

> Down with the Rosemary, and so
> Down with the Bais, & mistletoe,
> Down with the Holly, Ivie, all,
> Wherewith ye drest the Christmas
>   hall:
> That so the superstitious find
> No one least Branch there left behind:
> For look how many leaves there be
> Neglected there (maids trust to me)
> So many *Goblins* you shall see.
>   ROBERT HERRICK,
> "Ceremony upon Candlemas Eve," 1648

Cradlewort

St. Francis of Assisi first established our nativity scene tradition by using real people and live animals, in much the same vein as the medieval mystery plays, which enacted biblical stories for the illiterate peasants. It was not until the sixteenth century that the nativity scene depicting the birth of Christ in the stable of Bethlehem became widespread in churches. These early scenes involved a special group of plants lining the manger, upon which the sculpture of the Christ child would lie. While today we soften the manger with common straw, originally the plants used were symbolic herbs called cradle-grasses, cradleworts, or holy hay. Some of the plants still bear a common name which attests to their popular use in the nativity.

Not a true sage, sage of Bethlehem (*Mentha viridis*) was the most common cradlewort plant because it was plentiful, and all mints had been dedicated to the Virgin Mary in both Europe and Britain. Gerard listed the plant as Our Lady's mint in his famous herbals. Another mint, *Pulegium*, was also named churchwort or bishopswort as it was poplar for strewing before religious processions or in banquet halls. This plant was traditionally gathered at daybreak of the feast of St. John the Baptist, June 24, the Christian rite of the summer solstice. The herbs were dried and stored until Christmas, then placed upon the altar for the first mass to be said on Christmas Eve, when many believed a miracle would occur to revive the dried herb.

The Glastonbury Thorn

Hawthorn trees, long a part of pagan legend, were thought to be both protective and unlucky. Hawthorns sheared into hedgerows were believed a haven for witches and fairies. Such superstitions are still known in Ireland, where it is considered dangerous to cut down a hawthorn tree. The tree was also a sign of hope and joy, the flowers part of wedding bouquets, and branches hung above children's beds to ward off evil.

There is a curious Christmas legend about one famous hawthorn tree that was not native to Britain but the Holy Land, where its season of

THE MOVEABLE FEASTS

There are certain religious feast days known as "moveable feasts," which are a legacy of agrarian roots in the Holy Land. The dates are based upon the Hebrew lunar calendar, and thus fall relative to the full moon and spring equinox. Passover is celebrated on the first full moon after the spring equinox. The observance of Easter falls a bit later: on the first Sunday after the first full moon after the spring equinox. Because the calendar date of the equinox and the full moon vary by a few days each year, so do their related feasts.

We must use the Easter date to find the related feasts of Good Friday, Palm Sunday, Ash Wednesday, and Shrove Tuesday. Similarly, most of the Jewish observances are moveable, including Rosh Hashanah, Yom Kippur, Succoth, Purim, and, of course, Passover—each in relation to the lunar calendar. Moveable feasts offer us a very tangible link to the earthy roots of Judaism, the shining moon of myth and mystery, as well as the eternal cycle of the seasons.

bloom is much earlier than the British hawthorns. Its story begins after the Crucifixion, when Joseph of Arimathea set off to bring the message of Christianity to distant shores, carrying with him a staff made of the Palestine thorn tree. It was believed he did make it to Britain after a long, arduous journey, landing on the island of Avalon in Somersetshire, which at that time was still separate from the English mainland. Tired and discouraged, Joseph worried about failing his mission, and knelt down beside his staff to pray for strength and guidance. As he uttered the words "You green plants of the earth, bless the Lord," the staff began to grow buds. Joseph's staff took root there, and later the Abbey of Glastonbury was built beside it, where the tree grew very old and bloomed religiously on Christmas Day each year. The out-of-season blossoming was thought similar to that described in the German folk tale of the Christ child and the wood cutter. From that connection the Glastonbury thorn tree became a symbol of Christianity in Britain.

This unusual behavior imbued the Glastonbury thorn tree with supernatural character, and the Christmas flowers were carefully picked and sold at a very high price for those seeking holy talismans. Tales suggest that the original tree had two trunks, but an evil man cut one down. While he did so, a thorn flew off and blinded him as punishment for such sacrilege. James Howell in 1644 describes the event in *Dodona's Grove*: "He was well serv'd for his *blind* Zeale, who going to cut doune an ancient white *Hawthorne-tree*, which, because she was *budded* before others, might be an occasion of *Superstition*, had some of the *prickles* flwe into his eye, and made him Monocular."

Boughs of the Glastonbury thorn were carried in religious processions for many centuries, and it was propagated so that similar holy trees of winter bloom could be planted throughout the realm. The remainder of the tree is believed to have been cut down during the civil war of the reign of Charles I. A memorial was erected beside the stump in the eighteenth century, commemorating Joseph of Arimathea's landfall in A.D. 31. Two offspring reportedly still bloom at the Abbey right on schedule, at Christmas each year.

Plants of the Aztecs and Franciscans

No Christmas scene today would be complete without the poinsettia, a peculiar New World plant of the genus *Euphorbia* infamous for its latex sap, which can be highly toxic. The poinsettia is unique in that its red flowers are actually bracts, which change color as the length of day shortens. Commercial growers control exactly how much light their plants receive in order to ensure they are at peak color for the holidays.

Native to Mexico, this plant was too tender to grow in Mexico City, yet Aztecs still held it in highest regard before the conquest, calling it *Cuetlaxochitle*. They saw it as a symbol of purity due to the brilliant color and used it as a source for dye. It was found growing near present-day Taxco by a seventeenth-century Franciscan priest who tended a Catholic mission there. He discovered it blooming in its bright red glory during Advent, the four weeks preceding Christ's Nativity, and found it ideal for his church decorations.

A charming tale about the poinsettia explains its place in the church. On Christmas Eve long ago, a little Mexican girl was sad because she wished desperately to give the Christ Child at the church Nativity a suitable gift. Upon visiting the chapel one day, she explained her frustration to her uncle, who assured her that even the most humble gift would still be accepted with love by the little Savior. So the girl gathered a bouquet of flowering weeds from the roadside and brought them to the church. As she neared the altar with her little gift, she became elated and grew confident in her offering, which she laid at the feet of the Christ Child. Upon touching the altar her lowly weeds were miraculously transformed into brilliant red flowers. They became the *flores de noche buena*, "flowers of the holy night," and would forever be a part of the New World Christmas celebration.

LUNA, ESTO PERPETUA

The moon replenishes the earth; when she approaches it, she fills all bodies, while, when she recedes, she empties them.

PLINY

The sun's seasonal changes are relatively simple compared to those of the moon, although there remain remarkable similarities. This moon—the glowing orb of backseat lovers, the witch's torch, the harvest light—is a vastly beautiful reflector of the night that is, and will forever be, cloaked in myth and mystery. It is also a heavenly body which has been linked with plants and gardens since the earliest times, for it has many other powers, including the ability to turn tides.

We know that the universe is defined by opposites, and when these opposing forces are balanced, there is harmony. This, the fundamen-

Modern hybridization has produced poinsettia cultivars in many shades of white, pink, and red.

tal philosophy of many Eastern religions, is depicted by the black-and-white symbol of yin and yang. This harmony relates to many pairs of opposites, be they light and dark, hot and cold, sweet and sour. Extremes are important in life, because without them we have no idea where a harmonious equilibrium really exists.

The moon, whenever given a personality, has been considered feminine, probably because its monthly cycle is similar in length to that of women. There are a great number of female deities associated with the moon, compared with male gods, who more often represent the sun. Moon goddesses are frequently shown two ways, one dark skinned and one light skinned, symbolizing the two aspects of the moon. These moon goddesses govern the night sky and oversee rites carried out under its eerie light.

Artemis was worshipped under the full moon by dancing in forest clearings. Hecate also represented the moon but in a more malevolent way, reigning over the evil forces of darkness. Selene was the goddess of the full moon. Diana, a Roman goddess, was worshipped out in the open, where she could look down from the heavens upon her minions. Among the Aztecs there is Caotlicue, wife of the sun god and ruler of the moon. Mama Quilla, the Incan moon goddess, protected married women and was often depicted as a silver disk. The Yellow Woman is moon goddess of the Pueblo tribes.

The monthly cycle of the moon is divided into four phases, which range from the new moon, which is totally dark, to the full moon, which is totally light. Increasing light is known as the two weeks of the waxing moon. After the full moon, the process reverses itself, with the shadow portion growing larger every night, until no light is seen—the new moon has returned. This half of the cycle is known as the waning moon. The full circle of waxing and waning is about thirty days long, the basis for the period of time we know as the lunar month.

The lunar month provided early people with a schedule for organizing the multitude of tasks involved with farming. Each month's moon was dedicated to an aspect of life when people depended on their crops, hunting, and gathering

for sustenance. From these names we get a clear picture of how close to the land our ancestors really lived.

The phase of the moon governed everything from the time to slaughter livestock to the planting of seed. Much of the folklore surrounding the moon is related to the do's and don'ts during each quarter of the lunar month. In general, the following shows what plant-related tasks are appropriate during each of the four quarters of the lunar cycle.

New Moon to first quarter: *Beginnings, outward-going, germination, coming forth*
Plant varieties which bear their seeds on the *outside* of the fruit, such as strawberries or corn.
First quarter to full moon: *Development of things already started*
Plant varieties which bear seeds *inside* their fruits, such as tomatoes and peppers.
Full moon to third quarter: *Completion, maturity, fullness*
Plant varieties which bear the crop *underground*, such as carrots, potatoes, or bulbs.
Third quarter to new moon: *Rest, introspection, disintegration before rebirth*
Do not plant. This is the time to *destroy*: kill weeds, cut timber, plow, and harvest.

Sow peason and beanes in the wane of
the moone,
Who soweth them sooner, he soweth
too soone,
That they with the planet may rest
and aries,
And flourish with bearing most
plentiful wise.

Thomas Tusser,
Five Hundred Points of Good Husbandrie,
1562

A more complicated way of breaking down the lunar month is by the zodiacal sign. When primitive hunters looked up at the night sky, they saw the moon's position in the sky gradually shift from day to day. They would have begun to recognize certain groups of stars, and could see when the moon's position occurred in or around a particular constellation. As civilization advanced, a science was born out of these moon-constellation relationships. Ancient astronomers identified twelve constellations relating to our modern signs of the zodiac. They were eventually able to predict when the moon would appear under a certain sign, and the art of astrology used that information to develop a system of fortunetelling by the stars. For those seeking a glance at the future, the moon's presence in the constellation Pisces could foretell success or failure, and for farmers it designated allowable activities related to both the phase of the moon and its zodiacal sign.

The signs of the zodiac are expressed in a variety of ways. Early farmers, rarely literate, had to have means of establishing the moon signs, from which evolved the graphic depictions of an animal or similar image which a constellation resembled. The sign was indicated by the old graphic, a single symbol which is the same today as it was a thousand years ago, and farmers recognized them in the monthly charts in the almanacs. In local folklore the signs were expressed as parts of the body, and early American pioneers preferred this over the old zodiac depictions.

head—Aries
throat, neck—Taurus
shoulders, arms—Gemini
back, heart—Leo
breasts, stomach—Cancer
intestines, bowel—Virgo
kidneys, loins—Libra
sex organs—Scorpio
hips—Sagittarius
knees—Capricorn
ankles—Aquarius
feet—Pisces

The very ancient system of moon signs is still recognized today in the practice of astrology. New Age occult moon sign charts follow the old method, which never adjusted for irregularities, which are always part of the natural world. The actual zodiacal signs calculated by astronomers vary from the traditional ones by a few degrees, after corrections through advanced mathematical calculations. The calendar of moon signs recognized by American farmers is recorded in the annual, *Old Farmer's Almanac*, which is still in use today. However, it conflicts with astrologers' predictions, and there will always be a difference between the astrological moon signs and the mathematically correct astronomical moon signs.

LANDSCAPES OF THE MOON AND SUN

To create a garden or at least devote a part of a larger landscape to the mysteries of the heavens allows us to tap into its infinite majesty. Whether it is a nighttime outdoor living space or simply a plot devoted to plants of the sun and moon, the garden becomes your rejection of things that separate us from the skies. We may draw inspiration for this effort from Vita Sackville-West, creator of Sissinghurst. Although this massive garden has much to offer, we are here interested in just two separate garden rooms that speak volumes of her deep understanding of the sky's many moods. This is no doubt due to the fact that Sissinghurst is actually a collection of old buildings dating back to Tudor times, and Vita's family lived in some, while dining and working in others. This required all of them to take outdoor paths at all times, giving them a glimpse of the surrounding gardens day and night.

Vita preferred to write at night after spending the day in her garden, and to work out her writer's cramps or gain momentary inspiration, she would leave her medieval tower office and walk through the dark garden and out into the countryside with her dogs. Such nighttime activity had more impact on the evolution of this garden than most of its viewers will ever know.

Sissinghurst is famous for its white garden, which lies at the foot of Vita's tower. Vita wrote that on one of her earlier night walks, she discovered wild lilies blooming so brilliantly in the

A stunning garden made for the evening hours combines a diversity of white flowers—including *Rosa* 'Iceberg', grey foliage, and touches of blue and purple for interest during the daylight hours. *John Alexander Garden, Santa Barbara, California.*

moonlight they hardly seemed real, Henceforth, she set out to create a new garden that would be dedicated to this eerie scene and remain clearly visible from her rooms above that contained her office. The white garden is composed of a rigid parterre of boxwood hedges enclosing only plants with white and pale yellow flowers and those with gray-green or silver foliage. Although it may not be obvious in the sunlight, it's abundantly clear under the light of the moon that this garden was created for the nocturnal experience.

On the other side of the garden is South Cottage, where Vita slept. Before it, on the sunny south side, is the cottage garden, where Vita chose to plant in wild sunset colors, those hues of flame that often overwhelm more subtle palettes. With the climate of Britain so moist and rainy, often overcast, the sunset garden offered a sense of warmth that was surely welcome on the dreary days. In one of her gardening columns, she explained her love of this place of the sun:

> I see that this has turned itself into a symphony of all the wild sunset colors, a sort of western sky after a stormy day. The sunset colors are not always very good mixers in a garden, happily though they may consort

in the heavens. In a garden they should, I think, be kept apart from the pinks, and be given, if possible, a place to themselves.
>
> *A Joy of Gardening*, 1958

Just as Vita has acknowledged both the powerful heat of the sun and the soft light of the eerie moon, so too can we create gardens of equal focus. Our landscapes may be planted for visual beauty under certain light, or they may acknowledge special plants that are botanically significant due to their reactions to the sun or moon. Third is the garden of color, where we create a palette inspired by heavenly bodies.

Children of the Night

One of the first signs of spring are the moths that come fluttering around our windows after dusk, where they are drawn by the bright electric lights. What candles drew them before man inhabited the landscape? Did these moths live for the light of the moon and fly upwards forever? The answers to these questions open doors to rooms shared by science and mysticism, botany and the occult. Behind them lies an entirely separate world of wonders that many never see nor ever participate in.

Though we often see the night as simply dark, there is always light, no matter how faint. This is proven by the modern military night-vision goggles, which take the pale glimmer of far-off stars and magnify it enough to allow soldiers to move about freely without a single artificial light to guide them.

Flowering plants rely upon pollen vectors for reproduction, The vector is any organism which carries the pollen from one flower to another. The most common pollen vector is the honey bee, now crucial to our fruit crop production. Other vectors include bats, hummingbirds, butterflies, flies, and a host of other insects. A surprising number of flowers need the moth for such a task, and what better way to attract them than with light. The reason flowers bloom in white or pale yellows is because at sunset, as the light grows dim, the red, green, and blue colors fade away, while the pale ones grow relatively more iridescent by the minute. On moonless nights they remain faint but gain some benefit from starlight. During all but the few nights of the new moon, these flowers greedily capture the lunar light and reflect it brilliantly in an effort to lure the nighttime pollen vector: the moth, the bat, and night-flying beetles. Should this be insufficient, then they may add an alluring fragrance, the "scent of a woman," mimicking pheromones to draw them in, blindly guided by nothing more than the fragrance of sex.

Some of the most interesting secrets of the night are true nocturnally pollinated flowers, with some of the most fascinating native to North America. However, the majority of these prefer the tropics, where the cool night air is far more conducive to pollination than the brutal daytime heat.

The genus *Cereus* is an enormous group of cacti, with over 450 species that bloom at night. The early California fiestas were arranged around the flowering of a giant cereus called *reina de la noche*, or "queen of the night." Many other types of cacti and desert plants bloom after dark, when temperatures are cooler and flying insects more numerous. Bats help pollinate the giant saguaro cactus, the most easily recognized of all, with its massive size and humanlike arms.

High atop the plants there develops a wreath of fragrant white blossoms, each one up to four inches across when fully open. These are a favorite food of Sanborn's long-nosed bat, which literally buries itself in pollen while sucking out the abundant nectar deep inside each flower.

Another fascinating desert plant is the yucca, whose iridescent candles of blooms make it a fine garden specimen and a conversation piece after dark. This plant maintains a unique relationship with yucca moths (*Tegeticula yuccasella*), which play a key role in the plant's ability to reproduce. Although yucca flowers are open during the daytime and visited by bees, the pollen grains are large and too sticky for these insects to carry away. Yucca is a nyctitropic plant, a species that physically changes at nightfall. During the day each cuplike blossom hangs downward, but at dusk the yucca flowers turn upwards to face the sky and emit their fragrance. This artificial pheromone, or sexual scent, attracts the yucca moths, although different species of moth may be required for specific types of yucca.

A yucca must cross-pollinate with another plant to set seed. The moth not only picks up this rather heavy, moist pollen but rolls it into a ball, as well. She will carry the ball to another yucca plant, where she lays her eggs inside the

A white garden showing how multiple shades of green provide a nice contrast during the day but fall back into darkness as the sun sets.

Yucca whippeli bears a bloom spike with flowers that point downwards by day, but turn up after dark to invite pollination.

flower parts and plugs the hole with the pollen ball. Her offspring will hatch, feed upon the developing seed ovary, but always leave a suffi-cient number of mature seeds behind to sustain the species. Due to the unique, heavy nature of the pollen, the yucca would not be capable of pollination without the assistance of these moths

The saguaro and yucca rely on both flower color and fragrance to ensure pollination, and our night gardens may enjoy both these sensual experiences, as well. Many other garden plants offer the same characteristics, particularly those which originated in the tropics, where scent is an important means of drawing pollen vectors in the riot of jungle vegetation. With limited eyesight, many insect species will respond to scents over a much larger area than they do to color or other visual cues. Fragrances in cultivated garden flowers vary in their sweetness and intensity. In some cases the plants mimic insect pheromones, which may be too subtle for us to smell. Musty odors tend to resemble the natural odors of bats.

Most other plants of the night garden offer us a visual feast of reflected light. They pro-vide a palette that is far more familiar than the true night-pollinated plants, and thus are our most effective materials.

The Garden of Sun Worshippers

We picture gardens of the sun as being in the Desert Southwest, filled with cactus, agave, and other plants that thrive in the very hot, direct sunshine. Sun gardens are really most beneficial to people in cold climates like Vita, however, because the warmth and light of the sun is scarce and thus precious.

The ancients named flowers composed of a flat disk and petals "day's eye," or daisy, because many open and close with the sun. Most of these are members of the *Compositae*, or composite family, and their flowers not only open with the sun, they bear remarkable similarity to the shape and color of the sun. In fact, most early illustra-tions of the sun depicts it with rays that surround a central disk. From the composite family we may draw some of our best sun garden plants, ideal due not only to the flower shape but to the beautiful warm range of colors, from yellow to red. Among them are black-eyed Susan, chrysan-themum, Mexican sunflower, cosmos, dahlia, zinnia, coreopsis, aster, gazania, marigold, and calendula.

As discussed in the opening of this chapter, sunflowers, genus *Helianthus*, are the most obvi-ously phototropic plants you can grow. There are

Helianthemum, Iris, Lupinus, and *Meconopsi cambrica*—many of the plants making up Vita Sackville-West's sunset palette. *Ilmington Manor, Mr. D. and Lady Flower, Warwickshire, England.*

Poppies and iris in warm hues. *Barnsley House Garden, Rosemary Verey, Barnsley, Gloucestershire, England.*

many different types of sunflowers, most originating from the strains that were a natural part of the midwestern American prairie and plains. Native Americans living in these areas brought the sunflower into cultivation very early on in order to harvest the nutritious seed. Ethnographic studies indicate that they grew several varieties of sunflower, which they named for the colors of the seeds, black, red, striped, and white.

Pioneer farmers found this plant and began more selective breeding to produce ever larger seeds for the oil and feed industry. Such efforts finally yielded the mammoth sunflower, the one bearing that single, giant blossom. When the demand was for a better cutting flower or plants that are more attractive in the landscape, breeders returned to the original strains of wild plants, which allowed them to breed branching plants with smaller but more numerous flowers.

There are many strains of ornamental sunflowers to choose from in today's seed catalogs, ensuring you plenty of variety in your sun garden. These include flowers that are ruby red, cream colored, orange, some with green centers, and still others that have more than one shade on the same petal. Because all sunflowers are easy to grow from seed, you may create an entire garden of brilliant color with just this one familiar plant.

There are some really easy to grow plants that will offer you all the brilliant sunny colors your garden needs to suggest the bounty of this

𝒫LANETARY INFLUENCES OF PLANTS

In magic and herbal witchcraft, great emphasis is placed on certain heavenly bodies, which are believed to have special influences and symbolism. Virtually every magical and herb plant has its celestial counterpart which governs its use.

The SUN rules all acts of divine power and intervention: acacia, angelica, ash, bay, chamomile, carnation, celandine, cinnamon, eyebright, hazel, heliotrope, juniper, marigold, mistletoe, oak, peony, rosemary, rowan, rue.

The MOON rules the occult, spiritualism, and medicine: camphor, eucalyptus, gardenia, lettuce, lovage, poppy, willow.

MARS resolves conflict, aids strength, and gives courage: anemone, basil, broom, coriander, garlic, geranium, hawthorn, holly, hops, nettle, onion, pine, thistle, tobacco, woodruff, wormwood.

MERCURY governs learning, communication, and self-improvement: caraway, clover, dill, elecapane, horehound, lavender, mandrake, marjoram, pimpernel, valerian.

JUPITER rules the finances and all increase of wealth: anise, avens, betony, cinquefoil, geum, honeysuckle, hyssop, jasmine, meadowsweet, nutmeg, sage.

VENUS, the Roman goddess of love, intervenes in matters of the heart and relationships: burdock, catnip, cyclamen, elder, heather, hyacinth, lemon verbena, mugwort, myrtle, orris, pennyroyal, peppermint, periwinkle, primrose, rose, snapdragon, spearmint, thyme, vervain, violet, yarrow.

SATURN marks ending times, including that of human life: asafoetida, balm of Gilead (poplar), comfrey, cypress, fern, henbane, ivy, mullein, pansy, Solomon's seal.

Sheared boxwood hedges are the preferred method of creating either a labyrinth or maze in a garden. *Bourton House, Mr. and Mrs. R. Paice, Bourton-on-the-Hill, Gloucestershire, England.*

planet. They are reliable, and you need not be a master gardener to achieve success. Most of these do prefer plenty of summer heat, so be sure to grow them where exposures are south or west.

THE SPIRITUAL LABYRINTH

Mazes and labyrinths are often thought to be the same thing, when in fact they are quite different. A maze is a pattern that offers many different paths to the same point, while a labyrinth is a complex pathway that leads to only one point at the center.

Throughout early Britain, and on the Continent as well, there were once many large outdoor mazes and labyrinths cut into the sod. The purpose of these early patterns remains a mystery, but some believe they were part of early fertility rites. Others say the walking of a maze is the equivalent to the movement through life, with its twists and turns and the inevitable dead ends. Still others claim the mazes were sited upon places with supernatural power, sometimes

connected with the leys of Britain, though this is yet unproven. The concentric rings of the round Cretan maze may have also represented a fortress as illustrated by one of the surviving spring rites.

The custom of running the maze was most popular among rural farming communities as part of their spring equinox festivities, which was the Celtic New Year. A woman from the village was designated the earth goddess, and she stood at the center of the maze. A young man of similar age, assigned the role of the sky god, waited at the entrance. With the townspeople surrounding the maze he walked, ran or danced through the pattern until he reached the goddess. He carried her out back out, marrying sky with earth in a symbolic way. This is oddly similar to our modern computer games, where the player must travel through many different mazelike worlds to finally liberate the princess. Perhaps the Old World running of the maze was also just a game.

When the Christian world replaced the old religions, it took on these ancient mazes as part of the developing church rituals. During the time of the Crusades, it was believed to grant one a special place in heaven if he or she made a pilgrimage to Rome, or better yet, the Holy Land. This journey could take years, and most people had no chance of gaining such indulgences from the church. Therefore, the maze became the symbolic journey to Jerusalem, which is the purpose of the colored paving stone pattern in the floor of the great cathedral at Chartres. The practice was to travel this labyrinth on one's knees, praying the entire time, perhaps while saying the rosary or various litanies, in hopes of obtaining the same rewards in heaven as a pil-

This is an exact reproduction of the thirteenth-century labyrinth at Chartres Cathedral, and it is the design used today at Grace Cathedral.

grimage. The Miserere Psalms, 51, 56, and 57, were etched into the original stones along the Chartres labyrinth so that the monks could recite them as they moved through the path.

Today we are finding such labyrinths reappearing. Some are part of New Age spirituality, which relies on a reverence for nature and the notions of power places and earth energies. Perhaps the most unexpected applications are among Christian churches, inspired by the labyrinth at Chartes. Dr. Lauren Artress, a psychotherapist and now priest of Grace Cathedral in San Francisco, has spearheaded the movement to resurrect the spiritual labyrinth. Under her direction, a canvas replica of the Chartres labyrinth, forty-two feet in diameter, was created and laid out on the floor of the church. Portable, it could be taken up and used elsewhere. Later it was replaced by a more permanent, heavy wool tapestry, and now there is a corresponding outdoor paved labyrinth, as well.

Dr. Artress authored *Walking a Sacred Path: Rediscovering the Labyrinth as a Spiritual Tool* (Riverhead Books, 1995), an in-depth analysis of the Christian approach to using these pathways. The Grace Cathedral labyrinth has become very popular, and various programs at the church help members and visitors use the path. Artress is developing a labyrinth network in preparation for the celebrations at the end of the millenium, and asks that anyone developing a labyrinth register it with the network. Grace Cathedral offers a seed kit, which helps individuals and groups develop their own sacred paths.

Other churches are picking up the labyrinth as a spiritual tool, as well. The art teacher at Mercy High School on the San Francisco peninsula, Sister Jean Marie, painted a labyrinth on canvas, like the one at Grace Cathedral, which could be used in retreat houses to teach meditation techniques. Like the seed kit, these giant painted canvases are sold to retreat houses, where they can be laid out upon the floor, indoors or out, and walked upon.

The labyrinth represents a threefold mystical tradition, which is based on the universal understanding of meditation: to release and quiet, to open and receive, and to take what was

Boxwood hedge maze. *Bourton House, Mr. and Mrs. R. Paice, Bourton-on-the-Hill, Gloucestershire, England.*

gained back out into the world. Each of these three phases is represented in portions of the spiritual path of the labyrinth. The first part is purgation, which means cleansing. This is the letting go of your concerns as you walk the path, often on the knees. The second stage is illumination, in which you open the mind and heart to subtle answers from heaven. This path twists and turns and ultimately reaches the center, where you may find both revelations and truths. Finally, the third stage, union, begins when you leave the center and retrace the path that brought you in. Many consider this the most energized part of the experience, integrating the new discoveries into the real world. It is considered a stage which renews the creative energy within, empowers, and invites us to a more grounded, authentic union with God.

There are many opportunities to add the sacred path to the garden. Certainly, the Chartres labyrinth is large and complex, but there's no reason why you can't create a simpler pattern for the meditative experience. The size and detail of your labyrinth will depend on what you have available. It's common to create small berms, from twelve to eighteen inches tall, to give definition to the pattern outlines while the path remains at grade. This technique is often used in turf or meadow areas, and the natural grass and wildflowers cover the bare berms. You can also depress the path, leaving the pattern outlines at grade, thus defining the pattern in the negative. The down side to this method is that the paths may collect water, refuse to drain, and remain useless during the rainy season.

Labyrinth patterns, both simple and intricate, are ideal for rock gardens or raised planting areas. Stones make good retaining walls, surrounding narrow, linear raised beds. The entire layout appears to be irregular, whereas it is actually very controlled. The beds may be filled with any kind of plant, from veggies to cactus. Imagine watering such a garden by hand and at the same time walking the labyrinth. This garden, by virtue of its very pattern, is deeply rooted in the spirit.

THE CELESTIAL GARDEN DESIGN

Garden of the Sun and Moon

There is order to the universe, and a garden that reflects the sun and moon must also reflect this order. The layout is divided into four quadrants representing the four cardinal directions, and each is planted in schemes to illustrate the influences of night and day. At the center of the circle is a sundial to mark the passage of time. The sundial might also be replaced by a pole or obelisk, which could cast its shadow onto the circle and mark the passing hours on a grander scale. Icons may be marked or painted onto the circle to show specific times, such as the sunrise on the summer solstice or midwinter's day sunset.

The circle at the center is surrounded by eight mammoth sunflowers that can grow to well over ten feet tall in a single season. As the flower heads develop, all will turn with the passing sun

in unison, establishing the vital link between this plant and its favorite star. Between each pair of sunflowers is a field of annual flowers that may be changed with the season to create more variety.

You may choose one or more of these concepts for your own garden or create this exact layout, which provides plenty of variety and special effects day and night.

White Flowers for Moonlight

The plants in this quadrant bear large white flowers that will be quite visible, even under just a sliver of moon. At the center is the yucca with its glowing candelabra of waxy blooms—the most famous of white flowered plants.

Silver Foliage for Moonlight

Plants with gray or silver foliage become absolutely iridescent in moonlight, especially if there is dew or moisture on the leaves. Those with fuzzy foliage are even more beautiful, for they glitter like little jewels. Although they are separated here, these plants may be combined with those that have white flowers for a more diverse moonlight garden.

Daisy Flowers of the Compositae

Most plants that share daisylike flowers belong to the botanical family *Compositae*. They are truly flowers of the sun: the word *daisy* derived from the early Celtic "day's eye"—since many open and close with the sun.

Sunset Garden

The inspiration for this sunset garden comes from Vita Sackville-West's cottage garden at Sissinghurst. It is a garish assembly of hot colors, all drawn from the shades that streak across the evening sky. Such a garden is most appreciated in cooler climates, where the colors suggest warmth and comfort amidst fog and rain.

White Flowers for Moonlight

A. *Cerastium tomentosum*—Snow-in-Summer
B. *Cistus hybridius*—White Rockrose
C. *Chrysanthemum maximum*—Shasta Daisy
D. *Hemerocallis* spp.—White Daylily
E. *Iberis sempervirens*—Candytuft
F. *Moraea iridioides*—Fortnight Lily
G. *Spiraea prunifolia*—Bridalwreath Spiraea
H. *Yucca aloifolia*—Spanish Bayonet

Silver Foliage for Moonlight

A. *Artemisia albula*—Silver King Artemisia
B. *Buddleia davidii*—Butterfly Bush
C. *Lavandula angustifolia*—English Lavender
D. *Lavandula dentata*—French Lavender
E. *Santolina chamaecyparissus*—Lavendercotton
F. *Senecio cineraria*—Dusty Miller
G. *Stachys byzantina*—Lamb's Ears

Daisy Flowers of the Compositae

A. *Achillea filipendulina* 'Coronation Gold'—Fernleaf Yarrow
B. *Chrysanthemum maximum*—Shasta Daisy
C. *Coreopsis grandiflora*—Coreopsis
D. *Gazania* 'Clumping Hybrid'—Clump Gazania
E. *Gazania leucolaena*—Trailing Gazania
F. *Helianthus annuus* 'Chrysanthemum Flowered'—Red Sunflower
G. *Rudbeckia hirta*—Black-eyed Susan
H. *Senecio cineraria*—Dusty Miller
I. *Tagetes erecta*—African Marigold
J. *Tithonia rotundifolia*—Mexican Sunflower
K. *Zinnia elegans*—Zinnia

Sunset Garden

A. *Alcea rosea*—Hollyhock
B. *Centranthus ruber*—Red Valerian
C. *Gladiolus* Hybrids—Gladiolus
D. *Iris* Hybrids—Bearded Iris
E. *Kniphofia uvaria*—Red Hot Poker
F. *Papaver orientalis*—Oriental Poppy
G. *Rosa* 'Joseph's Coat'—Hybrid Tea Rose
H. *Rudbeckia hirta*—Black-eyed Susan
I. *Tropaeolum majus*—Garden Nasturtium

Nine

THE URBAN OASIS

AND WHETHER DOE THEY WITHDRAW THEMSELVES FROM THE TROUBLESOME AFFAYRES OF THEIR ESTATE, BEING TYRED WITH THE HEARING AND JUDGING OF LIGITIOUS CONTROVERSIES, CHOKED WITH THE CLOSE AYRES OF THEIR SUMPTUOUS BUILDINGS, THEIR EARES FILLED AND OVER-BURTHENED WITH TEDIOUS DISCOURSINGS. WHITHER? BUT INTO THEIR ORCHARDS? MADE AND PREPARED, DRESSED AND DESTINED FOR THAT PURPOSE TO RENEW AND REFRESH THEIR SENCES, AND TO CALL HOME THEIR EVER-WEARIED SPIRITS.

William Lawson, *A New Orchard and Garden*, 1618

The word *oasis* evokes visions of a lush, palm-shaded spring in the midst of a desert. In many ways this harsh landscape is similar to most urban environments, where a few plants and an occasional street tree provide scattered greenery on cold, hard surfaces. Just as the oasis provides relief from the desert, small pocket gardens amidst the concrete offer respite from the worst of city life.

In the philosophical writings of many faiths, we find examples of this need for an oasis of solitude where we may cultivate our gifts and allow the complexities of life to settle out. Certainly, Thomas Merton, the great Trappist monk who gave up the world in favor of his tiny hermitage, found truth there, sharing it through the abundance of his writings. We find those who live the creative life of

The natural recesses in this wall become the frame for an enchanting mural suggesting mystical, far-away realms. Coordinated plantings help to further the illusion. *Cawdor Castle, Highland, Scotland.*

Quail Botanic Garden, Del Mar, California.

literature and art seek out such oases, where they may exist in havens safe from the confusion and interruptions of more interactive living.

Even those who do not rely on solitude for their work benefit from daily meditations and escape from the urban environment. Though many do not realize it, each day is filled with thousands of small decisions, which combined create stress. We are often separated from nature, breaking the bond which centers us to the earth. Without these earthen ties, we float aimlessly through life, surrounded by the synthetic rather than the organic, so that our sense of self is often threatened.

A garden offers one of the most beautiful solutions to the problem, because a narrow strip of soil, a flower pot, or a postage stamp plot of earth is all that is required to recover our lost ties to nature. Even a small space surrounded by buildings can become a private refuge, a port in the storm that rages through cities, an oasis of calm. The Serenity Prayer, which helps thousands treading the road of recovery, clearly states the need for such internal peace. For those seeking enlightenment through meditative paths, the separation is as important to finding one's center. To those suffering wounds of the heart and body, gardens of peace enhance the healing process through living plants and quiet places. The urban oasis, by virtue of the fact that it is a garden, offers us all the benefits of the cultivated landscape. We may join farmers and kitchen gardeners everywhere by growing herbs, dwarf vegetables, and salad greens. The florist in us all may be assured fresh flowers and real greens for the winter holidays.

For many of us, life is an eternal struggle, and the overriding need in the garden is an idea or focus which suggests something meaningful. The preceding chapters suggest many ways to tap into our spiritual affinities. A garden that responds to our wonder toward the heavens, that links us to ancient history in a modern world, to fully understand the reverence for all life of the Native Americans, or simply to remind us of all things biblical is to make the garden more than mere things of beauty.

To inject a sense of your lifestyle goals into the garden is deeply personal. For some born-again Christians, a continual focus upon Scripture is essential to walk the path away from sin and despair. This is also the case with anyone in recovery from alcohol, drugs, gambling, and the other vices that can destroy lives. For them the oasis must be a part of their lifelong struggle to survive, whether it is based upon a religious, philosophical, or other lifestyle program.

An oasis which stresses a twelve-step program may be organized around the symbolic number twelve. Since such a program depends on recognition of a higher power, this too may be manifest in sign or symbol. If it is a religious deity, the appropriate image is important, be it a Buddha, a Star of David, or a crucifix.

Everyone is different, and in this most intimate aspect of life, spirituality, people seek answers in so many places. In seeking the meaningful in your urban oasis, beyond simply developing aesthetic beauty and separateness from the outside world, you will ultimately find the best choice by examining your thoughts in a sincere, thorough way. Never forget that gardens are indeed for people, and the landscape you create should be uniquely tailored to you, your loves, and your needs, so it indeed becomes your port in the tempest that is everyday life.

GARDENS FOR PEACE

During the Vietnam War, Laura Dorsey Rains's husband was wounded in action and hospitalized. Laura traveled from home in Atlanta, Georgia, to be at his side during the three-month convalescence in Japan, where she discovered Japanese gardens as places to separate herself from the stress and rigors of the military hospital. The peace and serenity so characteristic of Asian gardens left a deep, lasting impression upon Laura. Thus began her deep interest in developing gardens as more than just places of beauty but of healing, reflection, and renewal. Years later, while touring English gardens, she realized that "the sense of peace which comes to each of us through the experiences felt in gardens crosses all political and economic barriers."

Such was the seed that began her labor of love, the creation of the nonprofit organization Gardens for Peace. Its goal would be to identify and link established gardens throughout the world where contemplation and meditation by individuals and communities will foster respect for the environment and a climate for peace among all peoples. To be chosen as an official garden in the network, four characteristics are required. It must make use of expanses of water or surrounding woodland, provide a sense of enclosure with an overhead canopy, contain a diverse selection of vegetation, and display sufficient visual stimuli through line, form, color, and texture. Above all, it must lend a sense of safety and separation in order to shut out the conflict of the outside world.

The first designated garden was the Swan Woods Trail, dedicated in 1988, a ten-acre woodland in the heart of northwestern Atlanta. After a visit to Atlanta from officials of its sister city, Tbilisi, in Soviet Georgia, it was agreed that a second garden would be dedicated there, and the two cities would exchange bronze sculptures that would reside in the gardens to underscore this peaceful relationship. In 1991 the third official garden in the network was dedicated on the grounds of the Royal Botanical Garden in Madrid, Spain.

Today Gardens for Peace continues its efforts to educate the public on the significance and benefits of gardens in an ongoing program to use these expressions of nature as common ground upon which we all may escape conflict and experience true peace. (For more information contact Gardens for Peace, P.O. Box 7307, Atlanta, Georgia 30357).

PROBLEMS IN THE CITY

In cities nationwide, landscape architects have created marvelous gardens in the postage-stamp yards behind townhouses. These are the oases we all need, and such places enhance our lives and those of family and friends, but these places present unique challenges due to the many con-

The Atlanta Garden for Peace focuses upon the sculpture from Soviet Georgia. The location emphasizes the sense of separateness, succeeding very well, considering this woodland sits amidst Atlanta's most densely populated neighborhoods. (*Courtesy of Gardens for Peace, photograph by David Schilling*)

Built-in planters filled with plants are a good way to utilize every inch of space available. *Garden Valley, Petaluma, California.*

straints imposed by the surrounding buildings. Limited space also demands a special economy, and the knowledgeable designer knows many ways to obtain the greatest benefit from even the smallest urban garden. Perhaps most essential is the ability through design to block out the less desirable influences of congested life that surround the garden.

To create a truly effective urban oasis, it is essential to first identify the problems common to all cities. Landscape design is often called problem solving because it is these difficult issues which the layout must mitigate. Landscape design is a process, and solutions are found through a logical, ordered approach.

One of the greatest challenges of the small urban garden is lack of space. When some yards are no bigger than a good-sized swimming pool, every inch of landscape must be maximized to its potential. Above all it must be planned according to how people are to use the space.

What we see in nature offers inspiration in myriad ways. Nature can make us realize the great gift of colored skies offered by our Creator and can encourage positive reflection on our lives. Such enlightenment will inspire an artist to paint or a writer to capture the scene in words.

Imagine how a concrete wall influences our feelings, though, with its cold, impersonal face. Certainly, it is far different and less desirable than the sunset. In fact, surrounding multistory buildings may give the impression that the proposed garden area lies at the bottom of an elevator shaft. Other visual problems stem from other uses of adjacent land. For example, the yard of a residential dwelling next door to a parking lot may be separated by a transparent chain link fence. On the other side is a large area of paving and the cars themselves, which can cause extreme glare from shiny paint and reflective chrome and glass. Perhaps the problem is nothing more than neighbors who fail to tidy up their own yard. In every case the goal is to solve the visual problem through good design.

Privacy is also a visual issue, but it is based upon the ability of others to see into the garden, not what those in the garden see outside it. It's difficult to find privacy in the city, particularly when it is desired in an outdoor space. In the "elevator shaft" situation described above, the windows of all those apartments look down upon the site, which leaves very little privacy. No one wants to feel as though the urban oasis is a fishbowl. Perhaps most important is that if you feel as though you're continually being observed, you will not find the sense of oasis or separation from your surroundings.

Our sense of smell can be very acute, and the notion that scents can create a beneficial healing experience is manifest in aromatherapy. Have you ever smelled something that reminded you of your childhood, and with it comes the ghosts and memories of long ago? Perhaps it was your first-grade teacher's jungle gardenia perfume. Maybe it's the haunting earthen fragrance that comes with the first rainfall of autumn. To many the fragrance of lilac blossoms will forever remind them of Grandmother's room.

In the city we are assaulted with a variety of potent smells. There is the lingering aroma of diesel from buses or that of the garbage trucks, which is much like fermenting fruit. Every city has its own array of olfactory offenses, which can spoil the sensory enjoyment of the garden. For this reason, design must provide a means of masking such smells if the garden is to become a true sensual oasis.

The day will come when man will have to fight merciless noise as the worst enemy of his health.

DR. ROBERT KOCH,
Conservation Foundation Newsletter, 1910

The congested streets of London differ from those of New York in one way: the Brits have made unnecessary use of auto horns illegal. Here in the States the sound of horns, brakes, boom boxes, crashing lift gates, and human voices combine to create a continual din, which many notice only upon their return from a vacation in the quiet countryside. Noise is subtle, and after a while we cease to notice it. Yet the brain indeed registers the sounds, and they prey upon the peace of our subconscious.

That oasis in the empty desert is a place of quiet where nothing conflicts with our internal voices—not the distorted ramblings of schizophrenia, but the vital process of pondering, weighing choices, and creative thought. In biofeedback people learn to generate beneficial brain waves, helping them better control their

bodies and health. These are the waves that come only when deeply relaxed, while teetering on the verge of sleep or when loosened up by a hot bath, a creative mode in which we come up with some of our best ideas. The need to block out the sounds of the city make our oases so much more effective and indeed help in the ultimate goal of separation.

Anyone who has walked around Chicago's Loop knows how the buildings can channel the winds, turning some streets into virtual wind tunnels. During the winter months these winds can make city gardens unpleasantly cold and tatter plants to the point where they lose their foliage. On the other hand, lack of air movement can be equally difficult, leaving elevator-shaft spaces stale and hot during the summer months. Under such conditions many plants will be overcome with fungus diseases, limiting the choice of species.

An architect designing a large building must pay special attention to the shadow it will cast upon other buildings and spaces around them. A tall building can completely disable a solar heating system on top of an adjacent rooftop. It can also deny light from entering the windows of apartments next door. More than any other type, urban gardens suffer from lack of sunlight. The only real mitigation is to carefully choose shade-loving plants, which thrive under low light. It's also important to avoid any design elements which may increase this overabundance of shade.

The earth of city gardens can be hostile to plants. In places like San Francisco, many neighborhoods are built upon fill material of dubious origins, and other homes sit upon the rubble from earthquakes and fires. Many also fail to realize, until they begin excavation for a garden, that cities are honeycombed with underground utilities, both in use and abandoned. This can limit what you plant and where you plant, further influencing the layout of the design. The ground beneath your feet is the only lingering vestige of what existed before the city grew up there, and this should be treated gingerly and with sufficient care to avoid a lawsuit and make it fertile enough to support plants.

FINDING SOLUTIONS

Before finding solutions to city garden problems, it's important to understand just how difficult design is under such circumstances. When space is limited, planning the sizes of things in the garden and their relationship to one another—such as walls, paving, and structures—requires a certain degree of skill that only comes with experience. It is a good idea to consult a landscape architect or professional garden designer to assist with layout or to come up with a basic plan that functions according to your needs. This ensures you a workable plan that you can embellish with plants and creative materials, thus making it your own.

> Nor is the imagination so fastidious as to take offense at any well-supported deception, even after the want of reality is discovered.
>
> H U M P H R E Y   R E P T O N ,
> *The Art of Landscape Gardening*, 1795

Outdoor mirrors become a window to an imaginary garden just beyond the wall. *Linda Teague Garden, Del Mar, California.*

Creating the Illusion of Space

One of the most fun and creative challenges of urban gardening is creating space that really doesn't exist in order to make the garden seem larger. You've probably seen this done with interiors, large windows borrowing space from outdoors or mirrors appearing like doors to other rooms. Mirrors also reflect existing light from windows, fixtures, and candles back into the room, augmenting their illumination capability.

The creation of illusions, or *trompe l'oeil* among the French, can go outdoors, too, although most people don't realize it. There are very potent means of doing so, and in the process you can also make some of those ugly walls disappear.

You can use a mirror outdoors just as you would indoors, by attaching it to a wall. In order for the effect to be successful, the mirror must be properly framed so it looks as much like a gateway, door, or window as possible. That means a doorjamb, if that is the desired effect, or a wooden window sash, which is easier to work with. You can create more elaborate effects using a wrought iron frame or built-in masonry. If you don't want to build a wood framework around your mirror, the lazy gardener's option is to choose vines to train up and around as a leafy frame.

Note: Do not use an indoor mirror in the garden. The weather would cause the silvering to dissolve from the back of the glass. Be sure to order one designated for all-weather use and with sufficient thickness to avoid cracking.

Forced perspective is an old idea that got lost for a while and is coming back again. The French called it *trellage*, but it's really just the creative use of lattice to achieve false depth through manipulation of perspective lines. Forced perspective takes advantage of how the eye perceives depth, which artists know makes items in the foreground of a flat painting appear closer than those in the background. When lattice applied to a flat vertical surface is organized so the dimensions reflect a change in size appropriate to typical change in depth, your eye thinks there is depth where it does not exist. Forced perspective is an ideal way to make a focal point for the tiny garden or when attempting to enlarge the visual size of a side yard, as seen through doors or windows. To create trellage with forced perspective requires precise measurements and construction. In the past this required the skills of a very good carpenter working off a detailed drawing. Fortunately, today there are garden suppliers which prefabricate forced perspective trellage panels of wood, and some do so with modern plastics that require no painting or maintenance.

You can improve visual quality and increase the sense of space using the tricks of mirrors and forced perspective, but there is a third trick not often used because of its expense. In Britain and Europe wealthier city gardeners turn their blank walls of stucco, plaster, or concrete over to artists, who paint a realistic, scenic mural. This has been done on a very large scale or within the framework of just a false window or doorway which seems to open onto a landscape. Either way, it can be attractive but probably will never be quite as realistic as the mirror effect. If you have the artistic skill to paint your own mural, it's definitely worth the effort.

Vertical Gardening

Improving the vertical is related to improving the visual, since it is with vertical elements that we cover up or screen what is seen around the edges of a city garden. The best way to turn walls into positive elements is to transform them into vertical gardens, because the more plants trained to these surfaces, the more area is left for living space. Both types of improvements make walls seem less faceless and create space, but the vertical does not rely on illusion.

Vertical gardening is done with vines and plants that can be made to act like vines. Since there is great variety in the way vines climb and how or whether they attach themselves, the three groups detailed here will solve most urban design problems. They also solve other problems, such as masking smells with fragrance and absorbing noise.

The best way to cover unattractive walls is to plant self-clinging vines, which will grow high upon the walls on their own. There are just a few self-clinging vines, some of which are highly

The beauty of deciduous *Parthenocissus tricuspidata* is its variations in color. The first leaves of spring are lime green, then emerald in summer and scarlet in fall before finally shedding foliage for winter.

invasive, both in size and through aggressive holdfasts. English ivy *(Hedera helix*, zones 5 through 10), a family of large and small cultivars, can be the most damaging, but it is evergreen and covers quickly. This true ivy has variegated cultivars with white patches on their leaves, a feature which designers use to bring light into shaded spaces. A plain green leaf reflects very little light, but variegated leaves in sun-starved places provide the illusion of dappled sunlight.

Many seeking an evergreen alternative to ivy favor wintercreeper, or evergreen bittersweet *(Euonymus fortunei*, zones 4 through 8), for its fine texture and slower growth, which lessens the need for frequent trimming. Wintercreeper provides seasonal color not common in evergreens, when autumn frosts turn the foliage a purple hue.

Two popular clinging vines, Boston ivy *(Parthenocissus tricuspidata*, zones 4 through 10) and its cousin Virginia creeper *(Parthenocissus quinquefolia)*, are not true ivies but entirely different deciduous plants. They are found clinging to the walls at most Ivy League schools. They have beautiful, bright green spring growth and fiery fall color, and they are ideal candidates for

Vines for Covering Fences

Botanical name	Common name	Zone(s)
Clytostoma callistegioides	Violet trumpet vine	9–10
Gelsemium sempervirens	Carolina jessamine	7–10
Jasminum polyanthum	Chinese jasmine	8–10
Lonicera spp.	Honeysuckles	Vary
Passiflora spp.	Hybrid passionflowers	9–10
Tecomaria capensis	Cape honeysuckle	9–10
Trachelospermum jasminoides	Star jasmine	8–10

Colorful Accent Vines

Botanical name	Popular name	Zone(s)
Bougainvillea hybrids	Bougainvillea	9–10
Campsis radicans	Trumpet creeper	4–8
Clematis armandi	Evergreen clematis	8–10
Clematis hybrids	Clematis	4–10
Clytostoma callistegioides	Violet trumpet vine	9–10
Distictis buccinatoria	Red trumpet vine	9–10
Hydrangea anomala	Climbing hydrangea	5–9
Rosa spp.	Climbing roses	5–10
Wisteria spp.	Wisteria	5–9

covering city walls since they inflict little damage to masonry. While dormant, they are also much more easily cut back to a manageable size.

Another evergreen self-clinging vine is creeping fig (*Ficus pumula*, zones 9 and 10), favored for its tolerance of very shaded conditions in subtropical climates. It has two very distinct types of growth: the small, tightly knit juvenile foliage clings to the stems and vertical surfaces, but secondary growth juts out perpendicularly to the wall with big leathery leaves. The most beautiful creeping fig walls are regularly trimmed so they bear only juvenile foliage. If you keep an eye out for this plant, though, you'll discover lots of examples of vines well trimmed to the extent of the ladder's reach, then a bulge of uncontrolled secondary growth further up spoiling the effect. Tip: Never let your vines grow beyond the reach of your ladder.

Aggressive vines may invade roofing and attics to cause serious damage.

Another group of vines for vertical gardening are those which have widely varied growth habits and require some sort of support. The chain link fence adjacent to the parking calls for a vine that is capable of cloaking the fence in foliage and flowers. Virtually any vine will serve this purpose if it is leafy enough, but the species listed above are some of the most reliable for open fencing or framework lattice. If you are planning to screen off an unattractive view or improve security with a new fence, these same vines will help make it appear like a more expensive barrier. These plants may require some help at first but will eventually cover the entire fence line.

Many of the most beautiful landscape vines do not cling or effectively climb on their own, but they have the sort of growth habit that makes them graceful, or they may bring brilliant color or foliage into your vertical landscape. These too can be grown on vertical walls, but you must attach a trellis to the wall, onto which you tie the vine runners. If the wall surface is wood, train them to nails or screws, eliminating the need for a trellis.

Plant these vines at gateways, beside doors or windows, up the columns of overhead structures, or onto a balcony railing. They offer all the benefits and color of shrubs and trees, but they will grow out of very small openings in the pavement and rarely disturb underground utilities.

Sound Attenuation

City noise is a perpetual problem, and it can be serious if you live adjacent to a freeway or a major intersection. A good way to reduce the problem is to take advantage of sound-absorbing barriers, which may act in one of two ways. Those that reflect the sound turn it back toward its source, while barriers designed to refract sound dissipate, diffuse, and disburse it. Masonry sound walls now flanking many urban freeways adjacent to residential areas are an example of the former technique. They are designed to reflect noise, and can be over twenty feet high since sound travels upward and will breech the wall if it isn't tall enough.

Walls or fences adjacent to noisy areas are clearly effective in reflecting sound before it can reach your garden space. They are even more capable when you add the refraction ability of vines upon such barriers. Vines increase the overall thickness of the wall, and their foliage refracts the sound. This means the vines have the ability to dissipate sound energy in the layer of

ESPALIER

Espalier is a French term for the training of any plant to a vertical surface. For urban gardeners this means that certain trees and shrubs can be pruned while young to grow flat against walls. They require continual training for their entire life spans to maintain that posture. Espalier allows you to increase the plant palette of your vertical garden, which can be valuable in a shaded elevator-shaft garden, where the choices of plants are limited.

The most useful of all espalier techniques is applied to fruit trees, usually dwarf or semidwarf varieties. In Europe this has been used to increase solar exposure and allow trees to be planted much closer together for a greater crop on small farms. It was once a real art form, with grafting used to create elaborate geometric patterns of branches upon vertical walls. Books on vertical gardening and specialized pruning cover all the different methods in much greater detail.

Here firethorn, *Pyracantha*, has been trained to frame a window. The linear effect is achieved with wires strung tightly across the wall, to which the young, flexible limbs of the shrub are tied. *Bourton House, Mr. and Mrs. R. Paice, Bourton-on-the-Hill, Gloucestershire, England.*

Wall fountains are designed to provide a highly visible water feature without sacrificing living space. *Julia Price Warren Garden, Designed by Sydney Baumgartner, Santa Barbara, California.*

dead, unmoving air, which acts like insulation between the vine foliage and the wall.

In fact, the fewer bare surfaces you have in the urban oasis, the less likely you are to notice the urban din. To understand how this works, imagine an empty apartment with hardwood floors and bare walls, all highly reflective surfaces. When you walk around or speak, every sound echoes off the bare walls as it bounces around from one reflective surface to another. Once you bring in furniture and carpets, though, the entire acoustical climate changes, and the echo disappears. This is because the reflection is minimized while the refraction is maximized. The same concept applies to urban gardens, too, when well cloaked in vine-covered walls and fences or surrounded by dense evergreen hedges. A good deal of the ambient city noise is muffled by refraction before it reaches your ears.

A second approach to ameliorating the noise situation masks ambient noise but does nothing to reduce the noise itself. One of the most pleasant masking techniques is the sound of falling water. This doesn't mean you need a big waterfall to completely overwhelm city noise, but you'd be surprised at how the trickle of a small fountain catches your ear. We know there is something elemental about this sound, perhaps because it is a God-given tool for masking all

sorts of noises. The Arabs, who cherish every drop of water, use tiny jets to create sound, which to them evoked paradise through both audio and visual experiences. In fact, most Arab gardens are long on reflective masonry and tile while short on refraction plants, which served to enhance the sound of a little water through echo.

Until recently a fountain in the garden was a luxury, but today you can share in the benefits of falling water very cheaply. Various companies are now using molded concrete to create beautiful classical fountains that are relatively inexpensive and operated by a small internal electrical pump to circulate the water. All you need is a 110-volt electrical plug for power supply. If you are installing paving, be sure to install a flush-mounted, all-weather receptacle with a removable lid. It allows you to place the fountain in the middle of your paving without a visible cord. If the fountain is removed, you can put the lid back on the receptacle. Once the fountain is in place, simply fill it with the garden hose and switch on the pump for falling water. You can disassemble the fountain for storage during winter, rather than struggle with weather damage.

You can also mask sound with wind chimes. Today's wind chimes are much more sophisticated than their predecessors in a variety of ways. First, they are made with greater precision, so that even the slightest air movement will result in some sound. Most of the quality chimes lack strings or chains, which used to become tangled and break easily in the old-fashioned models. Best of all, they are made of a variety of remarkably resonant metals that are long lasting in even the harshest climate.

Wind chimes are usually made with a number of metal tubes, whose pitches can vary from a single pinging to a full garden harp, with a range of tones affected by different lengths and diameters. For example, the tone of a chime three or more feet long will be much deeper and resonant than that of a smaller chime. There's one which is over five feet long and mimics the bells of old cathedrals. On the other hand, a small chime with just one or two tubes gives off a much more delicate and whimsical sound. With tubular chimes ranging from $45 to $150, it's important to see and hear wind chimes before you buy. Be sure the tones are pleasing to you personally and are loud enough to function as a cover-up.

Outdoor Aromatherapy

Anyone who lives in the city knows the special smells of the streets, which are somewhat unavoidable with so many people living in such a small area. There is no way to reflect or refract this problem, for no one has yet invented a device for screening odors.

Even if there is no perceptual problem with city smells, though, a garden with pleasant fragrance is of universal appeal. The Romans knew this because they were fastidious about bathing and the quality of their living spaces. Offensive odors had no place in the Roman household, yet Romans often lived in conquered cities where the people did not take hygiene so seriously. They too found the odors of high-density living, then without sewage systems, somewhat offensive, and to mask it, the courtyards of Roman homes were planted with aromatic herbs, shrubs, and trees. Among their favorites were drought-resistant plants, such as rosemary, lavender, myrtle, and laurel. Frequently, the gardener, whose Latin title was *toparius*, would come in and gently shear the plants to release their aromatic oils, which then scented the entire courtyard. This is the beginning of what we know as the art of topiary.

From the Romans we learn that the most reliable source of garden scents are not with the flowers, because they bloom only in season. Aromatic plants are usually evergreen and will scent the space all year. To see how to increase their scent, simply pick a bunch of fresh sage leaves and crush them in your hand. You'll find the aroma is suddenly and potently released. In the urban oasis planted with aromatic foliage, all you need do is pull out the scissors, clippers, or hedge trimmer, shear the plants, and then sit back to enjoy an olfactory feast.

Fortunately, many aromatic plants are our most favored culinary and craft herbs, which shows how perfectly a kitchen garden fits into our urban oasis concept. In an effort to mitigate a problem with urban living, we find that the solution provides an opportunity to grow plants which are not only valuable for their ability to mask scents but for their beauty and utility, as well. The need to clip them to release fragrance ensures you a plentiful supply of material for home and kitchen. The following table is a list of the most common aromatic plants, whose exposure requirements will vary with climate.

Floral Scents

The scent of a flower exists for only one reason: to attract an insect pollinator. There has been much written about flowers and their individual perfumes, which can vary both in scent and the potency. Flowers pollinated by moths sometimes become more fragrant after dark. To use scented flowers as a cover-up for city smells, the plants must either be extremely potent or located right beside living spaces so their more subtle fragrances can still be effective.

Fragrant flowers in city gardens have much greater value than simply masking less pleasant odors. The power of scent can trigger feelings and thoughts that lead to a sense of tranquility. Such is the case with many types of incense, which suggests the divine when used to symbolize prayer rising to heaven.

Our flowers can evoke a similar spiritual response with their fragrance, particularly in people who live in the hearts of concrete jungles where plants are few and far between. The old

Even the smallest garden can grow herbs. Here a circle in the paving provides the gardener with plenty of seasonings and beautiful aromas. *Anne McIntyre Garden, Church Westcote, Oxfordshire, England.*

Aromatic Foliage Plants

Botanical name	Popular name	Type	Zone(s)
Achillea spp.	Yarrow	Perennial	3–10
Artemisia spp.	Wormwood	Shrub, perennial	Vary
Cinnamomum camphora	Camphor tree	Tree	9–10
Eucalyptus spp.	Eucalyptus	Tree	7–10
Lavandula spp.	Lavender	Shrub, perennial	Vary
Laurus nobilis	Sweet bay, laurel	Tree	8–10
Mentha spp.	Mint	Perennial	Vary
Myrtus communis	Myrtle	Shrub, Tree	9–10
Pelargonium spp.	Scented geranium	Perennial	9–10
Salvia spp.	Sage	Shrub, perennial	Vary
Santolina chamaecyparissus	Lavendercotton	Perennial	Vary
Thymus spp.	Thyme	Perennial	Vary
Umbellularia californica	California bay	Tree	7–10

phrase "stop and smell the flowers" illustrates how scent is often all around us, but few slow down enough to enjoy it. Therefore, a city garden planted with deliciously scented flowers invites the user to pause and experience each one in a sort of ritual, which helps keep us rooted in living gifts of the earth.

Hundreds of plants are considered fragrant, but some are easier to grow than others. To flower prolifically and emit sufficient fragrance, the plant must be happy and healthy in your garden, so sticking with a vigorous variety ensures a potent scent. Among them are permanent garden members such as vines, shrubs, and perennials. Seasonal plants—spring bulbs and annual flowers—have some of the most beautiful and easily obtained fragrances and make ideal window box plants. For an entire garden of fragrance, it's a good idea to purchase a book on the subject, which will discuss in detail all the scented flowers and how they differ. Some of the most popular fragrance plants follow.

Away from Prying Eyes

Obtaining privacy is one of the most challenging aspects of garden design in the city. Privacy must be looked at from both ground level and from windows above. On the ground we deal with visibility from neighbors, passing autos, and pedestrians. Solid barriers considered for visual rather than security purposes block out light, which can be vital to a building-shaded space. The reason lattice has remained popular for so long is because it offers an affordable, attractive visibility barrier which allows some light to pass through. In addi-

Climbing roses are excellent for walls that receive plenty of sunshine. *Cawdor Castle, Highland, Scotland.*

tion, the glimpses of light are sufficient to give a sense of greater space and thus do not compromise the visual roominess of a pocket garden.

Most people think there's only one type of lattice, the small diagonal design which is painted white to enhance country or cottage garden styles. Lattice is far more versatile, however, and can find a home in contemporary designs, as well, depending on the design, orientation, size of members and holes, and color, from hunter green to slate gray. It can also be used as panels in otherwise solid fences to create windows of light or be arranged in a band on top of a solid fence. There are literally dozens of variations to choose from, and when vines are added the possibilities are endless.

To screen the view from above is more difficult. The problem is, you don't want to screen off the visibility of the entire garden, or it will be forever dark with shade. The common solution is to create a small structure beneath which there is privacy for dining or a hot tub, the remaining garden still receiving maximum light. One key to making the structure work for you while under it is to hang the lattice to the undersides of the

Orene Horton Garden, Columbia, South Carolina.

cross beams. That way you see only the lattice, leaving the less attractive structural members for the upstairs neighbors to enjoy. A tree canopy also provides a certain amount of privacy within its dripline. If you want more light, the tree can be thinned out occasionally.

Trees can create a variety of problems in urban gardens, though. Their rooting ability can

Fragrant Flowering Plants

Botanical name	Popular name	Type	Zone(s)
Clematis armandi	Evergreen clematis	Vine	8–10
Daphne odora	Daphne	Shrub	8–10
Dianthus	Carnation, pinks	Perennial	2–10
Freesia spp.	Freesia	Bulb	9–10
Gardenia spp.	Gardenia	Shrub	8–10
Hyacinthus hybrids	Hyacinth	Bulb	7–10
Jasminum polyanthum	Chinese jasmine	Vine	8–10
Lathyrus odoratus	Sweet pea	Seed	Annual
Lilium, Asiatic hybrids	Lilies	Bulb	4–10
Matthiola incana	Stock	Seed	Annual
Narcissus hybrids	Daffodils	Bulbs	5–10
Paeonia hybrids	Peony	Shrub	5–9
Rosa, early hybrids	Old Musk roses	Shrubs	Vary
Syringa vulgaris	Common lilac	Shrub	3–8
Trachelospermum jasminoides	Star jasmine	Vine	8–10
Viburnum carlesii	Fragrant snowball	Shrub	5–10

ORNAMENTAL IDEAS

Wind is one of the most active aspects of the natural world and powerful enough to drive windmills to pump water and mill grain. It has long been popular in rural areas with persistent wind to install wooden whirligigs, which spin with the wind and turn to indicate its direction. The problems with them may be that their sound is not pleasant, and they do not hold up well to the elements. Today's versions of these works of art use metals and precision connections that move gracefully and without sound and provide us with a visual experience that is far more peaceful.

Wind also drives bells, as well as chimes. Bells have long been a part of Eastern religious temples, as well as every church and cathedral tower. Wind-bells are different in that the striker is connected to a larger piece that hangs down, where it is in contact with the breeze. Some of the most beautiful of these are long bells made out of old welder's gas tanks, which result in deep, resonant bongs rather than the busy sounds of a chime. If you already have a bell that would fit nicely in the garden, simply attach a piece of chain and a disk of metal to the end of the striker.

disturb adjacent paving and underground utilities. Surface roots make it difficult to garden around the base of the tree. Some roots, mostly those of fibrously rooted species, will actually travel up into raised planters seeking water. Trees create leaf litter, a nuisance where there is no room for a compost heap. Trees often grow to overwhelm a small garden, and their eventual removal comes at great expense.

One solution is to use smaller tree species that are well adapted to your climate. The best ones—laurel, privet, toyon, and a few others—are naturally small in stature and evergreen, so they ensure privacy year-round. While they don't offer the cover of large trees, they can be carefully placed for maximum benefit. Plus, these little ones look stunning in winter with white twinkle lights strung around their canopies.

Yet another screening idea is to use shade cloth, a sheet material designed to cast varying degrees of shade. You'll see this in garden centers as a large overhead covering which protects the plants from direct sun. Though it is somewhat transparent, shade cloth attached to decorative posts for the summer months can be a viable solution to lack of privacy. When all else fails, one of the most versatile options is the very large market umbrellas that are opaque, portable, and require no special construction.

THE URBAN OASIS GARDEN DESIGN

A Courtyard Garden

This garden is located in a courtyard bound by walls on all sides. It is divided into two sections with a brick wall separating them. A fountain is mounted on the wall to save space, but that does not diminish its effect. A chamomile lawn provides additional living space without sacrificing planting, and a secondary brick patio is arranged toward the rear. This smaller patio may serve as a meditative shrine separated from the rest of the garden. An altar or pedestal is located adjacent to the wall, upon which flowering vines create a leafy backdrop.

Plants chosen include two trees: the pink flowering dogwood and the tiny weeping mayten tree—one of the slowest growing species. It is rare that a mayten ever outgrows its space. On the walls hang a variety of vines trained to nails or a trellis, and Boston ivy, a self-clinging deciduous species, frames the fountain. Even when not in leaf, Boston ivy's spidery network of stems provides an attractive pattern against the brick. Other plants are chosen for their fragrance: daphne, peony, and gardenia offer scented flow-

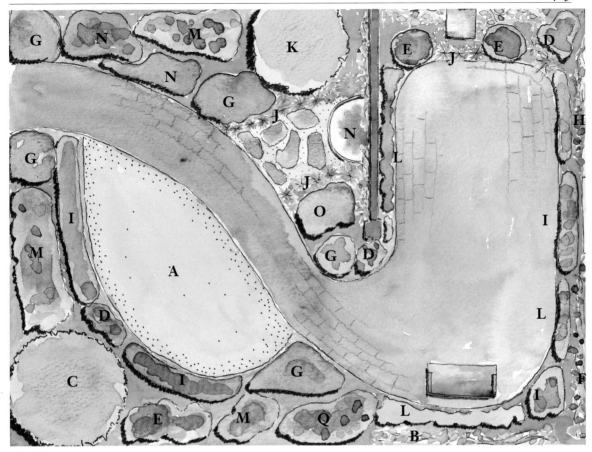

ers, and mint, lavender, scented geranium, and chamomile all release their aromas when walked upon or freshly pruned. Amidst the shrubs and perennials are many spaces to plant scented annuals, such as stocks, pinks, carnations, and sweet pea, as well as bulbs, such as hyacinth, jonquils, and freesias.

This garden shows how a diversity of materials and plants can create intense interest in even the most ordinary city yard. Cold, hard surfaces can be thwarted by a small patch of landscaping, complete with the sound of falling water and a shrine, and even a scented lawn can grow in moderate light. If every vacant lot and back alley was planted with flowers, herbs, or food crops, urban blight would become a thing of the past, and our downtown neighborhoods would flourish once again.

A. *Anthemis nobilis*—Perennial Chamomile
B. *Clematis armandi*—Evergreen Clematis
C. *Cornus florida* 'Rubra'—Pink Flowering Dogwood
D. *Daphne odorata*—Daphne
E. *Gardenia* spp.—Gardenia
F. *Gelsemium sempervirens*—Carolina Jessamine
G. *Pelargonium* spp.—Scented Geranium
H. *Jasminum polyanthum*—Chinese Jasmine
I. *Lavendula dentata*—French Lavender
J. *Liriope* 'Silvery Sunproof'—Lily Turf
K. *Maytenus boaria*—Mayten Tree
L. *Mentha* spp.—Mints
M. *Paeonia* spp.—Peony
N. *Parthenocissus tricuspidata*—Boston Ivy
O. *Rosa* 'Flower Carpet'—Everblooming Rose
P. *Wisteria sinensis*—Chinese Wisteria

SPIRITUAL GARDEN DESIGN

MAKE NO SMALL PLANS, THEY HAVE NO MAGIC TO STIR MEN'S BLOOD AND PROBABLY THEMSELVES WILL NOT BE REALIZED. MAKE BIG PLANS, AIM HIGH IN HOPE AND WORK. REMEMBER THAT OUR SONS AND GRANDSONS ARE GOING TO DO THINGS THAT WILL STAGGER US.

Daniel Burnham

reativity is in many ways an example of divine inspiration. No one really knows where our ideas and visions come from, and artists agree it is a somewhat mystical process. For those fortunate enough to be born with such talent, creation of any sort becomes an act of thanksgiving, and when it is applied to a spiritual garden, it verges on sacrament.

Design of gardens and buildings, or for that matter the simple act of planting a tree, satisfies the subconscious desire for immortality hidden in all of us. When asked about the reasons for their chosen courses of study, college students often explain a desire to leave their mark on the world, to make it better for their having lived and worked there. When we create a garden, chances are it will live long after we are gone as a living testament to our having been there.

The statement of architect Daniel Burnham opening this chapter points to one of the most profound truths of all creativity: that we should consider every garden, no matter how small, a great work with the power to "stir men's blood." It also shows that unless we view our efforts as being important, then our final product may be weak or never realized at all. American architect Philip Johnson has

Tsuga canadensis. Sharon Abroms Garden, Atlanta, Georgia.

Christ in the Garden by Nicholas Fiddian-Green. *The Hannah Peschar Sculpture Garden designed by Anthony Paul Landscape Designer, Ockley, Surrey, England.*

always emphasized that each and every building he designs is a "monument." This notion applies to gardens, as well, and suggests that these places of spiritual meaning should be considered with the same level of attention as a building that has the potential to alter a city's skyline forever.

It is also important to know that there are no new ideas in the world today. Only our applications of the ideas change with time. This is the reason history is so vital to garden making. In this book the ideas generated by cultures past are presented within separate threads in order to show the crucial relationships of religion, climate, and civilization.

Design of a spiritual garden adds a new dimension because the scheme must respond to the theme in every way. Gardens rooted in the spirit are places of deep meaning where the goal is not just creation of beauty, but space that suggests truths and mysteries of life through plants. This intent must be clear so that it may function as intended.

But just as a painter must learn his skill before rendering a work of art, so does the gardener require training in order to lay out a well-planned landscape. Landscape design of any kind is a skill that requires knowledge of much more than just plants, because you are organizing spaces that must function properly. It's unrealistic to think that all that needs to be said on this massive subject fits into a single chapter, but we can highlight the most essential concepts and criteria to help get you started.

In landscape architecture we have a few truths which will bear largely on the overall success of a project.

1. You must have a big idea or solid concept. You must know what you are trying to do before you can achieve it.
2. Design every inch of the garden. Areas left unresolved become nightmares in the field.
3. Make no small plans. A spiritual garden is a monument, so treat it as such and try to avoid watering down the design to simplify installation.

CHURCH GARDENS

A church is basically a community of people who all share a single faith. The church and its grounds become a temple to that community, providing a place not only of worship but education, recreation, and gathering for fellowship. These sites are rich with potential, particularly where there is plenty of space yet undeveloped. For those of Christian faith, the role of the church is central to their lives as a place where personal, social, political, and economic issues are shared and resolved.

Let us not become too focused on Christian needs, however, for there are others who follow different callings. There are as many different approaches to spiritual gardens as there are religions, so the best way to begin is to establish the purpose of the space. Everyone in your group must be in agreement on the proposed goals if the project is to run smoothly and produce a space that all find appealing.

Teaching gardens are generally associated with community churches and church schools charged with the ongoing religious education of children. They provide hands-on experiences which take the words of the Bible and Catechism and make them tangible through plants. A teaching garden provides all kinds of seasonal activities, from planting the winter wheat to harvesting palm fronds.

A teaching garden may also apply to adults, be they Christian, Jewish, or of one of the many other faiths and interest groups. A women's group learning about the use of herbs for healing may find a comprehensive herb garden of greatest value. A celestial garden designed to mark the solar and lunar points becomes an ideal means of learning about the annual cycles of these bodies and the constellations. Religious or secular, we all have something to learn in the garden, and if properly focused it may provide that ideal teaching environment your group has been seeking.

Traditional churches are always in need of outdoor activity spaces that can hold the entire congregation. Weddings, receptions, outdoor services, processions, festivals, and many other activities can be held outdoors if there is a suitable place to do so. This can be of particular

Chateau de Nacqueville, Cherbourg, France.

importance for a rapidly growing church which has to hold numerous services on Sunday to accommodate the entire congregation. The garden provides the ideal extension of usable space.

An assembly garden can be even more important with retreats and religious communities. Here the assembly place may be much more informal—a clearing in the woods, an outdoor theater, or simply a place in nature for spiritual exercises of intimate groups.

Prayer gardens have long been a part of the Catholic tradition, particularly at retreats, monasteries, and convents, where there is much time spent in silent or group prayer. These are interactive prayer spaces, most often linked to a series of prayers so that you, the user, may move around the garden as you work through the series. The garden design actually becomes part of the prayer ritual, as is the case with a spiritual labyrinth.

The rosary can be incorporated into the garden to replace beads. Stations of the Cross are composed of fourteen points to mark and often used in Holy Week processions. Although these two examples are Catholic in origin, the concept can be applied to any series of prayers, mantras, or formal meditations, be they philosophical or spiritual.

The origins of the Western meditation garden lies in the *paridaeza* garden of the early church. It is a small, walled enclosure separated

Betula, Robinia Pseudoacacia 'Frisia', and *Cedrus atlantica* 'Glauca Pendula'. *Limoges Cathedral, Limoges, France.*

from the outside world and specifically dedicated to God. In it are certain images, usually of Christ or Mary, which evoke curious feelings in those who comes upon this small sanctuary tucked away behind a very busy cathedral. Sometimes it is a tiny vision of paradise, a garden suggestive of Eden where we may stop and ponder, separated from life.

Although Zen Buddhism is not within the scope of this book, there is great emphasis in this faith upon quiet meditation. Frequently, Zen centers are set within beautiful natural environments or cultivated gardens, since these are the images of earthly peace and harmony.

Just south of San Francisco in the city of Burlingame are the grounds of Mercy Center, a high school and retreat center set within a sizable piece of property donated to the church many decades ago. It is the home of Father Tom Hand, a Catholic priest now in his seventies, who spent twenty-five years ministering in Japan. There he became intimate with the Eastern way of spirituality and learned to adapt its beneficial concepts to our modern Christian tradition. In a tiny strip of earth behind a large multistory building, Father Hand created a small Zen garden of white gravel, stone, and a few plants. He uses it as a place of meditation, explaining that "in the West we use symbolism to help us with meditation, while in the East meditation is the surrendering of one's mind in order to separate ourselves from the world." Father Tom insists that we try to read too much into Zen gardens, which is our attempt to apply symbolic spirituality to gardens not really designed that way. Instead, we should focus on the rock, the leaf, the water, as we empty our minds of extraneous thoughts. What results is an essential peaceful silence, which is the path toward enlightenment and the true connection with God.

While in Japan Father Hand spent six years carving a meditation path out of a rocky mountainside. At Mercy Center he has created other meditation paths that apply the same concept as his Zen garden, but in a far more natural way. "Meditation paths should separate us," he explains, "so we may become more in tune with the energy of all things, be it a stone or a pool of water." Father Hand created these paths so that the surrounding city is carefully camouflaged by vegetation. What may appear as a simple little walk through the woods is actually Father Hand's careful eye manipulating exactly what we see and what we don't see. Along the path he has enhanced stones or trees and other natural elements so that the walker may pause and better focus on them in order to initiate the meditative process.

What we learn from Father Hand's wisdom is that different faiths may have good things to offer our spiritual lives. It is essential that no one closes doors to good ideas just because they aren't exactly what we're used to. Ideas which have evolved over thousands of years may be easily adapted to our own outdoor spaces, no matter what faith you are. All that is required is a dedicated space that provides separation from the hustle and bustle of the outside world, so we may let go of stress and return our minds and hearts to God.

GUIDELINES FOR CHURCHES, RELIGIOUS GROUPS, AND RETREATS

Many retreat houses are located in rural areas where visitors can get away and rekindle the subtle aspects of faith and serenity. These sanctuaries are found all over the world, from monastic cloisters to Tibetan temples, drawing those seeking the spiritual with gentle promises of renewal. Sometimes the best retreat houses are the spare rooms in monasteries and convents, some almost self-sufficient with their own farms and compounds. These places are of growing interest in the United States, and the need for retreats has encouraged such lesser-known groups to offer any number of spare rooms for visitors wishing to experience firsthand the litanies and eternal prayer of such groups. Visitors can also furnish vital revenue to the hosts. A listing of retreat houses that allow guests can be found in the sanctuaries books in the Bibliography.

When we consider the development or

improvement of churches, communes, or retreats through plants and gardens of meaning, lofty ideas must be supported by nuts-and-bolts knowledge. There are a few issues you must consider before attempting to create a garden of any kind, be it public or private. Some problems are unique to the group approach and must be taken care of early on to avoid difficulties later. Most important is the preparation of a detailed design plan. Without one, or if the plan is vague, conflicts are bound to arise over interpretation. When working within a community, there is also a certain amount of passing the buck that goes on. If not resolved early on, a need can sometimes be overlooked entirely.

An antique clay or stone urn lends an ancient quality to the garden—here, cloaked in rosemary, a storied herb. *Bill Slater Garden, Santa Barbara, California.*

part of the learning experience. Assembly gardens can take a real beating, particularly during receptions or festivals where attendance is high enough to fill the space to capacity. This demands less creative gardening and more cleanup maintenance.

In general, you should always consider maintenance when planning such a garden, and that's why it is the first of these issues. A poor design can become a maintenance nightmare if the following are not fully considered beforehand:

- Plants must be suited to the climate, cold hardy, and long lived and require no special treatment. Avoid finicky plants and lean toward well-adapted native species.
- Permanently installed sprinklers on an automatic timer is preferable in climates where seasonal irrigation is required.
- Avoid plants that have berries or fruit that will ferment in the summer heat, stain paving, and create a hazard to foot traffic if not immediately cleaned up.
- Avoid plants that drop unusually large amounts of litter.
- Avoid hedges which must be sheared often to look good. Natural hedges are fine.
- Beware of planning too much lawn, which must be watered and mowed.
- Avoid leaving large areas of soil uncovered or unplanted, as these are havens for weeds.

Plants and gardens require a certain amount of care if they are to survive, and preferably thrive in order to look their best. This demands the community develop a plan to maintain the garden during days of the week when there are no on-site gatherings. The degree of care is dictated by the design of the garden and whether the plants require special treatment. For example, in temperate climates some plants may require winter protection, without which they will not survive their first year. Similarly, plants in arid climates must be watered during the dry season, or they will wither and die.

There are many creative ways to approach this, which will vary with the group and site, as well. Meditation and prayer gardens are often more beautiful than teaching or assembly spaces. These provide a greater opportunity for the gardener to express the personal love of flowers in an intensely intimate way. On the other hand, a teaching garden may change considerably throughout the year, with instructors leading their students in many of the seasonal tasks as

Gardens can become means of healing, and caring for them can fill the voids in lonely or depressed people's lives. For seniors, their efforts in caring for spiritual gardens can give them an important role in the community. Too often older folks are not as involved because they no longer have children at home that participate in church activities. So many have a lifetime of gardening skills, though, which they may bring to these gardens in a labor of spiritual love.

Such was the case at Notre Dame School in Maryville, California, where we restored an old grotto, containing a statue of the Virgin Mary, tucked away in the corner of the yard. We repaired the shrine and surrounded it with a small meditation garden. Adjacent to the school was a retirement home for Knights of Columbus, and among the men living there was a fellow who really needed something to care for. While restoring the site he came forward and offered to keep it looking beautiful for us free of charge as a way to show his devotion to the Blessed Mother. This arrangement provided the man with a spiritual purpose, and in turn the school was assured the little garden would blossom into a living form of devotion.

THE PROCESS OF DESIGN

A thorough examination of the proposed garden site will influence how you design your garden. From this assessment you can determine the site's benefits and liabilities and how best to work with them. In the process of analyzing the site, you'll develop a heightened awareness of its potential on many different levels.

Site Inventory

1. Site elements. The first step in the design process is to evaluate all the existing conditions which influence the area designated for the garden. This means acknowledging what is already there, whether it proves to be beneficial or not. Among the most important existing elements are buildings, and you should note where all the windows and doors are located. This helps you integrate the interior with the exterior where the two interface at the building wall. You must also identify all other qualities, such as walls, fences, changes in grade, steps, curbs, paving, and all existing trees, shrubs, and vines within the area. Also important are adjacent land uses and structures outside the site that influence your garden either visually, audibly, or in more subtle ways.

2. Solar exposure. All landscape plans indicate north to help with orientation and to show how sunlight reaches the designated space during winter and summer. A very hot, sunny site determines not only what species will grow there but whether you need trees or shade structures to make it usable during the summer months. Also consider any trees that are near the site which may cast shadows during certain seasons, such as winter, when the sunlight would be most appreciated.

A space with a southern exposure is ideal in many ways because it receives maximum sunlight in both summer and winter but lacks the searing afternoon heat from the west. A northern exposure tends to be cooler than all the others and may prove too cool for comfort during the winter months. It may only support shade-tolerant plants, as well. Eastern exposure is reached by the morning sun; spaces intended for Sunday morning services may benefit the most. It also ensures that the morning dew dries quickly, which reduces problems with fungus diseases, such as mildew and black spot. Western exposures tend to become very hot in the afternoon and unbearable to use without special shading mechanisms. Plants here must be rugged and heat loving to make it through the summer.

3. Adjacent land uses. Only a few home or church sites are surrounded by beautiful woods or meadows. The vast majority may be adjacent to residential, industrial, or commercial land, which can affect design. Screening devices—like fences, walls, and small structures—offer immediate, albeit expensive, solutions. Less costly are trees and shrubs planted in dense hedges or windrows, offering a suitable buffer that also absorbs unwanted noise generated outside the landscape. Mitigating off-site problems through good design is most essential for meditative and prayer gardens.

4. Existing plants and trees. If you are fortunate, there will already be plants and trees growing on site. Should they be attractive or vital in terms of shading and aesthetics, then your design must include them for an integrated garden plan. Some may not be worth saving if they are too old, damaged, or diseased, but remember that it takes decades to grow a tree and only a minute to cut it down.

5. *Utilities.* If the garden is to have irrigation, lighting, or outdoor electrical, you must know where your points of connection will be. This really helps the sprinkler designer and electrician do their jobs. People new to garden making always risk conflicts with unexpected underground utilities, which can foil even the best laid plan. If heavy equipment or even a strong rotary tiller is involved, you must avoid damage to water, sewer, electric, and gas lines and storm drains hidden below. Once broken, they can be very expensive to repair.

Spacial Layout and Focus

Spacial layout is not easy to do, but there is one trick of the trade that may be a big help. Remember the old Colorforms, little cutout images that you move into various combinations on a board to create pictures? Designers use the same technique to ensure they can accommodate tables, chairs, and other site furniture into the spaces they design. They simply sketch out the furniture to scale on a piece of paper, then carefully cut out each one and arrange them all on the plan.

I recently reviewed a small plan done for one of my clients by a backyard landscaper. His layout of three separate patios looked fine on paper, but when measured it was immediately clear that all failed to provide a place large enough to set a table and chairs comfortably. Although the patios would provide a good planting arrangement, it was a lousy people arrangement. The plan simply did not work. Had he cut out little templates and set them on the plan, it would have been clear that the patio areas were too small. Anyone can avoid guesswork by using this foolproof trick for virtually every element of a plan.

Certain basic dimensions used in landscape design will help you move toward a workable plan:

Walkway: 1 person: 3 feet wide minimum;
   2 people: 4.5 feet wide minumum
Gates: 3.5 to 4 feet wide
Fences: 6 feet tall maximum

Azalea 'Sherwood Red', forget-me-not, ajuga. *Connie Hansen Garden, Lincoln City, Oregon.*

Steps: riser: 6 to 8 inches tall; step tread:
   12 inches wide minimum

Warning: A garden open to the public must conform to the Uniform Building Code to avoid unnecessary exposure to liability. To ensure the design is laid out according to such codes of public safety, it is wise to hire a landscape architect or a similar professional for this basic layout.

Decoration

Some spiritual gardens are focused on a statue, a piece of sculpture, ornament, a water feature, or signage. Tile images upon a wall or virtually any meaningful image that may link the space to an inspirational theme. It is essential that all aspects of the layout be turned toward this focus so that the drama of the garden is clear. Vague, meandering, or hazy focus means the garden lacks the kind of bold impact needed to separate it from any other landscape. Sometimes structures such

Gordon Hayward Garden, Putney, Vermont.

as arbors or the alignment of walkways clarify focus.

Some of the most common religious images depict the Virgin Mary, the Sacred Heart, a crucifix, and angels. St. Francis of Assisi is by far the most popular image seen in gardens due to his relationship with nature and wildlife. Be sure to pick out items that work with the surroundings so that the statuary is enhanced rather than being in conflict with things around it.

Incorporating ornament into the garden helps underscore the fact that the space is meant for more than just growing flowers. We find more ornamental products on the market today than ever before, which makes it easier to add that mystical or historical character to the garden to enhance its focus. Perhaps one of the more difficult aspects of using ornament is selecting the most appropriate images for the focus of the garden.

Cast stone gargoyles, enjoying renewed popularity, make the perfect accent for a medieval monastic theme. For the celestial garden consider one of the more complex sundials that point to time and direction with remarkable precision.

Be it a water garden or simply a small electric pump fountain, the role of water in religious symbolism is widespread. The sound of water also helps disguise city noise in meditation gardens. Do not think that all fountains are made with Spanish tile, nor are all fountains natural waterfalls. A water feature must be designed to fit naturally into its garden setting.

Decorative signs for gardens with spiritual sources should be well suited to the garden, as well. Beware of making them so big they overwhelm the spaces around them; conversely, don't make them so small the lettering is illegible. Adjust the size of a sign to suit the distance from which it is viewed.

Amenities

Twelve-volt outdoor lighting systems allow garden use in the evening, when lighting can not only make them safer but will highlight focal points. Be aware of ambient lighting for an ethereal night garden. This technique hides every fixture so that the light is subtle.

Just as furniture provides us with a convenient place to rest indoors, seating and tables meet the same needs outdoors. However, there are many different styles of patio furniture at

Sally Cooper Garden, Charlotte, North Carolina.

vastly different price ranges. Furniture can enhance or fight the garden setting. The Lutyens benches so common in England and now available in America are timeless, simple, and blend into virtually any garden setting—but they are very expensive. Taking the same degree of care when choosing outdoor furniture as you do indoor pieces ensures that the landscape is wholly integrated.

CHOOSING PLANTS

Since a garden is a living thing, the most important task is to select plants carefully. The best plant for the garden will be one that meets two demands: it must respond to the theme or intent of the garden, and it must be well suited to conditions. It must be able to survive the winter, and live long enough to mature and express its ultimate beauty.

Plants with powerful associations and implications allow the planting to speak a silent message of symbolism. They should be prominent so that their mere existence reminds us of the original purpose of the space. There is also something deeply meaningful about plants with long histories of spirituality, such as the lily's link with the Virgin, datura and divination, the lotus and Egyptian immortality.

Creating a small shrine within a residential garden is not difficult. To create from scratch a larger garden with a spiritual theme and symbolic plant materials is another matter. Few people except design professionals have sufficient grasp of what will be successful on a larger scale, so if you are not well versed in planting design, it's important to hire a professional to help. Consulting early on in the planning process ensures that you or your group develop a workable design that is sure to thrive for decades.

To illustrate just how essential plant selection can be, you should know the answers to the following horticultural questions before choosing a plant for your garden or community project:

1. Does the plant fit in the space provided in both height and width?
2. Is the plant well suited to the exposure?
3. Will the plant survive the winter and summer without unusual protection?
4. Is the plant long lived?
5. Is it available from growers locally?
6. Does it have invasive roots or runners?
7. Does it create an unusual amount of litter?
8. Are there parts that can stain paving or cause a traffic hazard?
9. Is the plant—especially trees—vulnerable to specific diseases?
10. Is the plant aesthetically pleasing?

INSTALLATION AND PLANTING

There are two parts to installing a garden. First is the construction of permanent built-in features (paving, walls, etc.), or the hardscape, which requires special skills, equipment, and materials. The second is the softscape, which includes planting and irrigation. It's important for the leader, pastor, and elders to inventory the trades and talents of the congregation, because this will have some influence on the final design and material choices. You should also try to appoint one or two individuals to oversee the entire project, because a good contractor knows how to coordinate various work efforts and resources. If the project lacks this oversight, there are bound to be conflicts.

Look for two types of people vital to the creation of the garden. First are the skilled professionals who have materials and equipment at their disposal. For example, if one member of the church is an engineering contractor, he may offer heavy equipment and have access to bulk materials, such as topsoil and gravel. The second, equally important group are those who have no particular skill to donate but their labor.

It is essential that you know the order of tasks in landscape construction because the sequence is critical to making the whole project more efficient and the final product far more polished.

1. Demolition. Break up and remove all existing paving, structures, plants, and utilities

from the proposed garden site.

2. Grading. Level and contour the site to make it conform to specific uses or to ensure proper drainage.

3. Construction of structures, paving, walls, and fences.

4. Soil preparation. Most soils require some treatment to make them better suited to plant growth. This includes addition of plentiful humus and rototilling to work it in as deep as possible.

5. Irrigation, utilities. Do trenching, piping, and electrical connections for sprinkler systems in planters and lawn. Install any electrical conduits with 110-volt plugs and fixtures.

6. Finish grading. Do final contouring of soil after irrigation is completed and trenches are backfilled. Set sprinkler heads to appropriate heights.

7. Planting. Plant in this order: (1) trees, (2) shrubs, (3) vines, (4) perennials. Hold off on ground covers for now.

8. Mulch and lighting. Apply a layer of bark mulch to all exposed soils. Install 12-volt lighting. Plant ground covers through mulch.

9. Seed or sod lawn.

10. Clean up.

ENCOURAGING FUNDING AND DONATIONS

Building gardens these days can be very expensive. Costs are generated by purchasing materials, renting equipment, and hiring professionals, when necessary. When creating a church garden, funding is a most critical need because most communities don't have sufficient disposable income. Therefore, you must initiate a drive to raise money and obtain donations of both cash and materials.

You can often obtain a greater benefit through donations of materials and skills than of money, because with just the latter you would be forced to purchase the former two at market value. A good mason may charge you $40 per hour for his services if you were to hire him as a contractor, but he may be more than willing to donate piecework, which could involve many hours of labor and really add up.

Sometimes the most powerful way to encourage donations is to provide recognition. At Descanso Gardens, a large botanical landscape in Los Angeles, the old rose garden is filled with little teak arbor benches, each with a bronze plaque bearing the name of a donor. Donor recognition is particularly attractive to local business because they know that the plaque will remain as long-term advertising with a congregation of solid consumers. In fact, contractors and merchants who are members of the congregation or support the community are often willing to contribute if promised this type of recognition.

Some creative coordination is needed to know who to approach, when to do so, and what to ask for. This list shows some of the typical materials in garden making and who to ask for help or donations:

- Sand, gravel, topsoil: trucking company, engineering contractor
- Masonry units: brickyard, tile company, masonry contractor, home improvement store
- Sprinkler, plumbing: lumberyard, home improvement store, hardware store, wholesale plumbing supply, irrigation company
- Lighting fixtures: electrical contractor, electrical supply, wholesale lighting
- Furniture: home improvement stores, department store, lumberyard, patio store
- Plants: nurseries, both retail and wholesale, landscape contractor, botanical garden, school
- Decorative mulch and soil additives: landscape contractor, landscape supply, forest products plant, tree trimming company

APPENDICES

SIGNS AND SYMBOLS

Symbolorum et emblematum ex re herbaria
(Signs and symbols from the garden)

he early relationships of symbol, number, form, and orientation provide us with a design vernacular to use as means of organizing the sacred garden or space of any faith or belief.

Colors

Religions place deep significance on color, which adds greater dimension to the palette of flowers. Colors chosen for a spiritually inspired garden represents more than simply their relative positions on the color wheel.

Blue, *luteus* Truth is revealed under the clear blue sky and in the light of day. Blue is the hue of Mary. In early art the dark blue paint made of ground lapis lazuli, a gemstone, indicated richness. It is the color of the heavens and baptismal waters. Blue was chosen by Israel to depict the Star of David on its flag.

Flowers: Ageratum, aster, bellflower, bluebells, blue vervain, ceanothus, columbine, delphinium, forget-me-not, gentian, grape hyacinth, iris, larkspur, lupine, monkshood, pansy, periwinkle, petunia, phlox, plumbago, primrose, rose of Sharon, sage, scabiosa, veronica, viola, violet.

Green, *viridis* The color of plants in leaf, green symbolizes the triumph of spring over winter, as well as reproductive fertility. Representing hope, it was the color favored by Greek and Roman priests in their water rituals. But it is the specter of jealousy, as Shakespeare expressed in *Othello:* "O, beware, my lord, of jealousy; It is the green-eyed monster." Among the Irish this color stands not only for their nation but also for the folklore of fairies and the "little people."

Plants: Evergreens, lawn, foliage plants.

Red, *coccineus* Red is the color of power and the blood of the martyrs, of love and hate. The color of fire, it represents the pagan fire festivals as well as the fires of faith and of Pentecost. The term *red-letter day* came from the practice of printing saints' feast days on calendars to make them stand out.

Flowers: Aster, azalea, canna, chrysanthemum, clematis, currant, dahlia, red-flowering dogwood, geum, gladiolus, hollyhock, nasturtium, oriental poppy, peony, petunia, pink, flowering quince, rhododendron, roses, scarlet sage, snapdragon, stock, sweet pea, scarlet trumpet vine, tulip, red valerian, zinnia.

Yellow, *caeruleus* This color has two sides. One can suggest cowardice by calling another "yellow," which no doubt came down from an old French custom of painting the doors to felons' and traitors' homes yellow. Yellow is also the color of the sun and gold, however, and of rays and halos which represents the light of God.

Flowers: Azalea, basket of gold alyssum, black-eyed susan, California poppy, chrysanthemum, columbine, coreopsis, cosmos, crocus, dahlia, daylily, forsythia, gaillardia, gladiolus, golden chain tree, Iceland poppy, iris, kerria, yellow lupine, marigold, narcissus, nasturtium, peony, potentilla, pot marigold, rose, St. Johnswort, Scotch broom, tulip, viola, fernleaf yarrow, zinnia.

Purple, *purpureus* Always a sign of royalty, purple was the toga color of Roman emperors. The Babylonians, Greeks, and many other cultures arrayed their gods in purple. It became the predominant color of penance and fasting, which led to its later use in Lenten celebrations. It is also the color of expectation and the Advent candles.

Flowers: Aubretia, clematis, columbine, daphne, foxglove, iris, lavender, lilac, pansy, passionflower, penstemon, petunia, phlox, primrose, rose of Sharon, rosemary, scabiosa, statice, sweet pea, violet, sweet William, wisteria.

White, *albus* White has universal appeal as a

Flowers of the Saints

Saint	Common name	Botanical name	Feast day
St. Agnes	Christmas rose	*Helleborus niger*	January 21
St. Anne	Chamomile	*Matricaria chamomilla*	July 26
St. Barbara	Winter cress	*Barbarea vulgaris*	December 4
St. Barnaby	Thistle	*Dipsacus* spp.	June 11
St. Blaise	Teasel	*Dipsacus sylvestris*	February 3
St. Bridget	Anemone	*Anemone coronaria*	February 1
St. Clare	Lily	*Lilium* spp.	August 12
St. David	Leek	*Allium* spp.	March 1
St. Dominic	Rose	*Rosa* spp.	August 4
St. Dorothy	Apple blossom	*Malus* spp.	February 6
St. Elizabeth of Hungary	Rose	*Rosa* spp.	November 19
St. Faine	Viburnum	*Viburnum tinus*	January 1
St. Fina	White violets	*Viola odora*	March 12
St. George	Bluebell	*Scilla* spp.	April 23
St. Hilary	Wild strawberry	*Fragaria chiloensis*	January 13
St. James	Ragwort	*Senecio aureus*	June 25
St. John the Baptist	St. Johnswort	*Hypericum* spp.	June 24
St. Joseph	Oleander	*Nerium oleander*	March 19
St. Leonard	Lily of the valley	*Convallaria majalis*	October 6
Mary Magdalene	Costmary	*Chrysanthemum balsamita*	July 22
Michael, Archangel	Michaelmas daisy	*Aster novae-anglia*	September 29
St. Patrick	Shamrock	*Medicago lipulina*	March 17
St. Peter	Cowslip, marsh marigold	*Caltha palustris*	June 29
St. Phocas	Pink	*Dianthus* spp.	September 22
St. Thomas Becket	Canterbury bells	*Campanula medium*	December 29
St. Therese of Lisieux	Rose	*Rosa* spp.	October 30
St. Valentine	Crocus	*Crocus* spp.	February 14

sign of purity, as in wedding dresses and the habits of nuns. It speaks of truth and innocence and was the primary vestment color of the early church, preceding purple as the color of Lent. White was the original color of mourning before being replaced with black. Druid priests and those who honored the Egyptian god Osiris and the god Zeus always wore white. Druids sacrificed only white bulls during their ceremonies of cutting mistletoe.

Flowers: Aster, azalea, bridalwreath, candytuft, chrysanthemum, clematis, crape myrtle, crocus, dahlia, gladiolus, hyacinth, climbing hydrangea, jasmine, lilac, lily, lily of the valley, magnolia, mock orange, peony, petunia, pieris, rhododendron, rose, rose of Sharon, Shasta daisy, snowdrop, spiraea, star jasmine, stock, sweet pea, tuberose, tulip, fragrant snowball viburnum, weigela, yucca.

Black, *nigrun* Black is the color of evil and darkness. The term *black arts* refers to satanic ritual. It indicates the absence of light, first as the loss of the sun and later of the light provided by the Son of God.

SOURCES

Inspiration, Art, and Products for Spiritual Gardens
Bose, Inc.
The Mountain
Framingham, MA 01701
1-800-444-2673
Quality sound systems
Free color brochure
This may be the most well-respected and established source of reliable audio systems uniquely adapted to small-space use.

California Landscape Lighting
31260 Cedar Valley Drive
Westlake Village, CA 91362
1-800-457-0710
Outdoor speakers and rock lights
Free color brochure
This company distributes a unique series of artificial boulders by Rockustics, Inc. designed to contain and protect your outdoor speakers without sacrificing sound quality. Natural looking, they provide the ideal opportunity for incorporating sound systems into the outdoor garden.

Cotter Church Supplies, Inc.
1701 West Ninth Street
Los Angeles, CA 90015-1093
In California outside area codes 213, 818, 310: 1-800-446-3366
All other states: 1-800-421-9026
568-page color catalog $10
This is the most widely used church supply catalog

and is used by all Christian churches. The size of a small city telephone directory, all in full color, it includes everything from gold altar furnishings to choir robes. It contains an extensive selection of fine statuary for use outdoors and indoor, including massive, life-sized figures plus bronze Stations of the Cross images for outdoor devotional walks. A virtual treasure trove of religious art and ephemera, incense, holy candles, candle holders, and holy water fonts, this catalog may already be in your church office, so check before ordering a copy of your own. The company sells both wholesale and retail.

Design Toscano
17 East Campbell Street
Arlington Heights, IL 60005
1-800-525-1733
Historical European reproductions for home and garden
Color catalog $4
Without a doubt the finest catalog of outdoor art available today, and worth every penny. Designs draw from Roman, Greek, and Renaissance fine art. Toscano artisans put you in touch with pagan, classical, and Christian motifs sure to lend that special touch. Here you'll find the green men of Druid spring rites, gods and goddesses, Michelangelo's *Pieta*, a host of angels and gargoyles, plus attractive pedestals in durable cast stone and concrete.

Leaflet Missal Company
976 West Minnehaha Avenue
St. Paul, MN 55104-1556
1-800-328-9582
Full-color religious articles catalog $5
This is a fine resource for Christians of any denomination and anyone drawn to Christian art and artifacts, offering a wealth of *affordable* accoutrements for home and garden in traditional and modern styles. The company has a limited selection of outdoor shrine statues in terra cotta, cement, and metals, including angels, saints, wind chimes, bird feeders, and many other options for enclosed shrines. The catalog contains plaques, holy pictures, a large book section, jewelry, holy cards, and gifts for all occasions. Low prices make this a satisfying catalog, and supplements are mailed out seasonally.

The Mystic Trader, Whole Life Products
1334 Pacific Avenue
Forest Grove, OR 97116
1-800-634-9057
The Mystic Trader: New Age and ethnic mystical art and artifacts
Whole Life Products: spiritual healing aids
Both free color catalogs
The Mystic Trader is a beautifully designed catalog filled with spiritual ethnic art of Asia, India, and

Water garden catalogs

There is a place for water in every garden, and today we are lucky to be able to choose from many different types of water features, from self-contained fountains to entire habitats that include plants and fish. The two companies that follow each put out comprehensive catalogs that show just how easy it is to get started with liners, pumps, filters, and a broad assortment of other equipment; hundreds of lilies, lotuses, and other aquatic plants; and exotic fish.

Van Ness Water Gardens
2460 North Euclid Avenue
Upland, CA 91786-1199
1-909-982-2425
Color catalog $6

Lilypons Water Gardens
P.O. Box 1130, Dept GBM
Thermal, CA 92274-1130

Africa—Buddhas galore plus Hindu gods in stone, wood, and metal; books on Eastern mysticism; high-quality copal, frankinsence, myrrh incense; colorful batik flag panels; crystals; meditation benches; wind chimes; and much, much more. Whole Life Products offers the latest in spiritual as well as physical healing aids, from herbal remedies to meditation garments, wind chimes, desktop gardens, books, and aromatherapy supplies.

Native Seeds/SEARCH
2509 North Campbell Avenue #325
Tuscson, AZ 85719
Catalog $1
A nonprofit conservation research and education organization. Source of seed cultivated by Native Americans in the southwestern United States and Mexico.

The Pyramid Collection
P.O. Box 3333
Altid Park
Chelmsford, MA 01824-0933
1-800-333-4220
Free color catalog
This is a broad collection of New Age art, jewelry, books, and meditation aids, with emphasis on Eastern traditions.

Seeds of Change
P.O. Box 15700
Santa Fe, NM 87506-5700
505-438-8080
Color catalog
Source for organic seed—of both vegetables and ornamentals.

Shibumi Trading Limited
P.O. Box 1-F
Eugene, OR 97440
1-800-843-2565
Oriental gardening supplies
Free black-and-white catalog
Even though the catalog isn't flashy or in color, this

resource is the best source around for desktop Serenity Water Gardens. The company also offers temple gongs, bells, exquisite carved granite basins, lanterns, bamboo products, and fence panels. Prices are reasonable.

The Nature Company
750 Hearst Avenue
Berkeley, CA 94710
1-800-227-1114
Color catalog $1
The Nature Company has proven over time to have one of the most satisfying catalogs around. It offers an intriguing collection of tools for discovering the night sky, including telescopes and star charts. It also promotes wildlife habitats with butterfly feeders, orchard mason bee houses, bat houses, and plenty of stuff for avid bird-watchers.

Wind & Weather
P.O. Box 2320
Mendocino, CA 95460-2320
1-800-922-9463
Free color catalog
This catalog is a treasure trove of technical and artistic products that help us better understand what is going on in the garden. It offers an extensive line of weather-tracking items, such as thermometers and barometers. Some are just functional, while others are works of art. The company also carries an intriguing assortment of weather vanes, wind chimes, and the most creative and complex sundials available today. It also offers many colored gazing balls, garden art, and great gifts for the outdoor aficionado. A must-have catalog full of inspiring ideas.

BIBLIOGRAPHY

Arguelles, Jose and Mirriam. *Mandala*. Berkeley, California: Shambala, 1972.

Bailey, Brian. *Churchyards of England and Wales*. Wigstan, England: Robert Hale, 1987.

Bamford, Christopher, and William Parker Marsh.

Celtic Christianity: Ecology and Holiness. New York: Lindisfarne Press, 1982.

Bancroft, Anne. *Origins of the Sacred: Spiritual Journey in Western Tradition.* New York: Routledge & Kegan Paul, 1987.

Carmichael, Elizabeth, and Chloë Sayer. *The Skeleton at the Feast: The Day of the Dead in Mexico.* Austin: University of Texas Press, 1991.

Castaneda, Carlos. *The Teachings of Don Juan: A Yaqui Way of Knowledge.* Berkeley, California: University of California Press, 1968.

Cruz, Joan Carroll. *Relics.* Huntington, California: Our Sunday Visitor, 1984.

Cunningham, Scott. *Magical Herbalism.* St. Paul, Minnesota: Llewellyn Publications, 1989.

Davies, Caroline. *The Eternal Garden.* Melbourne: Hill of Content, 1989.

Demarest, Donald, and Coley Taylor, editors. *The Dark Virgin: The Book of Our Lady of Guadalupe.* Freeport: Coley Taylor, 1956.

De Montfort, St. Louis. *The Secret of the Rosary.* New York: Montfort Publications, 1973.

Dobelis, Inge N., editor. *Magic and Medicine of Plants.* Pleasantville, New York: Readers Digest Association, 1986.

Ferguson, George. *Signs & Symbols in Christian Art.* New York: Oxford University Press, 1961.

Ford, Julian. *The Story of Paradise.* Richmond, England: Hazell Watson & Viney, 1981.

Frazer, Sir James. *The Golden Bough.* Hertfordshire: Wordsworth Editions, 1993. Reprint.

Gasnick, Roy M, O.F.M., author-editor. *The Francis Book: 800 Years with the Saint from Assisi.* New York: Macmillan Publishing, 1980.

Gordon, Anne. *A Book of Saints: True Stories of How They Touch Our Lives.* New York: Bantam Doubleday Dell Publishing, 1994.

Gordon, Lesley. *The Mystery and Magic of Trees and Flowers.* London: Grange Books, 1993.

Gonzalez-Wippler, Migene. *Rituals and Spells of Santeria.* New York: Original Publications, 1984.

Green, Marian. *The Elements of Natural Magic.* Rockport: Element, 1989.

Hawkins, Gerald S. *Stonehenge Decoded.* New York: Dorset Press, 1965.

Heiser, Charles B., Jr. *The Fascinating World of the Nightshades.* New York: Dover Publications, 1987.

Heiser, Charles B., Jr. *The Sunflower.* Norman: University of Oklahoma Press, 1976.

Heselton, Philip. *The Elements of Earth Mysteries.* Rockport: Element, 1991.

Inman, Jack. *Floral Art in the Church.* Nashville: Abingdon Press, 1968.

Johnston, Francis. *The Wonder of Guadalupe.* Rockford, Illinois: Tan Books and Publishers, 1981.

Jones, Alison. *The Wordsworth Dictionary of Saints.* Ware, England: Wordsworth Editions, 1994.

Kelly, Marcia, and Jack Kelly. *Sanctuaries: The Northeast.* New York: Bell Tower, 1991.

Kelly, Marcia, and Jack Kelly. *Sanctuaries: The West Coast and Southwest.* New York: Bell Tower, 1993.

Kendrick, T.D. *The Druids.* London: Senate, 1994. Reprint.

King, Eleanor Anthony. *Bible Plants for American Gardens.* New York: Dover Publications, 1975.

Leeming, David, with Margaret Leeming. *A Dictionary of Creation Myths.* New York: Oxford University Press, 1994.

MacMath, Fiona, editor. *The Flora: A Celebration of Plants, Flowers and the Human Spirit.* Oxford, England: Lion Publishing, 1990.

McKenna, Terence. *Food of the Gods.* New York: Bantam Books, 1992.

Matthews, John, editor. *Paths to Peace: A Collection of Prayers, Ceremonies, and Chants from Many Traditions.* Boston: Charles E. Tuttle, 1992.

Metford, J.C.J. *The Christian Year.* London: Thames and Hudson, 1991.

Michell, John, and Christine Rhone. *Twelve-Tribe Nations and the Science of Enchanting the Landscape.* Grand Rapids, Michigan: Phanes Press, 1991.

Minter, Sue. *The Healing Garden: A Natural Haven for Body, Senses and Spirit.* Rutland, Vermont: Charles E. Tuttle, 1993.

Moldenke, Harold and Alma. *Plants of the Bible.* New York: Dover Publications, 1986. Originally published in 1952.

Osmen, Sarah Ann. *Sacred Places: A Journey into the Holiest Lands.* New York: St. Martin's Press, 1990.

Rodriguez, Jeanette. *Our Lady of Guadalupe: Faith and Empowerment among Mexican-American Women.* Austin, Texas: University of Texas Press, 1994.

Steele, Thomas J., S.J. *Santos and Saints: The Religious Folk Art of Hispanic New Mexico.* Santa Fe, New Mexico: Ancient City Press, 1994.

Stewart, R.J. *Celtic Gods, Celtic Goddesses.* London: Villiers House, 1990.

Stokstad, Marilyn, and Jerry Stannard. *Gardens of the Middle Ages.* Lawrence, Kansas: The University of Kansas, Spencer Museum of Art, 1983.

Tallant, Robert. *Voodoo in New Orleans.* Gretna, Louisiana: Pelican Publishing, 1994.

Tarostar. *The Spiritual Worker's Handbook.* Toluca Lake: International Imports, 1985.

Vaughan-Thomas, Wynford, and Michael Hales. *Secret Landscapes: Mysterious Sites, Deserted Villages, and Forgotten Places of Great Britain and Ireland.* Devizes, United Kingdom: Selecta Books, 1992.

Veltri, Raylene. *A Garden of Woman's Wisdom.* San Francisco: Halo Books, 1995.

Walsh, Michael, editor. *Butler's Lives of the Saints.* New York: HarperSanFrancisco, 1991.

Wheelright, Edith Grey. *Medicinal Plants and Their History.* New York: Dover Publications, 1974. Reprint.

Wright, Machaelle Small. *Behaving as if the God in All Life Mattered: A New Age Ecology.* Warrenton, Virginia: Perelandra, 1983.

INDEX

Note: Page numbers in *italics* indicate illustrations.